Annabel Karmel

FEEDING YOUR
Baby & Toddler

Annabel Karmel
FEEDING YOUR
Baby & Toddler

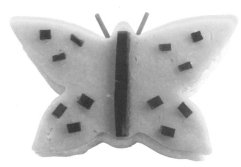

THE COMPLETE COOKBOOK AND NUTRITION GUIDE

DK

LONDON, NEW YORK, MUNICH,
MELBOURNE, DELHI

Revised edition
Senior editor Salima Hirani
Art editor Nicola Rodway
Project editors Jane Laing, Angela Baynham
Designer Christine Lacey
DTP designer Karen Constanti
Production controller Kevin Ward
Managing editor Anna Davidson
Managing art editor Glenda Fisher
Art director Carole Ash
Food photography Dave King
Model photography Vanessa Davies
Photographic art director Toni Kay
Category publisher Corinne Roberts

Original edition
Project editor Lorna Damms
Editor Lorraine Turner
Art editors Carmel O'Neill & Emy Manby
Senior art editor Carole Oliver
DTP designer Bridget Roseberry
Production controller Martin Croshaw
Deputy art director Carole Ash
Managing editors Corinne Roberts & Mary Ling
Consultant editor (child development) Caroline Greene
Food photography Ian O'Leary
Home economist Janice Murfitt

Note on the nutritional breakdowns of recipes
All information is approximate and based on figures from food
composition tables, not on direct analysis of made-up dishes. Thus
analyses should be used as a guide, not as guaranteed figures. As some
ingredients are not specified by weight, an estimated weight has been
used. No analyses have been provided for recipe variations. Analyses
are per portion.

As many vitamins are destroyed when exposed to air or light, the
guidelines on sources apply to dishes served immediately after
preparation. Where recipes are frozen immediately, they will, in
general, still provide a useful amount of the nutrients indicated.

First published in Great Britain in 1999 by Dorling Kindersley
Revised edition published in Great Britain in 2004 by
Dorling Kindersley, A Penguin Company
80 Strand, London, WC2R 0RL
Reprinted with corrections in 2010

A CIP catalogue for this book is available from
the British Library.

ISBN 978-1-4053-5978-8

Reproduced in Italy by GRB
Printed and bound in Hung Hing, China

Discover more at
www.dk.com

Contents

Weaning your baby

*This chapter explains all you need to know to wean your
baby successfully, showing how to prepare his first meals
and feed him for the first time, when to introduce more
advanced purées, and which foods provide a gentle introduction
to exciting new tastes and textures. Now is the best time to
establish sensible eating patterns and an enjoyment of good
food. There are 47 healthy and tasty recipes that are simple
to make and will start your baby off in the right direction.*

9 to 12 months

*Your older baby's dexterity is developing rapidly, as is his
sense of independence. With these comes his desire to start
feeding himself. This chapter shows you how to encourage
self-feeding with finger foods and includes 17 delicious recipes.*

12 to 18 months

*By now your baby's dietary needs are changing, along with
his attitude to food and mealtimes. This chapter discusses
how to encourage your lively baby to join in family meals
and includes 19 tantalizing recipes to keep him interested.*

18 months to 2 years

It's hard to get toddlers to sit down to eat, so you'll need plenty of good ideas for healthy, energy-boosting snacks to fuel your child's energetic explorations of the world. Most toddlers go through a phase of fussy eating, so you'll also need some sensible strategies to keep him well fed. This chapter contains 43 recipes that are ideal for growing toddlers.

2 to 3 years

This chapter contains constructive tips on planning easy and nutritious meals for young children with busy lives, along with 22 creative recipes designed to appeal to two year olds.

3 to 7 years

Encourage your pre-school child to follow a healthy, varied diet and enjoy family meals from around the world – there are 47 delicious recipes the entire family can enjoy in this chapter. There are also 21 recipes and further suggestions for healthy and tasty lunchboxes and snacks.

My children Scarlett (top), Lara (middle) and Nicholas (bottom) grew up on my recipes and now they enjoy eating a wide variety of healthy foods. Many of their favourite recipes are in this book.

Introduction

When it comes to the health and happiness of their children, I think that all parents will agree that only the very best will do. I lost my first child, Natasha, at the heartbreakingly early age of 13 weeks after she contracted a viral infection. Though this illness was not diet-related, Natasha's loss made me even more determined to give my second child, Nicholas, the best possible start in life. It was Nicholas who gave me my first experience of coping with a fussy eater. Indeed, my interest in the whole subject of child nutrition was born out of my own frustrations with feeding a child who for a time would eat only a limited range of foods. Thus the strategies and solutions for common feeding problems that are presented in this book are based not only on current nutritional guidelines, but on experience and a conviction that food is one of the best forms of preventative medicine.

At the time when diet is most crucial to health, we should not be reliant upon processed foods from jars and packets. After all, there is no great mystique to making baby food and there is nothing better for your child than home-cooked food made from fresh ingredients. Home cooking is an economical option and, as the recipes in this book show, it need not be time-consuming. There are many excellent purées that do not involve cooking and other recipes suitable for batch-cooking that enable a whole month's food supply to be prepared in just a couple of hours and then frozen. These homemade meals accustom babies to the natural variations in the taste of freshly cooked food, and this helps them adapt to family meals and grow up to be less fussy eaters. So while parents are giving their baby the best nutritional start in life, they are also helping to guard against future feeding difficulties.

Unfortunately, for many children convenience and junk foods are a regular part of their diet: fewer and fewer families are sitting down to meals together. Instead, children are often raised on a depressingly familiar repertoire of processed, packaged foods and "TV dinners" – pizzas, chicken nuggets, chips and spaghetti hoops. It can seem that "real" food is only for adults, and that children have a special diet consisting of some of the poorest quality, most unhealthy food on offer. Yet parents are the ones in charge of what their children eat, and it is up to parents to give their children the opportunity to follow a varied, healthy diet.

My three children, Nicholas, Lara and Scarlett, have been my constant inspiration over the years, but I am also grateful to all the babies and young children who have contributed to my research into nutrition and development, albeit unknowingly, and tested my new recipes. Children are exacting critics and while they are rarely interested in whether their food is healthy, they do care if it tastes good. Accordingly, the recipes in this book are designed to combine "child appeal" with sound nutritional principles.

Many parents have been kind enough to say how helpful they found the first edition of this book. In this new, extended edition, I have revised many existing recipes to make them even tastier than before and I have added more than 85 delicious new recipes. There are now two completely new sections in the book, providing recipes to tempt the fussy eater and ideas for healthy snacks, picnics and lunchboxes. There are more recipes to appeal to the whole family and more vegetarian dishes throughout. In addition, all the nutritional information has been completely updated in accordance with the latest research into child nutrition.

When you prepare food for your children using fresh ingredients you know you are giving them the very best start in life. I hope that many of my recipes will become firm family favourites for years to come.

Annabel Karmel

Early nutrition

"For his first six months all your baby's nutritional needs are fulfilled by breast milk or formula."

A balanced diet is one that perfectly suits your growing child's needs. Breast milk or formula is the essential source of nourishment throughout the first year of your baby's life, but from the time you begin weaning him, you should try to establish a diet that provides the five essential nutrient groups: carbohydrate, protein, fat, vitamins and minerals. Remember that your child's needs are different from your own. The under fives need significantly more fat and concentrated sources of calories and nutrients than adults in order to fuel their rapid growth during the early years.

Your baby's milk

During his first six months, your baby is dependent on breast milk or formula for all his nutritional needs. Although you may have begun weaning him at four or five months, his initial solid intake is so small that these "real" foods are little more than a taste experience, and it is vital not to reduce milk feeds.

Whole cow's milk can be used in cooking or with cereal from six months but should not be given as your baby's main drink before the age of one mainly because it is low in iron and vitamin C. Once he reaches his first birthday, cow's milk can become his usual drink, but until then he needs the vitamins and iron found in breast milk or formula. Do not give him skimmed milk before his fifth birthday as it provides too little energy. However, semi-skimmed milk can be given from the age of two if your child is eating well.

Benefits of breastfeeding

Current advice from the World Health Organization and the Department of Health is to breastfeed exclusively for the first six months. However, if you are uncomfortable about breastfeeding, or unable to breastfeed, you can still give your baby a good start with infant formula. Between four and six months, babies should be fed at least 600ml (20fl oz) of breast milk or formula a day. If you breastfeed you will know your baby is getting enough milk if he continues to grow along the same centile.

There are proven health benefits to breastfeeding for both child and mother in the short and long term.

• Breastfeeding helps strengthen your baby's immune system. Breastfed babies have a lower risk of respiratory or ear infections and gastroenteritis.

• Breastfeeding for six months has been shown to delay the onset, and reduce the severity, of allergies in children from families with a history of asthma, hayfever, eczema and food allergies.

• Breast milk is easily digested and lessens the risk of constipation.

• Breastfed children may be at lower risk of becoming obese.

• Breast milk provides a balance of essential fatty acids, which are important for brain development.

• Breastfeeding can help mothers lose excess weight gained during pregnancy.

• The risk of pre-menopausal breast cancer in mothers becomes lower the longer they breastfeed.

Water

Babies are vulnerable to dehydration and it is essential to maintain their fluid intake. If your baby is breastfed, your milk will supply the necessary fluids (he may need extra feeds on hot days). The same should be true for bottle-fed babies, although they may need sips of cooled boiled water on hot days.

Once your baby is on a mainly solid diet, you will need to top up his fluid intake. Cooled boiled tap water is accessible and the best thirst-quencher.

Young babies will need only a few sips of water, but it is wise to encourage your child to drink water from an early age: most herbal and fruit drinks marketed for babies contain sugar, which can harm developing teeth and give your baby a taste for sweet drinks.

Do not offer mineral water or use it to make up feeds: it is not bacteriologically safe unless boiled and may contain a higher level of sodium than is recommended for babies.

Carbohydrates

Carbohydrates are the body's main source of energy. The body breaks them down to release glucose, thereby providing itself with energy. There are two main types of carbohydrates: slow-burning and fast-burning. Complex carbohydrates, such as root vegetables and wholemeal bread, release glucose slowly to provide long-lasting energy. Simple carbohydrates, such as banana and white rice, release glucose quickly to provide a quick burst of energy. Although very useful at times, fast-burning carbohydrates cause a rapid rise in blood-sugar levels, which can cause the body to over-compensate. This results in a subsequent sudden dip in blood-sugar

levels and a low level of energy. Both types of carbohydrate contain vitamins, minerals and fibre that are useful to the body, and between them should make up about 40–50 per cent of your child's diet, depending on age.

Refined carbohydrates have usually been stripped of their natural fibre during processing and have decreased levels of their valuable nutrients. Cakes, sweet biscuits and sugary cereals (unless fortified) all fall into this category. Such foods are turned into glucose very rapidly, producing a short-lived energy "high" followed by an energy "low". Limit consumption of these types of food as they supply few nutrients but lots of "empty" calories.

What milk when

• From birth to one year, feed your baby breast milk or infant formula (cow's milk modified to resemble human breast milk).

• From six months to one year, your baby should be drinking around 600ml (20fl oz) of breast milk or formula a day. The Department of Health recommends that if your baby is being breastfed or is drinking less than 500ml (17fl oz) of formula a day, you should give him vitamin supplements from six months to two years of age.

• From six months, you can introduce whole cow's milk in cooking only.

• From one year give your baby whole cow's milk as a drink. One- to seven-year-olds should consume a combination of three servings of dairy products a day (milk, yogurt and cheese). A serving of miilk is 120ml (4fl oz).

Sources of slow-burning carbohydrates

• wholegrain breakfast cereals
• oats • wholegrain flour and bread • apples • carrots
• sweetcorn • pasta • lentils

Sources of fast-burning carbohydrates

• tropical fruit, such as melon, pineapple, kiwi fruit, banana • cornflakes • white bread • white rice • sugar
• sweetened breakfast cereals • most manufactured biscuits, cakes and pastry

Sources of protein
• red meat • chicken • fish
• eggs • milk • cheese (but
not cream cheese) • tofu
• pulses • nuts • grains

Protein

Protein is essential for growth and repair of body tissues. It provides the building blocks of all cells in the body and makes up a large portion of children's muscles, organs, skin and hair. If we have an inadequate level of protein our resistance to disease and infection is lowered. Protein is made up of amino acids, some of which the body can manufacture and some of which must be obtained from food. Animal proteins, including milk, contain all the amino acids the body needs. Soya is the only plant-based food that contains all of them. Other foods must be combined to provide complete proteins: for example, grains with pulses. These foods do not need to be combined at one meal, but can be eaten during the course of a day.

Children grow rapidly and need more protein in relation to their size than adults. However, protein-rich foods should not be the major part of a baby's meal as a high-protein diet can put strain on immature kidneys.

Because protein is not stored by the body, children need two portions of protein-rich foods each day. They should ideally eat meat three or four times a week and fish two or three times, of which one portion should be an oily fish, such as salmon, tuna or sardines. Protein foods such as cheese or eggs are good for breakfast. Try to introduce some vegan protein foods, such as beans and lentils, into the diet as they contain important minerals and phytochemicals, and are a good source of fibre.

Sources of saturated fat & trans fats
• meat • butter and hard margarine • lard • cheese
• hydrogenated vegetable fat or oil, found in processed foods, such as biscuits and pastries

Sources of unsaturated fat
• olive oil • sunflower oil
• corn oil • sesame oil
• rapeseed oil • safflower oil
• oily fish

Sources of omega-3 EFAs
• oily fish, such as salmon, fresh tuna, mackerel, trout, sardines • linseed or walnut oil • pumpkin seeds
• rapeseed oil • Columbus eggs (from hens fed on omega-3-rich seeds) • fish oil supplements

Sources of omega-6 EFAs
• sunflower, safflower and corn oil • soft polyunsaturated margarine

Fat

Fats provide the most concentrated source of energy and babies need proportionately more fat in their diet than adults. They need energy-dense foods such as cheese, meat and eggs to fuel their rapid growth and development. Up to the age of one, children should derive 40–50 per cent of their energy from fat (breast milk contains more than 50 per cent fat). After that they should derive around 35 per cent of their total energy from fat. However, all fats are not equal and it is important to distinguish between different fats when ensuring there is enough fat in your child's diet.
• **Saturated fat** is derived mainly from animal sources and is solid at room temperature. Butter, lard and the fat in meat and dairy produce are mainly saturated. Saturated fats can increase blood cholesterol levels, and high intakes are linked to heart disease in adults. Limit these fats in your child's diet: choose lean meats, use vegetable oils rather than butter for frying, and grill,

griddle, steam or stir-fry food whenever possible. Milk and cheese contain saturated fats but are also a good source of calcium, protein and vitamins.
• **Monounsaturated fats** tend to be liquid at room temperature. Olive oil, rapeseed oil and also the fat found in most nuts and avocados are mainly monounsaturated. These types of fat can help lower cholesterol levels and so can offer some protection against heart disease, as studies of the traditional Mediterranean diet, which is high in olive oil, have shown. Olive oil and rapeseed oil are also the safest for cooking at high temperatures.
• **Polyunsaturated fats** are found in corn, safflower and sunflower oils; these also lower cholesterol levels but it's good to get a balance between different unsaturated fats for good health, so don't just use these types.
• **Trans fats** are unsaturated fatty acids that have been hardened in the manufacture of commercial foods.

they can be found in some margarines, low-fat spreads, biscuits and cakes. They no longer have the properties of unsaturated fat and are nutritionally similar to saturated fats. Many experts believe that trans fats are even more harmful than saturated fats and should be avoided whenever possible.

• **Essential fatty acids (EFAs)** are essential for brain and visual development. There are two types of EFAs: omega-3 and omega-6. Both should be included in the diet because, unlike other fats, they cannot be made in the body. Currently we eat around 10 times more omega-6 fats than omega-3 fats. DHA, found in oily fish, is an omega-3 essential fatty acid that makes up a significant proportion of human brain tissue. It is important for regulating attention and controlling behaviour. Some research suggests that a diet rich in EFAs may improve the performance of children with dyspraxia (a condition impairing movement), dyslexia and attention deficit disorder.

Vitamins

Vitamins are essential for maintaining health. They are either water-soluble (B complex and C) or fat-soluble (A, D, E and K). Water-soluble vitamins can be destroyed by heat and, as their name indicates, dissolve in water, so do not overcook foods rich in these vitamins. Fat-soluble vitamins are stored in the body and may be harmful in large doses. Children aged six months to two years may be deficient in vitamins A and D. A baby may need supplements if he is breastfed after six months or taking less than 500ml (17fl oz) formula a day.

• **Vitamin A**, including beta-carotene and retinol, is essential for growth, fighting infection, healthy skin, good vision and strong bones.

• **B complex vitamins**, including folate, are essential for growth, energy, the development of a healthy nervous system and to aid digestion.

• **Vitamin C** is required for growth, tissue repair, healthy skin and to aid iron absorption.

• **Vitamin D** is manufactured by skin exposed to sunlight and is needed to absorb calcium and phosphorous for healthy bones and teeth.

• **Vitamin E** is needed for the maintenance of the body's cell structure: it helps the body to create and maintain red blood cells.

Remember
If you leave the skin on roast chicken but cut the visible fat off roast beef, the chicken will contain more fat than the beef.

Sources of vitamin A
• carrots • red peppers
• sweetcorn • sweet potatoes
• tomatoes • melons
• apricots • mangoes • liver
• butter and margarine

Sources of B complex vitamins
• meat, especially liver
• tofu • sardines • eggs
• nuts • dark green vegetables
• dairy produce • wholegrain cereals • yeast extract
• avocados • bananas

Sources of vitamin C
• citrus fruits • strawberries
• blackcurrants • kiwi fruit
• dark green leafy vegetables
• potatoes • peppers

Sources of vitamin D
• salmon • tuna • sardines
• milk • cheese • eggs

Sources of vitamin E
• vegetable oils • wheatgerm
• avocados • nuts

"A carefully balanced vegetarian diet can be perfectly adequate for babies and small children, as long as meals do not contain too much fibre."

Calcium

Calcium is important for the formation and health of bones and teeth. 400ml (14fl oz) of milk a day provides an adequate amount for children between the ages of one and five years.

Zinc

Zinc is essential for normal growth and for the efficient function of the immune system. A varied diet should provide all the body's daily zinc requirements.

Iron

Iron is needed for both physical and mental development. Babies are born with a store of iron that lasts for about six months. After this time it is important to make sure that they get the iron they need from the solid food they take in because iron deficiency, which can lead to anaemia if unchecked, leaves children feeling run-down and tired and can make them more prone to infection. Premature babies are especially vulnerable to iron depletion as their store of iron may last for only six weeks. If your baby was born prematurely, you may be advised by your doctor to give him an iron supplement until he is one year old.

A baby's iron requirements are particularly high between the ages of six months and two years. This is a critical time for brain development and a lack of iron in the diet can lead to impaired mental development and lack of concentration. Follow-on formula, which contains more iron than standard infant formula, can be given to babies between six months and two years of age. Follow-on formula is not necessary for most babies but can provide a useful nutritional safety net if your baby is a very picky eater.

Identifying iron deficiency

Iron deficiency is the most common childhood nutritional deficiency – 25 per cent of children do not have enough iron in their bodies. Iron deficiency can be difficult to spot as the physical symptoms are not so readily identifiable as those of an infectious illness. If you notice symptoms of pallor, listlessness and fatigue in your child, he is probably deficient in iron. You can rectify the problem quickly by providing adequate dietary sources of iron – talk to your health visitor or doctor too.

Dietary sources of iron

Iron from animal sources, such as red meat, particularly liver, or oily fish (salmon, sardines, mackerel or pilchards, for example), is easily absorbed by the body. Plant food

...urces, such as pulses and green leafy vegetables, and iron added by manufacturers to foods such as fortified breakfast cereals is absorbed less easily. However, if foods or drinks containing vitamin C are eaten at the same meal as a plant-based source of iron, then the iron is better absorbed. Offer kiwi fruit, citrus fruit or berries, or some diluted pure fruit juice, with the meal. Alternatively, serve a few chunks of vitamin C-rich sweet red pepper or cauliflower florets with an iron-rich spinach or lentil dish. In both cases, the vitamin C will improve iron absorption in your child's body.

Protein-rich foods also aid iron absorption. By serving fish, lean red meat or chicken with dark green leafy vegetables or lentils, you will improve the absorption of the vegetable sources of iron by about three times.

Vegetarian diet

Parents who follow a vegetarian diet sometimes worry that it may not be suitable for their children. In fact, only a bulky, high-fibre vegetarian diet is unsuitable for growing young children because it is too low in calories and essential fats, and hinders the absorption of iron. However, a vegetarian diet can be perfectly adequate for babies and small children as long as the meals are carefully balanced and do not contain too much fibre.

Boosting protein
Animal proteins, including those found in egg and dairy products, are high quality and contain essential amino acids. Vegetable proteins, such as those found in beans, pulses and seeds, provide a lower-quality protein. Soya is the only plant-based food that contains all the amino acids.

So, if your child is following a vegetarian diet, ensure that he receives enough high-quality protein by serving cereal or vegetable proteins such as pasta, bread, rice or lentils, with small quantities of dairy foods or eggs. Alternatively, you could include two vegetable-protein food groups. There are three groups: pulses, such as beans, lentils and chickpeas; grains, such as wheat, rice, oats, bread and pasta; and nuts and seeds.

A good way to improve the protein in a baby's diet is to make up some cheese sauce and freeze it. Then, when you give your baby some vegetable purée, simply add cheese sauce.

Here are some examples of good vegetarian dishes for babies and young children:
• lentil and vegetable purée with cheese
• peanut butter sandwiches
• baked potato with cheese and milk
• pasta with cheese sauce
• baked beans on toast
• rice and lentils.

Improving iron absorption
Children brought up on a vegetarian diet can sometimes be deficient in iron, since red meat provides the best and most easily absorbed source of iron. Plant food sources of iron are more difficult to absorb. So it's especially important to remember that vitamin C-rich foods given with your child's meal (see under Iron) greatly increase the absorption of iron from non-animal sources.

Vegan option
If you wish your child to follow a vegan diet (that is, without meat, dairy products or eggs), you will need to plan his diet carefully, in consultation with your GP or a paediatric dietitian.

Sources of calcium
• milk • cheese • yogurt
• leafy vegetables • tofu • nuts
• sardines • sesame paste

Sources of zinc
• shellfish • red meat
• peanuts • sunflower seeds
• fortified breakfast cereals

Sources of iron
• liver and red meats • egg yolk • oily fish, fresh or canned
• pulses, such as lentils and baked beans • fortified breakfast cereals • bread and rusks • dark green leafy vegetables • dried fruits, such as apricots

Vegetarian sources of iron
• fortified breakfast cereals
• egg yolk • wholemeal bread
• beans and lentils • dark green leafy vegetables • dried fruits, such as apricots

Healthy eating

"95–99 per cent of all food products advertised during children's television are high in fat, sugar and/or salt."

The most common nutritional disorder in the Western world is obesity. Obese children as young as five are displaying early-warning signs of heart disease. Type 2 diabetes – once called adult-onset diabetes – is now appearing in teenagers. There are other dietary concerns. Too much salt is linked to high blood pressure, which can lead to heart disease and strokes, and most children eat two to three times the daily recommended salt intake. Most children fall far short of the five daily portions of fruit or vegetables recommended to boost the immune system and reduce the adult incidence of cancer.

Reducing obesity

In the UK more than one in five children under the age of four is overweight and nearly one in ten is classified as obese. Thanks to the popularity of computer games, television and DVDs, children are only too happy to stay in their rooms moving nothing more than a few fingers on a keyboard. A couch potato generation of junk food addicts is storing up serious health problems for the future – ultimately one-third of these sedentary youngsters will die from a diet-related disease.

Children do not make food choices in a vacuum; they are influenced by the products they see advertised on television, what their favourite sports or pop stars are seen eating or drinking and peer pressure. Advertising and promotion that produce the phenomenon of pester power are ultimately dangerous since the label "children's food" has come to represent some of the worst quality, most unhealthy food on offer. Whether it's packs of chicken nuggets or the "special children's menu" in a restaurant, children's food is generally over-processed and high in saturated fat; it is often high in sugar and salt, too. Most children have intakes of saturated fat that exceed the maximum level for adults.

A balanced diet

Children who are overweight should not be put on a restricted diet. Unlike adults, children are still growing and it is important that they eat a broad variety of healthy foods that provide plenty of calcium, protein, iron and other essential nutrients.

By adopting a long-term approach to healthy eating, it should be possible for your child to maintain a static weight rather than losing weight and, as he grows taller, he will "grow into" the weight rather than lose weight and appear slimmer.

Encourage exercise

Overweight children are often embarrassed by their bodies and dislike taking part in school sports. They are usually the last to be picked for team sports.

Set a good example yourself – children of active parents are much more likely to be active themselves. Limit television and computer games and find a sport or physical activity your child enjoys.

Provide play equipment, such as a climbing frame or trampoline. Encourage family activities, such as trips to the pool, bicycle rides, roller blading, ball games or racket sports. It's a good idea to introduce a regular time for such a family exercise, even if it's just walking in the park, to help make regular exercise a habit. Consider enrolling your child in gymnastics, swimming or dancing classes.

Watch the salt

Over half of all children eat twice as much salt as they should. It is estimated that by reducing salt intake by just 3g a day for adults, 14 per cent fewer people would suffer strokes and there would be 10 per cent fewer heart attacks. Bones would benefit, too, as excess salt causes a loss of calcium, which could lead to bone thinning, a higher risk of fractures and osteoporosis.

The liking for salt and salty foods is a learned taste preference. During the first year babies are not given any salt in their diet and they don't miss it. However, after this more and more salt creeps into your child's food. There is hidden salt in foods such as bread and breakfast cereals. In fact, cornflakes contain as much salt as seawater. Approximately three-quarters of the salt children consume comes from processed foods. So, to reduce your child's salt intake you must limit the amount of processed foods, snacks and fast food, such as pizzas, chicken nuggets, spaghetti hoops and crisps, that your child consumes. As far as possible, ensure that your child eats freshly cooked food that does not contain added salt.

Most foods are labelled with grams of sodium per 100g. One gram of sodium is equivalent to 2.5g of salt, so anything with more than 0.5g sodium per 100g is too high in salt. Try to buy foods with less than 0.2g of sodium per 100g.

Eating more fruit & vegetables

Researchers estimate that a diet filled with fruit and vegetables instead of unhealthy fats and refined foods, combined with increased exercise, could reduce the incidence of cancer by at least 30 per cent. Health experts recommend that we eat at least five portions of fruit and vegetables each day.

Fruit and vegetables are packed with powerful natural compounds called phytochemicals. Many of the bright colours in fruit and vegetables come from phytochemicals, and they can help to protect the body from heart disease and cancer, boost immunity and fight harmful bacteria and viruses.

Fruit and vegetables also contain antioxidants, which protect the body by neutralizing free radicals that can damage cells and lead to poor health.

In general, the more colourful the food, the more nutritious it is. For example, spinach rates more highly than lettuce, and sweet potato is better for you than an ordinary potato. Lycopene gives fruits such as tomato and watermelon their red colour. It is a very powerful antioxidant that can protect against heart disease and some forms of cancer. Different coloured fruit and vegetables contain different nutrients so aim for a mix of colours.

Salt issues
- Recommended salt intake per day is 2g for one to three year olds, 3g for four to six year olds, and 5g (or 1 teaspoon) for seven to 10 year olds.

- Potassium's relationship with salt is like a see-saw: if your potassium intake is high, your body's level of sodium (the key element in salt) will be healthier. Dried fruits, nuts, bananas, onions, potatoes and pulses are all good sources of potassium.

- Some food labels list the salt content of food per serving, but currently this applies only to a few foods. Other labels give the amount of sodium in grams per 100g. To convert this to the salt content, multiply the amount of sodium by 2.5.

Rainbow fruit & vegetables
Try to include different coloured fruit and vegetables to provide a wide variety of nutrients.

Orange/yellow: carrots
- mangoes • papaya
- sweet potatoes

Red: tomatoes • red peppers
- strawberries • raspberries

Green: broccoli • spinach
- peas • kiwi fruit

Purple/blue: blueberries
- grapes • blackberries
- purple figs

White: cauliflowers • onions
- garlic • potatoes • pears

Food allergies

"Most babies who suffer a particular food allergy or intolerance will outgrow it by the time they are three years old."

An allergic reaction occurs when the immune system perceives a harmless substance as a threat and overreacts, triggering unpleasant, occasionally dangerous, side-effects. If you have a family history of allergy, such as hay fever, asthma, or eczema, your baby will be at increased risk. If this is the case, you will need to be more cautious when introducing new foods and wait a little longer between each to see if there is a reaction. There is no evidence that weaning later or avoiding introducing potentially allergenic foods will affect the likelihood of developing allergies.

Common allergies

The foods that most commonly carry a risk of allergic reaction in babies include: • cow's milk and dairy products • nuts and seeds • eggs • wheat-based products • fish and shellfish • soya. Sesame seeds, berries, citrus fruits and kiwi fruits can sometimes cause a reaction in susceptible babies.

Cow's milk (protein) allergy

An allergic reaction to one of the proteins found in cow's milk, cow's milk-based infant formulas and dairy products can give rise to diverse symptoms, namely diarrhoea, vomiting, abdominal pains, eczema and lactose intolerance (see opposite). Babies who experience this allergic reaction can be given a soya-based or hypoallergenic formula milk, on the advice of a doctor, if breast milk is not an option. Older children need a dairy-free diet (consult your GP or a dietitian).

Nut allergy

Although allergy to tree nuts is relatively rare, the peanut can be a trigger for one of the most severe allergic reactions, anaphylactic shock (in which the throat swells and breathing becomes difficult). In families with a history of any kind of allergy, including hayfever, asthma and eczema and food allergy, watch your baby carefully when introducing nuts. Otherwise it's perfectly fine to introduce very finely ground nuts and nut butters from six months. Research indicates that early introduction may even help to prevent allergies, although more research is required. Whole nuts should not be given to under fives because of the risk of choking.

Symptoms of food allergy

Allergic reactions usually manifest as:
• swelling of the lips or tongue with a runny nose
• persistent diarrhoea
• vomiting
• wheezing or difficulty breathing
• abdominal pain

in extreme cases, anaphylactic shock – a sudden and life-threatening reaction with wheezing, hives, swelling of the throat and shock (peanuts are the most common cause).

Diagnosing a food allergy

The most accurate way to diagnose a food allergy is to eliminate all the suspected foods from your child's diet, wait for the symptoms to cease and, after a period of several weeks, start to reintroduce these foods one by one until the symptoms reappear. The last food to be reintroduced is usually the one producing the allergic reaction. This process should be carried out under medical supervision only.

Do not remove key foods from your child's diet. If you suspect she is allergic to a common food, such as milk or wheat, seek expert advice (from your GP or a dietitian) to confirm the diagnosis and help plan a balanced diet before taking any action yourself.

Children who do experience a food allergy may well outgrow it by the age of three, but occasionally an allergy will persist and the only option is avoidance.

What is food intolerance?

A person is said to have an intolerance to a food or food substance if eating that food leads to an adverse reaction not involving the immune system. The body is temporarily incapable of digesting certain foods. This is generally short-lived, unlike a true food allergy.

Lactose intolerance

Children who suffer permanent lactose intolerance lack a substance called lactase, an enzyme needed in order to digest the lactose (milk sugar) in milk. Affected babies cannot drink breast milk or cow's milk formula and need a special low-lactose (sometimes labelled "LF") infant formula (available only on prescription). Lactose intolerance may cause diarrhoea and gassiness after taking milk or dairy products.

Temporary lactose intolerance – usually caused by gastroenteritis from bacteria or viruses damaging the gut, where lactase is produced – is more common. Once the gut repairs the damage (which may take from a few days to a few weeks), the enzyme is produced once more and the intolerance disappears. While the condition lasts, it can be managed with a soya-based formula or a low-lactose infant formula.

Gluten intolerance

Wheat, barley, rye and possibly oats and their products contain gluten, a type of protein. Intolerance to gluten causes coeliac disease, a genetically linked, lifelong condition, that can appear at any age. Foods containing gluten should not be introduced into a baby's diet until he is six months old. If there is a family history of gluten intolerance, advice is to introduce gluten at six months, as normal, so it can be clearly diagnosed.

In most cases, the condition disappears once the gut has had time to recover from the gastroenteritic illness. Symptoms of gluten intolerance include frequent, bulky, pale, foul-smelling stools, loss of appetite, failure to thrive, distended stomach, stick-like limbs, irritability and lethargy and saggy, flat buttocks.

If coeliac disease is diagnosed proper dietary and medical management will be required. The good news is that there are a whole host of gluten-free grains that you can give your child, such as rice, quinoa, millet, corn and buckwheat, as well as gluten-free alternatives to favourite foods, such as pasta and bread.

A family history of allergies

If your family has a history of food allergy or atopic disease (such as hay fever, asthma, hives or eczema), the risk of developing an allergy is increased. Introduce each new food one at a time and wait to see if there is a reaction, and talk to your doctor or health visitor for individual advice. If there is no family history of allergic conditions, you can introduce new tastes each day.

• Do not start weaning before 24 weeks.

• Begin weaning with low-allergen foods, such as baby rice, potato and sweet potato, carrot, cauliflower, broccoli, pear, apple, melon, peach and nectarine purées.

• There are no foods that need to be avoided while breastfeeding, but keep an eye out for foods that may cause your baby discomfort. If he appears to be uncomfortable after feeds, crying, vomiting, drawing his knees up to his chest, or experiencing "wind", it may well be that something you have eaten doesn't agree with him. Removing the offending food should make a difference instantly.

Gluten-free cereals

• rice • millet • corn
• quinoa • buckwheat

Full-size processor with mini bowl attachment

Mouli

Collapsible steamer   *Stacking steamer*

Kitchen basics

There are many kitchen tools and shortcuts you can learn to help make the entire process of food preparation for your baby or young child quick, simple and fuss-free. There are certain pieces of equipment, store cupboard essentials and cooking techniques that are invaluable, and you'll need to know how to freeze baby food safely if you want to avoid cooking every day. A little knowledge of food hygiene will also help you keep your baby healthy.

Equipment

You will probably find that you already have most of the equipment needed to make home-cooked meals for your child, but certain items will facilitate food preparation and prove useful for general family cooking. Equipment need not be expensive or complicated, but you should look for items that will make preparing solids easy for you and that will later help your baby learn how to feed himself.

Sterilizing equipment
Warm milk is the perfect breeding ground for bacteria, so bottles must be scrupulously washed and sterilized. Sterilize all bottles, teats and feeding cup spouts up to one year, and sterilize feeding spoons for the first six months. You can use an electric, steam or chemical sterilizing kit, or simply boil feeding equipment in a pan of water for 10 minutes, or wash it in a dishwasher on a hot programme.

Processors & blenders
Electric food processors, liquidizers or hand blenders make it easy to purée large quantities of food quickly. Some foods, such as cooked apples, will purée to a smooth consistency; other, coarser foods, such as peas or dried apricots, should be strained through a metal sieve after puréeing to remove the fibrous, indigestible material.

• **Mini processors** are useful for making baby foods in small portions.
• **Full-size processors** facilitate cooking food in large batches, but a mini bowl attachment will work better if you are mainly preparing small quantities.
• **Moulis** purée foods while holding back any indigestible husks or skins. This is ideal in the early stages when serving nutritious foods such as dried apricots and peas, the skins of which are indigestible for young babies.
• **Hand-held blenders** are easy to clean and ideal for puréeing small quantities in the container provided with the blender.
• **A metal-mesh sieve** can be used to eliminate any fibrous material from purées for babies.

Steamers
Steaming vegetables preserves maximum nutrients so it's well worth buying a steamer. There are two types.
• **A multi-layered steamer** allows you to stack several foods on the same pan so that you can cook them simultaneously. You can boil one ingredient in the bottom and steam others in the layers above.
• **A collapsible steamer** slots into an existing pan that has a lid. It fits various sizes of pan and is a versatile alternative to a stacked steamer.

Freezer containers

Tiny portions of purée can be spooned into ice-cube trays, then frozen (see page 22). You can buy small freezer-proof pots with snap-on lids that hold larger portions. These are particularly useful as they can be transferred straight from the freezer to the microwave.

• **Several ice-cube trays** will allow you to freeze meal-size portions of a variety of purées. Flexible rubber trays can be twisted to release the cubes easily.

• **Freezer pots** with snap-on lids are useful – use them as extra feeding bowls. They are also easy to transport.

Baby chairs

A good bouncy chair that supports the back is ideal for babies who cannot yet sit unaided. A baby car seat can double as a feeding chair. Once he can sit up, your baby can progress to a rigid highchair with safety harness. A clip-on chair with safety harness is a light, transportable, space-saving alternative.

• **Bouncy chairs** are lightweight and may recline in different positions. Wipe-clean or washable finishes are useful.

• **Highchairs** should be wide-based and sturdy, with a wipe-clean tray.

• **Clip-on chairs** may be clamped to a sturdy table that can take the extra weight. Do not clamp them over a cloth.

Feeding kit

There are many varieties of feeding bowls and spoons available. All that is needed to start with is a small weaning bowl and a shallow plastic spoon, preferably made of soft, flexible plastic that will not hurt tender gums. Later on, bowls with suction pads or thermal linings, feeding cups and children's cutlery become useful.

• **Weaning bowls** should be made of heat-proof plastic. Choose one with a hand-grip.

• **Heat-sensitive bowls** and spoons quickly change colour to indicate if the food is too hot.

• **Suction-pads** on bowls allow them to be secured to highchair trays.

• **Weaning spoons** should have a small, shallow bowl with no hard edges.

• **Feeding cups** enable babies to learn to take fluids independently. Most babies graduate from bottles to cups with a spout and snap-tight lid and then to an open cup. Non-spill multi-way beakers are ideal.

Bibs

Feeding can be a messy business, for young babies, parents, and even the surrounding walls. Protect your baby's clothes from the worst of the mess with a bib, and place a large square plastic splash mat, or an old plastic tablecloth, under feeding chairs.

• **Soft cotton bibs** should have a plastic backing and a Velcro fastener.

• **Bibs with sleeves** and ties at the back give the best all-over protection when your baby starts to feed himself.

• **Soft plastic pelican bibs** with a shallow trough are suitable for older babies. Their wipe-clean surface makes them a very practical alternative to cotton bibs.

Weaning bowl

Heat-sensitive bowl

Bowl with suction-pads

Weaning spoon

Graduated feeding cup

Feeding cup

Store cupboard

"A well-stocked larder is the best form of preventative medicine known to man."

A well-stocked store cupboard is invaluable in any kitchen. It should work as a fail-safe so that if you haven't had time to go shopping, you can use ingredients already to hand to make a quick and nutritious meal for your children, or indeed for the whole family. While the lists of foods on this page are by no means exhaustive, they represent a useful and highly versatile selection of stand-by foods. Check the ingredients lists on canned foods as some common commercial additives, such as the food colourings annato and tartrazine, can provoke an allergic reaction in sensitive young children.

STORE CUPBOARD ESSENTIALS

Dried staple foods

Bread and other grain products, such as pasta and rice, are invaluable sources of carbohydrate that can be used as the basis for many quick, healthy meals. Although dried beans and pulses generally require some advance preparation, they are both nutritious and economical. Keep flour and cornflour in the cupboard too.

Bread products Stock wholemeal and white bread, bread sticks, muffins and taco shells.

Beans & pulses Include red kidney beans, red and green lentils and haricot beans.

Dried fruit Include apricots, mangoes, peaches, prunes, apple rings, raisins and pineapple.

Rice Stock baby rice for purées, white and brown long-grain rice and risotto rice.

Pasta Include soup pasta, farfalle, fusilli, spaghetti, lasagne, cannelloni and Chinese egg noodles.

Couscous & other wheat products Include semolina and bulgar wheat.

Breakfast cereals

Choose low-sugar cereals made with rice, oats or wheat. A wholegrain variety is preferable, but for children avoid bran-based products with added fibre.

Commercial cereals Stock cornflakes, puffed rice, wheat biscuits and malted mini wheat biscuits. Check sugar content.

Muesli Make with a mixture of rolled oats, mixed grains, toasted wheatgerm and chopped dried fruit.

Eggs & dairy products

Eggs Choose organic or free-range eggs and store in the refrigerator. They make a nutritious meal in minutes.

Dairy products Choose full-fat, pasteurized products for children under five years old.

Cheeses Stock soft cream cheese for dips and spreads, mild or medium Cheddar, Edam or Gruyère, cottage cheese and fresh Parmesan.

Milk Choose full-fat and pasteurized, whether cow's or goat's milk. Keep a pint of long-life milk in the cupboard.

Yogurt Choose full-fat natural yogurt, low-sugar fruit or vanilla yogurts (preferably a live, organic variety) and fromage frais.

Butter Choose unsalted or lightly salted butter or a good-quality margarine for spreading on bread and for shallow frying and baking.

Sauces, oils & seasonings

A plentiful supply of bottled sauces and oils, herbs and spices will give plenty of culinary scope.

Sauces & flavourings Include soy sauce, oyster sauce, tomato purée, Worcestershire sauce, pesto, vegetable and chicken stock cubes.

Oils & vinegars Include olive oil, sunflower oil, vegetable oil, sesame oil, balsamic and wine vinegars for cooking and salad dressings.

Herbs Include mixed dried herbs, bay leaves, oregano, thyme, bouquet garnis, fresh basil, fresh and dried parsley.

Spices Include powdered cinnamon, mixed spice and ginger for baking, nutmeg (buy the whole spice), fresh root ginger and mild paprika.

Frozen foods

Many vegetables and fruits, such as peas and sweetcorn, are frozen within two to three hours of being picked, ensuring that they retain valuable nutrients. In fact, fresh vegetables that are stored for several days often contain fewer nutrients than frozen vegetables.

Frozen chicken portions and fish fillets are good stand-bys. If buying fish pieces in breadcrumbs, choose larger portion sizes as there will be less coating in proportion to the fish.

Freeze bread and butter for emergencies, and stock dairy ice-cream for quick puddings.

Canned foods

Some canned processed foods are high in sugar and salt, and all contain additives, so always read the labels carefully before you decide what to buy. However, many canned products are valuable nutritionally. Make sure you keep the following stand-bys in stock: tuna, sardines, baked beans, kidney beans, plum tomatoes and sweetcorn.

Preparing baby food

The ingredients of most commercial baby foods have been heated to very high temperatures and then cooled, giving them a very long shelf life (usually two years) but destroying the flavour and some of the nutrients in the process. By making baby food yourself, you can be sure of using only the best-quality ingredients to create fresh-tasting, nutrient-packed purées without thickeners or additives. You can also introduce a wide range of foods to your baby and make up your own combinations to suit his taste. The cooking methods shown here are useful for making the smooth purées suitable for the early stages of weaning (see pages 36–39 for recipes).

Choosing produce carefully

Babies are far more susceptible than adults to pesticide residues and other harmful artificial chemicals found in conventional food.

• **Organic agriculture** uses minimal antibiotics, no artificial fertilizers or pesticides and no genetically modified organisms. However, although environmentally friendly, organic produce is more expensive to buy. In addition, as it contains no chemical preservatives, you will need to buy fresh fruit and vegetables several times a week.

• **The use of pesticides** is controlled by law, so a non-organic diet is not necessarily unhealthy. Most residues in fresh produce are in the skin, so peel fruit and remove and discard the outer leaves of cabbages and lettuces.

Different cooking techniques

You don't need any special expertise to prepare baby foods, but there are ways to streamline the process so that even busy parents can produce meals that perfectly suit their babies' needs. Many first foods, such as mashed banana and avocado, make excellent baby purées and do not require any cooking at all. For other meals, you can either set aside unseasoned portions of food, such as vegetables, that are being cooked for the rest of the family, or cook batches of puréed foods just for your baby and freeze them.

• **Steaming** helps to preserve the taste and nutrient content of fresh produce. It preserves more antioxidants than boiling. Water-soluble vitamins B and C can be destroyed by overcooking: broccoli loses 60 per cent of its vitamin C if boiled, but just 20 per cent if steamed.

• **Boiling** can destroy nutrients, so ingredients should be cooked just until tender in the minimum amount of water. Be careful not to overcook.

• **Microwaving**, like steaming, leaves nutrients relatively intact and is preferable to boiling. It's a safe and easy way to steam.

• **Baking** is a nutrient-retaining, labour-saving cooking method. Potatoes, sweet potatoes and squashes can be washed, pricked with a fork and baked until tender. The flesh can then be scooped out and mashed.

Blending purées

Blending uncooked soft fruits or steamed harder fruits or vegetables in a food processor is the quickest and easiest way of making smooth purées.

"Making baby food at home is more economical than routinely buying commercial brands and means that you can establish a varied and healthy diet from the start."

Cook small pieces of vegetable or fruit until tender. Drain, retaining a tablespoon or two of the cooking liquid, then pour into the bowl of the food processor. Engage the food processor motor until a smooth, even-textured purée is produced. If necessary, add a little of the cooking water to thin the mixture, and then pulse briefly.

The final texture should be smooth. It can be thinned with breast milk, formula or cooled boiled water.

To blend fibrous ingredients, such as peas and dried apricots, use a mouli. Fit the fine mouli blade, then place the ingredients in the mouli and set over a bowl. Turn the mouli handle to rotate the blade. Continue the grinding until most of the ingredients are pushed through the mouli, then discard the fibrous pulp left behind.

The finished purée has a smooth, uniform texture.

Freezing & reheating

"Preparing large quantities of purées and freezing them in batches makes it easy and practical to feed your baby homemade food."

Batch-cooking and freezing purées is by far the most time-economical way to make food for your baby. Only a few first purées – banana, avocado, melon and aubergine, for example – do not freeze well.

Food should be stored in a freezer that freezes food to -18°C (0°F) or below in 24 hours. Food that has thawed should never be refrozen, although defrosted raw food, such as frozen peas, may be cooked and then frozen again for later use.

Freezing purées

Allow freshly cooked purée to cool to room temperature, then spoon it into clean ice-cube trays. Wrap in a freezer bag and transfer the trays to the freezer. When frozen, remove the trays from the freezer and push out the cubes of frozen purée on to a plate. Transfer the cubes to a fresh freezer bag, seal tightly, then label and date the contents. Return to the freezer and store for up to six weeks.

When you wish to use the frozen purée, take the required number of cubes from the freezer and heat in a pan or microwave until piping hot. Stir and allow to cool before serving.

Reheating rules

It is safe to thaw purées in a microwave or saucepan, as long as the food is then heated all the way through until piping hot. If using a microwave, be particularly vigilant as microwaves can heat food unevenly, producing "hot spots" but leaving other parts of the food cold. Let the purée cool after heating, and test the temperature before offering it to your baby. A baby's mouth is more sensitive to heat than an adult's, so food should be given at room temperature or lukewarm. If you are worried about gauging the temperature, try using a heat-sensitive weaning spoon, which changes colour according to the temperature of the food.

Food hygiene

Babies and young children are especially vulnerable to the effects of food poisoning, so it is essential that great care is taken in the storage and preparation of their food. In the first few months of a baby's life extra care must be taken (see page 18), but once your baby is mobile and exploring objects with his mouth, there is little point in sterilizing anything except bottles and teats. Attention to food safety rules, however, remains crucial.

Food safety

• **Keep raw meat, fish and eggs away from other foods.** Wash hands well after contact with any of these foods. Keep two chopping boards – one for meat and fish and another for fruit and vegetables.

• **Only reheat food once,** and ensure that it is reheated to a high temperature to kill off bacteria.

• **Do not keep your baby's half-eaten food for a later meal** because the saliva introduced from your baby's spoon will breed bacteria. If you are feeding from a jar that contains more than one portion, transfer a serving portion into a weaning bowl and feed from the bowl.

• **Always date frozen food** so that it is never offered if it is past its best.

• **Do not leave food unrefrigerated** as bacteria multiply rapidly at room temperature. Cool food quickly if it is to be refrigerated or frozen. You can accelerate cooling by placing a bowl full of cooked baby food in iced water.

• **Use up baby food** that is stored in the fridge within 24 hours.

• **Cover all food and drink** securely to protect it from contamination by germ-carrying insects, and keep pets away from food and work surfaces.

Kitchen hygiene

Adhering to a few simple rules will minimize the likelihood of food contamination.

• Always wash your hands before preparing food, and make sure your child's hands are washed before eating.

• Wipe daily, using an anti-bacterial agent, any surfaces that come into contact with your baby's food.

• Wash chopping boards and kitchen knives immediately after use, and leave equipment to air-dry.

• Use only perfectly clean tea towels to dry your baby's feeding equipment.

TIP When batch-cooking, cool food as quickly as possible and then freeze it. Don't leave it in the fridge for several days before freezing.

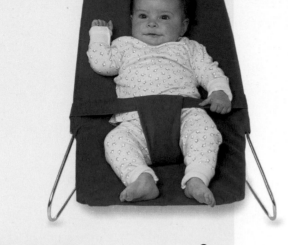

Weaning your baby

Starting solids

The first year of life is a period of rapid growth and development, with most babies at least doubling their birthweight by the time they reach six months. Don't be in a hurry to wean your baby on to solids. Solids should not be introduced until at least 17 weeks after your baby's due date. A young baby's digestive and immune systems are not sufficiently developed before this time and there is a greater risk of allergy occurring. Until six months or so, breast milk or formula provides all the nutrients your baby needs, but after six months, her digestive system will be ready for solids, and so will her appetite!

When does my baby need solids?

At around 26 weeks your baby will reach a stage when she needs solid foods as well as milk in her diet. For example, the iron inherited from her mother will have been used up. This is when the World Health Organization recommends that you introduce your baby to solids. Her first taste of solid food will be a significant milestone and mark the beginning of a gradual shift to a solid diet.

While sucking is a natural reflex, so too is gagging on unaccustomed solids. And if weaning is delayed beyond six months, some babies have difficulty learning to swallow and chew food.

"Begin with 1 tablespoon of single-ingredient fruit or vegetable purée that is the consistency of runny yogurt."

All babies need to learn the skill of pushing food to the back of the mouth with their tongues and swallowing.

Recognizing that she's ready
Your baby may show signs to indicate she's ready for solids.

• She may seem dissatisfied by her milk feeds and become unsettled.
• She may start waking in the night, demanding a feed when previously she was sleeping through.
• She might start showing an interest in the things you eat.

Ideal first foods
(see pages 34–35)
• baby rice • sweet eating apple
• pear • papaya • banana
• avocado • broccoli • carrot
• potato • sweet potato
• butternut squash or pumpkin

Foods for weaning

Plain baby rice, mixed with expressed breast milk or formula, is a good starter food, but you can also introduce single-ingredient purées during the first four weeks of weaning. Simple purées enable you to assess how each new food has suited your child, and accustom her to a wide range of single fruits and vegetables before they are mixed together. Avoid any foods that might cause early allergies (see page 16).

Root vegetables tend to be the most popular with young babies because of their naturally sweet flavour and smooth texture once puréed. Dessert apples and pears are ideal first fruits but taste them yourself before cooking as they must be ripe and naturally sweet. Remember that baby rice is an excellent mixer too, as it can make strong-flavoured foods more palatable to some babies. Alternatively, foods such as mashed banana, papaya or avocado make nutritionally excellent no-cook purées.

Why homemade is best
If you make baby food yourself, you can be sure of using only the best ingredients, without the need for thickeners or additives. It is also more economical and easier to establish a varied diet with food combinations designed to suit your baby. Homemade food has a fresher taste than commercial baby food, which may contain preservatives. Bought baby purées tend to be uniform and bland.

Remember
• Always wash your hands thoroughly before preparing or offering food, and wash your baby's hands before every feed.

• For thinning purées to the desired consistency of runny yogurt, use cooled boiled tap water, a little cooking water, or your baby's usual milk.

• Do not use bottled mineral waters in feeds as they are not sterile and also tend to have a high sodium content.

• All your baby's feeding equipment should be washed in water that is hotter than 80°C/176°F (you will need to wear rubber gloves). Alternatively, wash them in a dishwasher. Dry with a clean, dry cloth.

Getting started

Preparing tiny amounts of purée is time-consuming, so batch-cook and freeze portions in ice-cube trays, perhaps once a week (see page 22). At first your baby will manage only a "solid" consistency similar to runny yogurt, so the thickness of your purées will change over the weeks.

Alternatively, your baby's food can be prepared alongside the rest of the family's: if you are cooking vegetables for your supper, for example, simply cook without adding any seasoning, set aside a small portion for your baby and purée it in a blender when she is ready for her meal.

Special equipment
You will find suggestions for food preparation equipment on page 18. Your baby can take her first taste of solids from the tip of your finger, but once she is more accustomed to solids, you can use a small plastic weaning spoon and bowl.

Some weaning spoons are made of soft plastic that is kinder to tender gums. The spoon should be shallow so your baby can easily suck the food from it. The bowl may have a handle that allows you to hold it up to your baby. Cover her clothes with a bib and have wipes or a damp cloth on hand.

Introducing your baby to solids

"Don't worry if your baby refuses solids to begin with – many babies take a little while to get used to the idea. Simply try again the next day."

Pick a time of day for your baby's feed when you are not rushed or likely to be distracted. If possible, choose the same time every day (perhaps lunchtime) so that you can begin to establish a routine. You may want to give your baby half her usual milk feed before her solids so that she is not frantically hungry.

Judging quantities

All babies' appetites and needs are different, but you will probably find that your baby initially takes one to two teaspoons of purée, so allow one tablespoon (15ml) or one ice-cube portion. As she develops, offer a little more and continue the feed until her interest starts to wane. When she has had enough of the solid food, finish off with the second half of her milk feed.

Taking it slowly

Even though your baby may relish her solid food from the start, it will still take time for her to master the art of swallowing it. Let her enjoy her mealtimes by being relaxed yourself and taking things at your baby's pace. Avoid times when she is over-tired or restless. Talk to her encouragingly and make sure she is comfortable, whether she is in a bouncy seat, or cuddled on your lap. Show her that the experience is enjoyable by smiling and making eye contact and be prepared to get a little bit smeared with baby rice, too.

Foods to avoid

It is best to avoid giving your baby the following foods to minimize the risk of infection and allergic reaction and to set up a healthy eating pattern.

- **Salt** Babies under a year should not have any salt added to their food as this can strain immature kidneys and cause dehydration. A preference for salt can become established at an early age and eating too much salt may lead to high blood pressure later in life. You should also avoid smoked foods.
- **Sugar** Unless food is really tart, don't add sugar to it. Added sugar is habit-forming and increases the risk of tooth decay.
- **Raw or lightly cooked eggs** Due to the risk of salmonella infection, eggs should be cooked until the yolk and white are both solid.
- **Unpasteurized cheese** To avoid the risk of listeria infection avoid cheeses such as Brie and Camembert.
- **Foods containing gluten** Do not introduce wheat, oats, barley or rye before six months (see page 17).
- **Nuts** Government advice has recently changed. Very finely ground nuts can now be offered from six months. If you have a family history of allergies or eczema (see page 16),

FIRST TASTES

Wash your hands thoroughly then dip the tip of your finger into the food to test its temperature – it should be room temperature or lukewarm. If it is cool enough, let your baby suck the food from your finger to accustom her to the taste. The feel of your finger is probably familiar to her and lessens the strangeness of tasting "solids". You can then introduce a spoon.

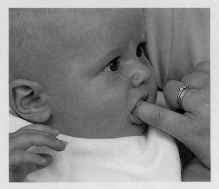

▶ To begin with, offer a small amount of purée from the tip of your scrupulously clean finger and let her suck the food off it.

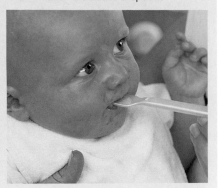

▶ Coat the tip of a soft, shallow weaning spoon with purée. Place the spoon between her lips and let her suck the food off. If she spits the purée out, scrape it up and offer it again.

watch your baby carefully. Whole nuts should not be given before the age of five due to the risk of choking.

• **Honey** Very occasionally, honey can contain a type of bacteria which, if eaten by a baby under the age of one, can produce toxins in the baby's intestine. This can result in a potentially serious illnesss called "infant botulism".

• **High-fibre foods** Excessive amounts of high-fibre foods may interfere with the absorption of important minerals.

If your baby rejects food

Your baby may be one of the many who refuse solids at the first try. Be patient, it doesn't mean that she will never eat them. Wait and try again the next day. Initially, you are offering solids purely to introduce your baby to different foods. It is vital not to cut down on the amount of milk you give as, at this point, solids are not replacing any part of her milk diet. If your baby seems to dislike a certain purée, try mixing it with a familiar or bland taste, such as breast milk, baby rice or puréed potato, to make a gentler introduction. If this does not work, simply stop offering that food and try it again at a later date.

Weaning is unlikely to take an uninterrupted course; there may be days when your baby refuses solids, perhaps if she is feeling unwell or is in an unfamiliar environment, and wants only her comforting milk feed. Don't be anxious about this: a short break from solids will not harm your baby. Try reintroducing solid food after a few days, or prepare a runnier purée that is easier for your baby to swallow. At this early stage, as long as your baby is getting her nutrition from milk, and as long as she continues to gain weight over a period of several days, she is probably getting enough food.

Remember

• Babies are born with a tongue-thrust reflex – if you introduce solids too early your baby will poke out both the food and her tongue almost immediately. This reflex clears any foreign bodies including food out of her mouth and protects her from choking. Some time between four and six months this reflex will disappear.

• Test the temperature of all food. If using defrosted food, reheat until piping hot and leave to cool. Stir well and check that the temperature is lukewarm before offering it to your baby.

• Do not reheat food more than once. Use a small quantity and leave the rest refrigerated.

• Use only breast milk, formula, or cooled boiled tap water to make up purées or to dilute them if they seem too thick.

• Do not save your baby's half-eaten food, as bacteria-carrying saliva from the spoon will have been introduced.

• Do not overload the spoon with purée as this will make your baby splutter.

• When freezing food try to fill containers right to the top without too much of an air pocket above and seal well to maintain the quality of baby purées.

"Gradually introduce coarser textures and new flavours to your baby: mash, grate and finely chop food rather than purée and combine sweet with savoury ingredients."

Exploring tastes

Between six and nine months is a time of rapid development and your baby will spend many more hours awake than previously. It is a good idea to introduce plenty of new flavours, in addition to the ones she already knows. Since everything is new for her, she will be receptive to these changes. This is the stage when solids should become a fixed part of your baby's daily diet.

Moving on from purées

Learning to chew

Every baby develops at her own pace, but your baby's first tooth (a front incisor) will probably be cut at around six to seven months; the remaining incisors usually follow in the next five months. As teeth begin to emerge, you can introduce coarser textures. Your baby will mostly use her gums to chew, so mashed and finely chopped food will provide ample chewing practice. It is not a good idea to offer smooth purées for too long as your baby may become lazy about chewing and have difficulty developing the tongue movements needed to deal with real solids. If she refuses lumpy food, make the transition easier by introducing a little mashed or grated food into her usual purées, or perhaps make a favourite meal in a thicker or coarser form. Introduce wider combinations of ingredients and don't be afraid to mix sweet with savoury: fruit combined with vegetables, fish or meat often appeals to babies.

Milk & dairy products

From the age of six months to one year, babies should have around 600ml (20fl oz) of milk each day, mostly in the form of breast milk or formula. While you can use cow's milk in cooking and with breakfast cereals, breast milk or formula should remain your baby's main drink as these contain nutrients that cow's milk lacks, such as iron and vitamin C.

If your baby is breastfed or if she is taking less than 500ml (17fl oz) a day of a fortified infant milk, the Department of Health recommends a vitamin supplement from six months to two years of age.

A portion of the milk intake can come from dairy products, such as cheese and yogurt or milk used in cooking, such as a cheese sauce. If your baby is not hungry at mealtimes you may find that cutting down on the amount of milk she drinks helps.

With the introduction of solids your baby may become more thirsty than she was on her milk-only diet. If you think this is the case, offer her some water or very dilute fruit juice in a cup at mealtimes once she is six months or older.

New tastes & textures
• wholegrain low-sugar breakfast cereals • rusks • rice cakes • whole-milk fromage frais • hard-boiled eggs • oily fish, such as salmon • organic liver • chicken puréed with carrot • green vegetables • tofu • mangoes • lentils

New foods for your baby

• **Bread and cereals**, including wholemeal bread, rusks, wholegrain low-sugar breakfast cereals (mini wheat biscuits, porridge and hot oat cereal) can now be given. Remember not to introduce gluten before six months. Avoid large amounts of high-fibre foods, such as high-fibre bread or bran flakes – this may fill her up without giving her the nutrients she needs for healthy growth and development.

• **Dairy products**, such as pasteurized whole-milk Greek yogurt and fromage frais; cottage cheese, cream cheese and mild hard cheeses, such as Cheddar and Edam, are excellent nutrient-rich foods. Low-fat foods, such as reduced-fat spreads, are not suitable as they are too low in calories for a growing baby.

• **Eggs**, if hard-boiled, and dishes made with well-cooked eggs, such as eggy fried bread, omelettes, frittatas or scrambled eggs, are fast to cook and nutritious. Do not serve raw or lightly cooked eggs to babies under one year old (there is some risk of salmonella). The white and yolk should both be cooked until solid.

• **Fish fillets**, such as plaice or cod, may be made into a purée with root vegetables or green vegetables such as courgette or broccoli, or perhaps blended into a homemade cheese sauce. Oily fish, such as sardines, salmon and tuna, are good sources of essential fatty acids, which are important for brain development. Carefully check all fish for bones before serving.

• **Red meat**, such as lean minced beef or lamb, can be combined with sautéed onion, potato and mushrooms then finely chopped in a blender. Organic liver, which is easily digested, provides the best source of iron. Slow-cooked lamb, pork or beef casseroles make good purées.

• **Chicken** is generally popular with babies because of its mild taste. Serve it chopped or puréed, casseroled or poached. It combines well with root vegetables, such as potato and carrot, and with fruits such as dessert apple, grapes, mango or papaya.

• **Vegetables**, including onions, leeks, cabbage, kale, green beans, spinach and other leafy green vegetables, red peppers, tomatoes, sweetcorn, peas and mushrooms, greatly expand the dietary repertoire. Frozen vegetables often retain as many nutrients as fresh ones.

• **Fruits**, particularly mangoes, grapes (peeled, deseeded and halved), citrus and berry fruits, can be served. Remove the pith from citrus fruits and sieve out seeds from berries. Be aware that berry and citrus fruits can cause redness around the mouth in babies and children with eczema. This is an irritant effect, however, and rarely due to allergy.

• **Beans and pulses** are ideal for boosting meat purées, and are especially valuable for vegetarian babies. Lentils and dried pulses (such as split peas or butter beans) are a good source of protein and iron. Tofu (soya bean curd) is a good meat alternative.

Remember
• If you begin weaning before six months, do not introduce gluten to your baby's diet before she is six months old.

• Do not serve raw or lightly cooked eggs to babies under one year old.

• Berry and citrus fruits can cause redness around the mouth in babies and children with eczema. This is an irritant effect, and rarely due to allergy. As always, consult a doctor if you are concerned.

First tastes

Very first foods must be easy to digest and made of ingredients that will gently accustom your baby to new flavours and textures. Although your baby may like quite strong flavours, such as sweet potato, parsnip or carrot, many babies prefer to begin with blander tastes, such as milky baby rice or a potato purée. To begin with, purées should be runny and absolutely smooth, similar to runny yogurt in consistency, and made up of only one or two ingredients.

1 Baby rice
Baby rice has a fine texture and is easily digested. Its milky taste makes for an easy transition to solids. Mix with cooled boiled tap water, breast milk or formula.

2 Potato purée
The mild taste of potato makes it a good weaning food. Boil and mash floury textured potatoes and press through a sieve. (See First vegetable purée, page 37.)

3 Carrot purée
The sweet taste of carrots appeals to babies. Steam or boil, and blend with a little cooking water. (See First vegetable purée, page 37.)

4 Broccoli & potato purée
Broccoli is a good source of vitamins. Combine with sieved boiled potato or puréed sweet potato for a creamy purée. (See page 39.)

5 Baby rice & dried apricot
Dried apricots are rich in iron and beta-carotene. Purée with baby rice for a gentle introduction to the fruit. (See Dried apricot purée, page 38.)

6 Apple purée
Sweet eating apples make a smooth apple sauce. Try combining with some puréed pear for a tasty combination. (See First fruit purée, page 36.)

7 Banana purée
A fully ripe banana makes an instant purée when well mashed. Make it less sticky by adding a little breast milk or formula. (See First fruit purée, page 36.)

8 Pear purée
Ripe pear, steamed until soft or cooked in a heavy-based pan, is an ideal first food. Combine with baby rice for a creamy finish. (See First fruit purée, page 36.)

9 Papaya purée
A fully ripe papaya needs no cooking. A rich source of antioxidants, it has a naturally sweet flavour. (See First fruit purée, page 36.)

10 Parsnip & carrot purée
Parsnip has a distinctly sweet taste that babies enjoy. Cook in the same way as carrots. It combines well with apple, too.

11 Butternut squash or pumpkin purée
Both these vegetables are good sources of vitamin A. Steam or boil until tender, then purée. (See page 39.)

12 Sweet potato purée
Orange-fleshed sweet potato is an excellent source of vitamin A and babies like its naturally sweet taste. Steam or boil until tender.

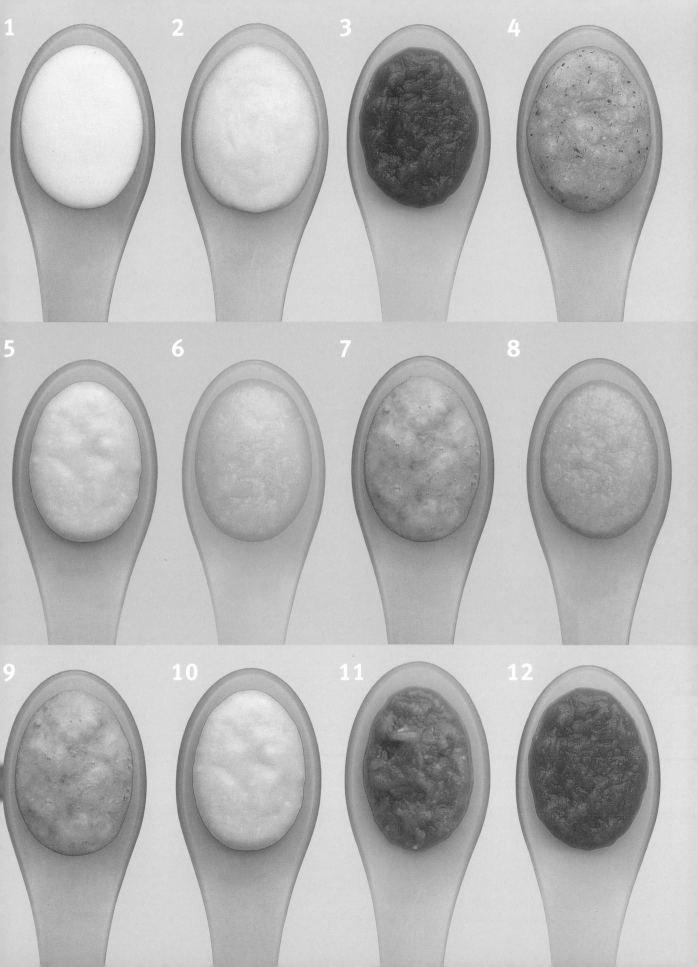

First fruit purée

⟳ Preparation: 5 minutes; cooking: 8 minutes for apples, 3–4 minutes for pears

◔ Makes 6 portions   ❄ Suitable for freezing

Fruit purées make ideal first meals. Choose only sweet fruit that is completely ripe for your baby. Once he is accustomed to eating an apple or a pear purée on its own, try combining the two fruits to give him a taste of a mixed flavour. This purée will be a little thinner than vegetable purées.

▶ Chop your chosen fruit into small, even-sized pieces. Put these pieces into a heavy-based saucepan with the water or apple juice. (If the pears are ripe, you may not need water or juice.) Cover the pan and cook over a low heat until the fruit is tender. Or steam the fruit for the same length of cooking times (see above).

▶ Blend the fruit to a smooth purée using a hand blender. Add a little boiled water, apple juice or water from the steamer to thin the purée (see page 22).

▶ Spoon a little purée into your baby's bowl and serve lukewarm. Pour the remainder into an ice-cube tray and freeze (see page 22).

Variation

▶ Mash a raw banana or half a papaya and purée with a little breast milk or formula. If necessary, the banana can be heated in a microwave for a few seconds to make it easier to mash. These variations are not suitable for freezing.

2 medium **sweet eating apples** or ripe **pears**, peeled and cored

3 tbsp **boiled water** or **pure apple juice**

TIP All fruits for very first purées, except for banana, papaya and avocado, must be cooked. A month after beginning to wean your baby, you can use raw pear, peach, mango, plum and melon, if they are ripe and juicy.

TIP You can thicken pear purée by stirring in a little baby rice.

First vegetable purée

⟳ Preparation: 5 minutes; cooking: 15–20 minutes ⊘ Makes 8 portions
❄ Suitable for freezing

Your baby's first foods should be mild in taste, easy to digest, completely smooth and unlikely to provoke an allergic reaction. Begin with single-ingredient purées in the first week or two, then progress to combinations of root vegetables (see pages 26–29).

▶ Chop the vegetables into small pieces. Put in a steamer or colander set over boiling water and cook for about 15–20 minutes, or until tender. Alternatively, place in a pan, pour over just enough boiling water to cover and simmer, covered, for 15 minutes, or until soft.
▶ Blend the vegetable to a purée using some of the liquid from the bottom of the steamer or the pan (see page 22).

▶ Spoon a little purée into your baby's bowl and serve lukewarm. Pour the remainder into an ice-cube tray and freeze (see page 22).

Variation
▶ Substitute other root vegetables, such as parsnip or swede. Chop, cook and blend as described above.

250g (8oz) **carrots, potatoes, sweet potatoes, butternut squash** or **pumpkin**, peeled

TIP The amount of liquid needed when blending depends on whether your baby finds swallowing difficult. A general rule is to make an absolutely smooth, very runny purée, akin to runny yogurt.

TIP Do not purée potato or sweet potato in a food processor as the mixture will become starchy and gluey. Use a mouli or sieve.

Creamy vegetable purée

⟳ Preparation: 5 minutes; cooking: 2 minutes ⊘ Makes 6 portions
❄ Suitable for freezing

Strong-tasting root vegetable purées, such as parsnip or carrot, may be made milder with the addition of baby rice. Baby rice also combines well with steamed and puréed broccoli and cauliflower.

▶ Mix together the baby rice and milk, according to the packet instructions, and stir into the vegetable purée until thoroughly combined.

▶ Spoon a little purée into your baby's bowl and serve lukewarm. Pour the remainder into an ice-cube tray and freeze (see page 22).

1 tbsp sugar-free, vitamin- and iron-enriched **baby rice**

3 tbsp **breast milk** or **formula**

4 tbsp **first vegetable purée** (see above)

Fruity baby rice

⟳ Preparation: 5 minutes; cooking: 2 minutes ⊘ Makes 6 portions
❄ Suitable for freezing

Baby rice is a valuable first food: it is easily digested and has a milky taste that helps to ease your baby's transition from a purely milk diet to solids. It may be served plain or combined with a purée.

▶ Mix together the baby rice and milk, according to the packet instructions, and stir into the fruit purée to give it a slightly creamy texture.

▶ Spoon a little purée into your baby's bowl and serve lukewarm. Pour the remainder into an ice-cube tray and freeze (see page 22).

1 tbsp sugar-free, vitamin- and iron-enriched **baby rice**

3 tbsp **breast milk** or **formula**

4 tbsp **first fruit purée** (see opposite)

TIP Pear, peach or plum purée mixed with baby rice are often popular with babies.

Simple fruit & vegetable purées

"Start with single, bland purées then gradually introduce stronger flavours and combinations of foods."

Once first tastes have been accepted, you can introduce a wider variety of fruits and vegetables to your baby. Some babies may find certain foods, such as dried apricot, mango or cauliflower, indigestible. If this is the case, try mixing them with other foods such as banana or root vegetables or leave them out of your child's diet until he is a little older.

Melon

Take a small wedge of melon, remove the seeds and cut the flesh away from the skin, discarding the greener flesh near the skin. Blend to a purée of the desired consistency. Combines well with mashed banana or avocado. Makes 1 serving.

Peach or nectarine

Score a cross on the base of a small, ripe peach or nectarine, then submerge in boiling water for 1 minute. Skin and chop the peach flesh, then purée in a blender. (Ripe, sweet peaches and nectarines can be used raw.) Makes 2 servings.

Dried apricot

Simmer a handful of dried apricots in a little water for about 5 minutes, or until tender. Blend to a purée of the desired consistency with as much cooking liquid as is needed to make a smooth pulp. Work the pulp through a mouli or strong-meshed sieve to remove the fibrous skins. Dried apricot purée is also good mixed with baby rice or puréed apple or pear. Makes 4 servings.

Avocado

Choose a soft, ripe fruit and prepare when your baby is ready to eat (to avoid discolouration). Halve one avocado, scoop out the stone and mash the flesh from one half with a folk or purée to the desired consistency with about 2 tablespoons of breast milk or formula. Makes 1 serving.

Cauliflower or broccoli purée

Place 250g (8oz) of small cauliflower or broccoli florets in a steamer and cook until tender, about 10 minutes. Drain and blend to a purée. Mix with potato purée (see First vegetable purée, page 37) or baby rice. Makes 6 servings.

Courgette

Place 250g (8oz) trimmed and sliced courgettes in a steamer and cook until tender, about 12 minutes. Alternatively, put in a pan with water to cover, bring to the boil and simmer for 6 minutes. Blend to a purée. Makes 8 servings.

Butternut squash or pumpkin

Peel and deseed a 500g (1lb) squash or slice of pumpkin, then cut into small pieces. Cook as described for First vegetable purée on page 37, then blend to a purée, adding a little cooking water if necessary. Alternatively, cut the squash in half, or cut a wedge of pumpkin, scoop out the seeds and brush with melted butter. Cover with foil and bake in the oven preheated to 180°C/350°F/ gas 4 for 1½ hours, or until tender. Makes 8 servings.

Sweet potato

Scrub 300g (10oz) sweet potatoes, pat dry and prick with a fork. Bake in the oven preheated to 200°C/400°F/gas 6 for 45 minutes to 1 hour. Scoop out the flesh and mash with 1–2 tablespoons of breast milk or formula. Alternatively, peel and cube the sweet potatoes and cook as described for First vegetable purée. This purée blends well with apple, peach or broccoli purées. Makes 8 servings.

Nutrition matters

- **Cantaloupe melons** are the most nutritious of all the melon varieties – they are rich in vitamin C and also provide beta-carotene and potassium.

- **Peaches** provide vitamin C.

- **Nectarines** provide vitamin C and potassium.

- **Dried, ready-to-eat apricots** provide beta-carotene, iron and potassium, and are particularly useful when seasonal fruits are scarce.

- **Avocado** provides potassium and vitamins B6 and E. It has a buttery flavour and texture that is usually popular with babies.

- **Cauliflower** provides folate, potassium and vitamin C.

- **Broccoli** provides beta-carotene, folate, potassium and vitamin C.

- **Courgette** provides beta-carotene, potassium, vitamin C and magnesium, but most of the nutrients lie in the skin, so do not peel.

- **Butternut squash** provides beta-carotene, potassium, and vitamins C and E.

- **Pumpkin** provides beta-carotene and vitamin C.

- **Orange-fleshed sweet potato** is an excellent source of beta-carotene, potassium, and vitamins C and E.

New tastes & textures

Once your baby has adjusted to simple purées, you can begin to introduce a broader range of flavours and textures. Keep textures smooth until your baby can cope well with chewing and swallowing. Then, gradually introduce purées with thicker or lumpier textures, beginning with familiar flavours. Try adding just a little grated or mashed food to a smooth purée, or make your baby's favourite purée in a lumpier form. You can also combine more ingredients to make interesting flavours. Don't be afraid to mix sweet with savoury: fruit with puréed chicken or fish, for example, is a favourite with many babies.

1 Tomato & cauliflower gratin
This blended gratin makes a good introduction to cauliflower. Cheddar cheese and deseeded tomatoes boost the flavour. (See page 49 for recipe.)

2 Spinach, potato, parsnip & leek purée
It's a good idea to combine stronger-tasting vegetables such as spinach with root vegetables or cheese sauce. (See page 48 for recipe.)

3 Fish with carrots & orange
This purée made with fresh white fish has a delicious combination of flavours and is bursting with useful nutrients. (See page 51 for recipe.)

4 Peach, apple & strawberry purée
Make this purée when peaches are in season and soft fruit is perfectly ripe and sweet. It can be mixed with baby rice for a milder taste. (See page 45 for recipe.)

5 First chicken casserole
Combining tender chicken breast with sweet root vegetables gives it a flavour and smooth texture that appeals to babies. (See page 53 for recipe.)

6 Banana with mango or papaya
Sweet ripe mango or papaya blended with banana makes a fruity, nutritious no-cook meal. (See page 42 for recipe.)

Remember

• Foods such as mashed banana or papaya make perfect fresh baby food in no time at all.

• Raw fruits are best since none of the nutrients are lost in cooking. Do make sure that the fruit is ripe and sweet – it is a good idea to taste it yourself.

Nutrition matters

• **Bananas** provide potassium and vitamin B6.

• **Papaya** provides beta-carotene, magnesium and vitamin C.

• **Mangoes** provide beta-carotene and vitamins C and E.

• **Blueberries** provide vitamin C.

• **Apples** provide vitamin C.

• **Plums** provide potassium.

• **Fresh apricots** provide beta-carotene and vitamin C.

• **Pears** provide vitamin C.

• **Strawberries** provide folate and vitamin C.

• **Cottage cheese** provides calcium, protein and vitamins B2 and B12.

• **Yogurt** provides calcium, protein and vitamins B2 and B12.

• **Chicken** provides iron (especially dark meat), protein, potassium, B vitamins and zinc.

TIP It is best to prepare these purées just before your baby is ready to eat.

Instant no-cook purées

There are many fast, no-cook purées that are both delicious and nutritious for your baby. Here are some good fruit combinations to try. Each recipe on these two pages makes one portion. For the apple purée plus three fruits recipe, you can mix and match fresh fruit with some unsweetened apple purée, either homemade (perhaps defrost a couple of ice-tray cubes) or bought. If you don't have apple purée in the freezer you could use pear, or apple and pear purée.

Mango & banana

Purée or mash the flesh of a quarter of a small, ripe mango together with half a small, ripe banana, peeled and sliced. Serve immediately.

Avocado & banana or papaya

Mash a quarter of a small avocado together with half a small, ripe banana and 1–2 tablespoons of breast milk or formula. You can substitute the flesh of half a papaya for the banana in this recipe – the milk is then optional.

Banana & blueberry

Cut a medium-sized, ripe banana into pieces and simply blend together with 30g (1oz) blueberries. Serve immediately.

Apple purée plus three fruits

Combine one ripe peach, skinned and cut into pieces, one small, ripe banana, peeled and sliced, 30g (1oz) blueberries and 2 tablespoons of apple purée, and purée in a blender. For older babies simply mash the fruit and mix with the apple purée.

Plum or apricot & pear

Peel and stone a ripe apricot or plum. Slice the fruit and purée or mash the flesh with the chopped soft flesh of a ripe pear. This purée is suitable for freezing.

Cantaloupe melon & strawberry

Blend together half a ripe cantaloupe melon, peeled and cut into chunks, with two strawberries, hulled and cut in half. Stir in 2 teaspoons of baby rice.

Papaya & cottage cheese or yogurt

Cut a small, ripe papaya in half, remove the black seeds and purée or mash the flesh of one half with 1 tablespoon of sieved cottage cheese or Greek yogurt.

Papaya & chicken

Cut a small, ripe papaya in half, remove the black seeds and purée or mash the flesh of one of the halves with 30g (1oz) of cooked, boneless, skinless chicken. This purée is suitable for freezing.

"Once your baby is happily taking her first pureés, you can start to experiment with different combinations. Fruits blend well together and are always popular."

2 ripe **pears**, peeled, cored and chopped

2 stoned **prunes**, chopped

1 tbsp **baby rice**

Juicy pear & prune purée

↻ Preparation: 5 minutes; cooking: 5 minutes ✓ Makes 2 portions

⚡ Provides fibre, potassium and vitamin C ❋ Suitable for freezing

This tasty combination of fresh and dried fruits is a useful source of fibre.

▶ Simmer the fruit in a saucepan with a little water for 5 minutes. Purée to the desired consistency, using as much cooking water as needed. Sieve to get rid of the tough prune skins.

▶ Stir in the baby rice while warm.

1 **sweet eating apple**, peeled, cored and chopped

1 ripe **pear**, peeled, cored and chopped

50g (1³⁄₄oz) **strawberries**, hulled and cut into quarters

40g (1¹⁄₂oz) **blueberries**

2 tbsp **baby rice**

Apple, pear, blueberry & strawberry purée

↻ Preparation: 3 minutes; cooking: 5 minutes ✓ Makes 2 portions

⚡ Provides fibre, potassium and vitamin C ❋ Suitable for freezing

▶ Put all the fruit into a heavy-based saucepan, cover and cook over a low heat for about 5 minutes. Purée in a blender and stir in the baby rice.

Variation

Instead of baby rice you could, if you prefer, mix with banana.

Apricot, pear, peach & apple compôte

⏱ Preparation: 5 minutes; cooking: 10 minutes 🥄 Makes 4 portions

🥕 Provides beta-carotene, fibre and vitamin C ❄ Suitable for freezing

3 ready-to-eat **dried apricots** or **fresh apricots**, chopped

1 **sweet eating apple**, peeled, cored and chopped

1 large, ripe **pear**, peeled, cored and chopped

1 large, ripe **peach** or **plum**, peeled, stoned and chopped

▶ Place all the chopped fruit in a saucepan and simmer with a little water until soft, about 8–10 minutes.
▶ Blend the mixture to a purée of the desired consistency.

Variation

For a creamier finish to this compôte, mix 2 tablespoons of baby rice with 4 tablespoons of breast milk or formula and blend this with the fruit purée.

Peach, apple & strawberry purée

⏱ Preparation: 5 minutes; cooking: 9–12 minutes 🥄 Makes 4 portions

🥕 Provides fibre and vitamin C ❄ Suitable for freezing

1 **sweet eating apple**, peeled, cored and chopped

1 large, ripe **peach**, peeled, stoned and chopped

3 large **strawberries**, hulled

This is a delicious fruit purée to make in the summer. It can be combined with some baby rice mixed with a little milk or water.

▶ Steam the apple for about 6 minutes, or until tender. Add the peach and strawberries to the steamer, and continue to cook for about 3 minutes. Blend the fruits to a smooth purée.

NOTE Strawberries occasionally provoke an allergic reaction in sensitive babies.

Peach & banana purée

⏱ Preparation: 5 minutes; cooking: 3 minutes 🥄 Makes 1 portion

🥕 Provides potassium and vitamins B6 and C

1 small, ripe **peach**, peeled, stoned and chopped

1/2 small **banana**, peeled and sliced

1 tbsp freshly squeezed **orange juice**

Instead of peach you could use a nectarine or two sweet, juicy plums to make this purée.

▶ Put all the ingredients into a small saucepan, cover and cook over a low heat for 2–3 minutes, or until the fruit is slightly mushy. Blend to a purée. Allow to cool before serving.

Apple & pear, with raisins & cinnamon

⏱ Preparation: 5 minutes; cooking: 8 minutes 🥄 Makes 4 portions

🥕 Provides fibre, potassium and vitamin C ❄ Suitable for freezing

1 **sweet eating apple**, peeled, cored and chopped

1 ripe **pear**, peeled, cored and chopped

1 tbsp **raisins**

1 tbsp pure **apple juice**

a generous pinch of **cinnamon**

▶ Put all the ingredients into a saucepan, bring to the simmer, then cover and cook for 5 minutes. Blend to a purée and allow to cool a little.

Yogurt & mango purée

½ small, ripe **mango**, peeled and chopped

3–4 tbsp mild, full-fat **natural yogurt**

🕐 Preparation: 5 minutes 🥄 Makes 2 portions 💉 Provides beta-carotene, calcium, fibre, potassium, protein and vitamins B2, B12, C and E

Always choose whole milk yogurt for babies – Greek or live natural yogurts are good. Fresh peach or dried apricot purée both also work well mixed with yogurt.

▶ Purée the mango using a hand-held blender and mix together with the yogurt.

Banana, prunes & yogurt

1 small, ripe **banana**, peeled

2 ready-to-eat, stoned **dried prunes**, chopped

2 tbsp mild, full-fat **natural yogurt**

🕐 Preparation: 2 minutes 🥄 Makes 1 portion
💉 Provides calcium, fibre, potassium, protein and vitamins B2, B6, B12 and C

▶ Simply chop the banana and prunes into pieces.

▶ Purée together using a hand-held blender and stir in the yogurt.

Apricot & banana custard

50g (1¾oz) **semi-dried apricots**, roughly chopped

100ml (3½fl oz) **boiling water**

1 small, ripe **banana**, peeled and sliced

1 tbsp **custard powder**

🕐 Preparation: 5 minutes; cooking: 5 minutes 🥄 Makes 2 portions
💉 Provides beta-carotene, iron, potassium and vitamins B6 and C

Check the label of the semi-dried apricots to make sure they have not been treated with suphur dioxide (E220) to preserve the bright orange colour, as this substance can trigger an asthma attack in susceptible babies.

▶ Put the apricots into a small saucepan and pour over 50ml (1¾ fl oz) boiling water. Simmer for 2–3 minutes. Blend the apricots and cooking liquid together with the banana.

▶ Put the custard powder in a small saucepan and mix in a little of the boiling water to make a paste. Pour over the rest of the boiling water and stir briskly over a medium heat until smooth and creamy.

▶ Mix the custard together with the apricot and banana purée.

Butternut squash & apple

500g (1lb) **butternut squash** or **pumpkin**, peeled, deseeded and chopped

1 **sweet eating apple**, peeled, cored and chopped

🕐 Preparation: 5 minutes; cooking: 17 minutes 🥄 Makes 4 portions
💉 Provides beta-carotene, fibre, folate and vitamin C ❄ Suitable for freezing

Mixing vegetables with fruit is a good way to encourage babies to eat vegetables.

▶ Put the butternut squash in a steamer and cook for about 7 minutes. Add the apple to the steamer and continue to cook for 10 minutes, or until the squash is tender. Blend to a smooth purée.

Variation

▶ Omit the apple and blend the cooked squash or pumpkin with a large, juicy, skinned raw peach.

Homemade vegetable stock

⏱ Preparation: 10 minutes; cooking: 1 hour 10 minutes   🥄 Makes 850ml (29fl oz)
🥄 Provides beta-carotene, folate and potassium   ❄ Suitable for freezing

It's easy to make a homemade vegetable stock that will keep in the fridge for up to a week. Use this to form the basis of your purées, rather than relying on salt-filled, shop-bought stock cubes.

▶ Roughly chop all the vegetables. Heat the olive oil in a large, thick-bottomed pan and add the vegetables and garlic. Sweat the vegetables in the oil without colouring for 5 minutes – cover with a lid if you like.

▶ Add the cold water and bring to the boil. Add the herbs, bay leaf and peppercorns. Reduce the heat, cover and simmer for 1 hour.

▶ Leave to cool for a couple of hours, then strain through a sieve. Squeeze remaining juices out of the vegetables by pushing them down in the sieve with a potato masher.

1 **onion**, peeled

1 **garlic clove**, peeled and roughly chopped

2 large **carrots**, peeled

1 large **leek**, washed

1 stick **celery**

1 tbsp **olive oil**

850ml (29fl oz) **water**

1 sprig of **parsley**

1 sprig of **thyme** (optional)

1 **bay leaf**

4 **peppercorns**

Cheesy leek, sweet potato & cauliflower

⏱ Preparation: 5 minutes; cooking: 15 minutes   🥄 Makes 5 portions
🥄 Provides beta-carotene, calcium, folate, potassium, protein and vitamins A, B2, B12 and C
❄ Suitable for freezing

As well as fruit and vegetables, it's good to add foods such as cheese to your baby's meals. Babies grow very rapidly in their first year and cheese provides a concentrated source of calories, which is important for growth.

▶ Heat the butter in a pan and add the leek. Sauté for about 3 minutes until softened. Add the sweet potato, pour over the water and cook for 5 minutes.

▶ Add the cauliflower and continue to cook for 5 minutes.

▶ Strain the vegetables, reserving the cooking liquid. Blend the vegetables together with about 100ml (3½ fl oz) of the reserved cooking liquid and the grated Cheddar cheese.

15g (½oz) **butter**

25g (¾oz) **leek**, washed and sliced

1 **sweet potato**, peeled and cut into chunks

225ml (8fl oz) **boiling water**

75g (2½oz) **cauliflower**, cut into florets

25g (¾oz) grated **Cheddar cheese**

Trio of root vegetables

⏱ Preparation: 5 minutes; cooking: 21 minutes   🥄 Makes 6 portions
🥄 Provides beta-carotene, fibre, folate and potassium   ❄ Suitable for freezing

Babies tend to love root vegetables because of their naturally sweet flavour.

▶ Put the vegetables into a saucepan and just cover with boiling water. Cook over a medium heat for about 20 minutes, or until tender. Alternatively, steam them until tender.

▶ Blend the vegetables to a smooth purée with about 125ml (4fl oz) of the cooking liquid, or use boiled water from the bottom of the steamer.

175g (6oz) **carrots**, peeled and chopped

175g (6oz) **potatoes**, peeled and chopped

125g (4oz) **parsnips** or **swede**, peeled and chopped

30g (1oz) **butter**

1 **leek,** white part only, washed and sliced

175g (6oz) **potatoes,** peeled and chopped

250ml (8fl oz) unsalted **vegetable stock** (see page 47) or **chicken stock** (see page 52) or **water**

60g (2oz) **frozen peas**

Potato, leek & pea purée

⟳ Preparation: 5 minutes; cooking: 24 minutes ⚥ Makes 4 portions
⚡ Provides fibre, folate and vitamins A and C ❄ Suitable for freezing

Use only fresh unsalted stock for this recipe, bought or homemade. To make this purée into a delicious soup for the family, simply add extra stock and seasoning.

▶ Warm the butter in a pan, add the leek and sauté until just golden, 5–6 minutes. Add the potatoes and pour over the stock. Bring to the boil, then reduce the heat, cover and simmer for 10 minutes.

▶ Add the frozen peas and continue to cook for about 6 minutes, or until the vegetables are tender. Blend to a purée using a mouli or sieve.

30g (1oz) **butter**

50g (1³⁄₄oz) **leek,** white part only, washed and finely sliced

250g (8oz) **potatoes,** peeled and chopped

100g (3¹⁄₂oz) **parsnips,** peeled and chopped

250ml (8fl oz) **boiling water** or unsalted **vegetable stock** (see page 47)

100g (3¹⁄₂oz) **fresh spinach,** washed and tough stalks removed, or 50g (1³⁄₄oz) **frozen spinach**

40g (1¹⁄₄oz) grated **Cheddar cheese**

Spinach, potato, parsnip & leek purée

⟳ Preparation: 10 minutes; cooking: 30 minutes ⚥ Makes 6 portions ⚡ Provides beta-carotene, fibre, folate, potassium, protein and vitamins A and C ❄ Suitable for freezing

▶ Melt the butter in a saucepan, add the leek and sauté for 2–3 minutes. Add the potatoes and parsnips, sauté for 1 minute, then pour over the boiling water or stock. Cover and simmer for 12 minutes.
▶ Add the fresh spinach leaves, if using, and continue to cook for 3–4 minutes. If using frozen spinach, cook it separately, according to the instructions on the packet, drain and then mix with the potato, leek and parsnip. Drain the vegetables, reserving the cooking liquid.
▶ Blend the vegetables together with about 50ml (1³⁄₄fl oz) of the cooking liquid and the grated Cheddar. Add more liquid if necessary to thin the purée.

Lentil & vegetable purée

🔄 Preparation: 10 minutes; cooking: 40 minutes 🥄 Makes 8 portions
🍴 Provides beta-carotene, fibre, folate, protein and vitamin C ❄ Suitable for freezing

Lentils are a good source of protein. However, some babies find lentils indigestible and so they are best not given before eight months.

▶ Melt the butter in a saucepan, add the leeks and sauté for 2–3 minutes. Stir in the celery, carrots and lentils, and cook for 2 minutes more.
▶ Add the sweet potatoes and bay leaf, and pour over the stock or water. Bring to the boil, then reduce the heat, cover and simmer for about 30 minutes, or until the vegetables and lentils are tender. Remove the bay leaf.
▶ Blend to a purée for younger babies. Older babies can eat it as it is.

30g (1oz) **butter**

125g (4oz) **leeks,** washed and finely sliced

30g (1oz) **celery,** chopped

125g (4oz) **carrots,** peeled and chopped

60g (2oz) **red lentils**

250g (8oz) **sweet potatoes,** peeled and chopped

1 **bay leaf**

475ml (16fl oz) unsalted **vegetable stock** (see page 47) or **chicken stock** (see page 52) or **water**

Sweet potato, carrot & broccoli purée

🔄 Preparation: 5 minutes; cooking: 18 minutes 🥄 Makes 6 portions
🍴 Provides beta-carotene, fibre, folate and vitamin C ❄ Suitable for freezing

It can be a good idea to combine popular vegetables with varieties that children tend to favour a little less. In this recipe, I have used carrot and sweet potato, which babies usually love to eat, to tone down the strong flavour of broccoli.

▶ Put the sweet potatoes and carrot in a steamer and cook for 10 minutes. Add the broccoli and continue to cook for about 7 minutes, or until all the vegetables are tender.
▶ Blend the vegetables with 6–7 tablespoons of water from the bottom of the steamer to make a purée.

300g (10oz) **sweet potatoes,** peeled and chopped

1 large **carrot,** peeled and sliced

125g (4oz) **broccoli,** cut into florets

Tomato & cauliflower gratin

🔄 Preparation: 5 minutes; cooking: 20 minutes 🥄 Makes 4 portions
🍴 Provides beta-carotene, folate, protein and vitamins A, B12 and C ❄ Suitable for freezing

▶ Put the cauliflower florets in a steamer and cook until soft, about 12 minutes.
▶ Meanwhile, warm the butter in a pan, add the tomatoes and sauté until mushy. Remove from the heat and add the cheese, stirring until melted. Mix the cauliflower with the tomato and cheese sauce, then blend to the desired consistency.

Variation

▶ Steam the cauliflower until soft, then blend it with 3 tablespoons of cheese sauce (see page 77), omitting the seasoning from the sauce.

150g (5oz) **cauliflower,** cut into florets

30g (1oz) **butter**

250g (8oz) **tomatoes,** skinned, deseeded and roughly chopped

30g (1oz) grated **Cheddar cheese**

1 small **onion**, peeled and chopped

1 medium **carrot**, peeled and chopped

25g (1oz) **red pepper**, cored, deseeded and chopped

1 tbsp **vegetable oil**

2 tbsp **red lentils**

250ml (8½fl oz) **boiling water** or unsalted **vegetable stock** (see page 47)

50g (1¾oz) grated **Cheddar cheese**

Lentil purée with carrot & sweet pepper

↻ Preparation: 10 minutes; cooking: 34 minutes   ⌀ Makes 3 portions   ⚷ Provides beta-carotene, calcium, fibre, potassium, protein and vitamins B12 and C   ❆ Suitable for freezing

▶ Sauté the onion, carrot and red pepper in the vegetable oil for about 3–4 minutes. Rinse the lentils, add them to the pan and pour over the boiling water or vegetable stock.

▶ Cover and simmer for 25–30 minutes or until the lentils are quite mushy. Top up with a little more water if necessary but there should be only a little liquid left in the pan at the end.

▶ Stir in the Cheddar cheese and purée using a hand-held blender.

125g (4oz) **potatoes**, peeled and chopped

125g (4oz) **carrots**, peeled and sliced

125g (4oz) **cod fillet**, skinned

3 **peppercorns**

1 **bay leaf**

1 sprig of **parsley**

100ml (3½fl oz) **milk**

15g (½oz) **butter**

1 **tomato**, skinned, deseeded and chopped

Fillet of cod with a trio of vegetables

↻ Preparation: 10 minutes; cooking: 25 minutes   ⌀ Makes 4 portions   ⚷ Provides beta-carotene, protein, B vitamins including folate and vitamin C   ❆ Suitable for freezing

Because the proportion of fish to vegetables is quite small, this dish has a fairly mild taste and it makes a gentle introduction to fish for your baby.

▶ Put the vegetables in a saucepan and cover with water. Bring to the boil, then reduce the heat, cover and cook for 20 minutes, or until tender.

▶ Meanwhile, put the fish in a pan with the peppercorns, bay leaf and parsley. Pour over the milk, then poach the fish for about 5 minutes, or until it flakes easily. Strain the milk from the fish and reserve. Discard the flavourings.

▶ Melt the butter in a pan, add the tomato and sauté until mushy. Flake the fish with a fork, checking carefully for bones. Drain the vegetables, then add to the fish with the tomato and 60ml (2fl oz) of the reserved milk. Blend to a purée.

150g (5oz) **plaice fillet**, skinned

3 **peppercorns**

1 **bay leaf**

1 sprig of **parsley**

150ml (5fl oz) **milk**

50g (1¾oz) **broccoli**, cut into florets

30g (1oz) **butter**

1 tbsp **plain flour**

45g (1½oz) grated **Cheddar** or **Edam cheese**

TIP Use spinach or courgette instead of broccoli if you prefer.

Plaice with cheese sauce & broccoli

↻ Preparation: 5 minutes; cooking: 15 minutes   ⌀ Makes 4 portions   ⚷ Provides beta-carotene, calcium, potassium, protein, B vitamins including folate and vitamin A   ❆ Suitable for freezing

▶ Put the fish in a pan with the peppercorns, herbs and milk. Bring to the boil, then simmer, covered, for about 3 minutes or until the fish flakes easily. Strain the milk and reserve. Discard the flavourings. Flake the fish with a fork, checking carefully for bones.

▶ Meanwhile, steam the broccoli for about 5 minutes or until tender.

▶ Melt the butter in a saucepan, stir in the flour and cook over a gentle heat for 1 minute. Gradually add the reserved milk, bring to the boil and cook, stirring until thickened. Remove the sauce from the heat and add the cheese, stirring until melted. Purée the fish with the broccoli and cheese sauce.

Fish with carrots & orange

Preparation: 5 minutes; cooking: 20 minutes ▪ Microwave on high or conventional oven at 180°C/350°F/gas 4 ▪ Makes 6 portions ▪ Provides beta-carotene, calcium, protein and B vitamins including folate ▪ Suitable for freezing

This purée is rich in vitamins and calcium, and bursting with flavour. Plaice is an excellent fish to choose for young babies as it has a very soft texture.

▶ Put the carrots and potatoes in a pan, cover with water and boil until soft. Alternatively, place them in a steamer and cook until tender.

▶ Meanwhile, place the fish in a gratin dish, pour over the orange juice, scatter over the cheese and dot with butter. Cover, leaving an air vent, and microwave on high for 3 minutes, or until the fish flakes easily. Alternatively, cover with foil and cook in the preheated oven for about 20 minutes.

▶ Flake the fish with a fork, checking carefully for bones. Add the vegetables to the fish and its juices, then blend to a purée of the desired consistency.

175g (6oz) **carrots**, peeled and sliced

125g (4oz) **potatoes**, peeled and chopped

175g (6oz) **plaice fillets**

juice of 1 **orange**

60g (2oz) grated **mild Cheddar cheese**

knob of **butter**

1 large **chicken** with **giblets**, cut into 8 pieces and trimmed of excess fat, or 1 or 2 cooked **roast chicken carcasses**, cut into pieces (no giblets)

3 litres (100fl oz) **water**

2 large **onions**, peeled and roughly chopped

3 large **carrots**, peeled and roughly sliced

2 **parsnips**, peeled and roughly chopped

2 **leeks**, washed and sliced

1 **celery stalk**

2 sprigs of **parsley**

1 sprig of **thyme** (optional)

2 or 3 **chicken stock cubes** (for babies over one year old only)

NOTE *Do not use stock cubes or paste in food for babies under one year as these products contain large amounts of salt.*

Grandma's chicken soup & stock

🕐 Preparation: 10 minutes plus 4 hours refrigeration; cooking: 2 hours
🥄 Makes 1.85 litres (65fl oz)   💊 Provides beta-carotene, folate and potassium
❄️ Suitable for freezing

I use fresh chicken stock as the base for many of my recipes. It isn't difficult to prepare and will keep in the fridge for two days. This also makes a delicious soup for older family members if you add some seasoning and chicken stock cubes and maybe some cooked pasta, such as vermicelli or tiny pasta shapes. Chicken soup, sometimes known as Jewish Penicillin, is well known for its medicinal properties, so is good to give to your children when they are unwell.

▶ Put the raw or cooked chicken pieces into a very large pan and cover with the water. Slowly bring to the boil and skim off any scum that comes to the surface.
▶ Add all the remaining ingredients, including the stock cubes if making for older children. Cover and simmer for about 3 hours, checking it occasionally and adding more water as necessary.
▶ Remove the pan from the heat and allow to cool. Chill for at least 4 hours or overnight in the fridge, and skim off the layer of fat from the surface.
▶ Strain the stock through a sieve into a clean bowl and use to make baby purées. If desired, make a purée by blending a little of the stock with some of the cooked vegetables and pieces of chicken.

30g (1oz) **onion**, peeled and chopped

1 tbsp **olive oil**

125g (4oz) **chicken breast fillets**, cut into chunks

1 **sweet potato**, peeled and chopped

250ml (8½fl oz) unsalted **chicken stock** (see above)

6 **seedless grapes**, peeled

Chicken with sweet potato & grapes

🕐 Preparation: 5 minutes; cooking: 16 minutes   🥄 Makes 6 portions
💊 Provides beta-carotene, potassium, protein and B vitamins   ❄️ Suitable for freezing

Sweet potato tends to be very popular because of its naturally sweet taste and smooth texture, so combining chicken with sweet potato makes a good introduction to chicken for your baby. Chicken also blends well with many fruits. Chicken with grapes or apple makes a good combination.

▶ Sauté the onion in the olive oil until softened but not coloured. Add the chicken and sauté for 3–4 minutes until sealed. Add the sweet potato and pour the stock over the top.
▶ Cover and simmer for about 12 minutes or until the chicken is cooked through. Add the grapes and purée in a blender until it is the desired consistency.

First chicken casserole

⟳ Preparation: 10 minutes; cooking: 22 minutes   ✎ Makes 6 portions   ⚗ Provides beta-carotene, potassium, protein and B vitamins including folate   ❄ Suitable for freezing

Babies tend to like the mild taste of chicken. Here I have combined it with vegetables that have a naturally sweet taste. Root vegetables are also good as they help to give a smooth texture.

▶ Warm the oil in a pan, add the carrots and leeks, and sauté until softened, about 6 minutes. Add the chicken and sauté, turning occasionally, until sealed.

▶ Add the potatoes and parsnips and just cover with boiling water. Cover and simmer for about 15 minutes, or until everything is tender and cooked through. Blend to a purée, or leave as it is for older babies.

1 tbsp **vegetable oil**

100g (3½oz) **carrots**, peeled and chopped

60g (2oz) **leeks**, white part only, washed and sliced

75g (2½oz) **chicken breast fillets**, cut into chunks

250g (8oz) **potatoes**, peeled and chopped

75g (2½oz) **parsnips**, peeled and chopped

Tasty minced meat with swede & tomato

⟳ Preparation: 10 minutes; cooking: 40 minutes   ✎ Makes 8 portions   ⚗ Provides iron, protein, vitamin A, B vitamins including folate and zinc   ❄ Suitable for freezing

This makes a good introduction to minced meat as it has a nice soft texture and a natural sweetness provided by the swede.

▶ Heat the oil in a frying pan, add the onion and sauté for a few minutes until softened. Add the minced beef and chicken livers, if using, and sauté, stirring occasionally, until the meat is browned all over.

▶ Add the swede and tomatoes, pour over the stock, holding back a little if a thicker consistency is preferred, and bring to the boil. Reduce the heat, cover and cook for 30 minutes. Blend to a purée of the desired consistency.

½ tbsp **vegetable oil**

30g (1oz) **onion**, peeled and finely chopped

125g (4oz) **lean minced beef**

125g (4oz) **organic chicken livers** (optional)

250g (8oz) **swede**, peeled and chopped

2 **tomatoes**, skinned, deseeded and chopped

250ml (8fl oz) unsalted **chicken stock** (see opposite) or **beef stock**

Braised beef with carrot, parsnip & potato

⟳ Preparation: 10 minutes; cooking: 1¾–2¼ hours   🔥 180°C/350°F/gas 4   ✎ Makes 10 portions   ⚗ Provides beta-carotene, potassium, protein, B vitamins including folate and zinc   ❄ Suitable for freezing

This combination of root vegetables and beef has a smooth consistency that appeals to young babies.

▶ Heat the butter in a flame-proof casserole, add the leeks and sauté for 5 minutes, or until softened. Add the beef and sauté until browned.

▶ Add the carrots, parsnips and potatoes to the casserole and pour over the beef or chicken stock. Bring the mixture to the boil.

▶ Transfer the casserole to the preheated oven and cook for 1½–2 hours, or until the meat is soft. Blend to a purée of the desired consistency.

30g (1oz) **butter**

125g (4oz) **leeks**, white part only, washed and sliced

175g (6oz) **lean beef stewing steak**, cut into cubes

150g (5oz) **carrots**, peeled and sliced

125g (4oz) **parsnips**, peeled and chopped

250g (8oz) **potatoes**, peeled and chopped

450ml (15fl oz) unsalted **chicken stock** (see opposite) or **beef stock**

9 to 12 months

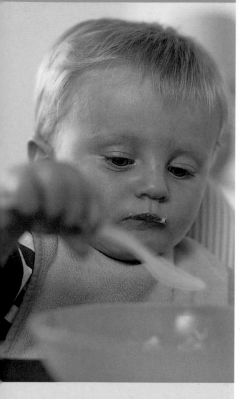

Growing appetites

Solid foods should now be the focus of your child's meals. This is a time of growing independence and your baby may insist on feeding himself. This may be a messy stage for a while but the more you allow your baby to experiment, the quicker he will learn to feed himself. He will probably be much more proficient at chewing now, which means that chopped or mashed food can replace purées. Recipes from the previous chapter can still be served; simply adjust the texture as necessary.

Exploring texture

At this age, your baby may well be on the way to eating three main meals a day, so that he receives a combination of starchy food, vegetable or animal protein, and fruit or vegetables. He will manage coarser textures (see pages 60–61), especially with the arrival of teeth to improve his chewing abilities (see page 59). He can master finger foods (see page 58), so keep up his energy levels between meals with healthy snacks of sandwiches or fruit or vegetable slices.

His diet can now include virtually all the foods the rest of the family eats, except lightly cooked eggs, unpasteurized or soft cheese, low-fat or high-fibre products, salt and, until the age of one year, honey. Indeed, many dishes can be shared by all the family as long as your baby's portion is unseasoned.

Keeping up his milk

Your baby may be drinking less milk as his appetite for solid food increases, but he still needs around 600ml (20fl oz) of his usual breast milk or formula per day (see page 30). If your baby has used bottles up to now, aim to decrease their use gradually, so that you can dispense with them altogether by the time your baby is one year old.

It helps if you give most milk feeds in a beaker or cup, perhaps reserving a soothing bottle feed before bedtime.

Once a bottle is no longer available, some babies aren't so keen on drinking milk. If this is the case with your baby try to make sure that you give cereal with milk at breakfast, include dairy foods, such as milk and cheese, and serve dishes such as cauliflower cheese and rice pudding.

You may need to reduce the amount of milk you give your baby if he is not hungry at mealtimes. Although he still needs around 600ml (20fl oz) of milk a day, some of this can be given as dairy products such as yogurt, or mini cheeses, which also make an excellent finger food. Ensure milk and dairy products you offer your child are full fat rather than low fat.

Maintaining his energy levels

Babies have small stomachs, so they cannot take in too much at mealtimes. Light meals that are full of protein and slow-release carbohydrates, such as vegetables or fish in cheese sauce, are ideal for fuelling his rapid growth.

Snacks are also important. Give your baby nutritious, healthy snacks such as cheese, carrot matchsticks or rice cakes to supplement his small meals.

Remember

• Your baby's hands should always be washed before and after eating.

• Honey should not be given to babies under the age of one because in rare cases it can contain bacteria that cause infant botulism. However, if it is an ingredient in processed food, it is perfectly safe.

• As your baby starts crawling, he will need more energy-rich foods such as cereals, fresh and dried fruit and pasta.

• To make it easier for your baby to feed himself, try to make sure that his bowl has a strong suction pad on the base so that it sticks to the table. It is also a good idea to give plenty of finger foods.

New independence

Your baby is now acquiring new physical skills: rolling, crawling, sitting or even walking. Improved muscle power and hand-to-eye coordination skills allow him much more independent movement. Your baby will be delighted by the freedom his body is giving him and he will want to take the lead at mealtimes by feeding himself; he may even become impatient when you try to spoon-feed him, and prefer to be helped with just the occasional spoonful of food. He will probably be following a more predictable sleeping pattern, which helps to regulate mealtimes.

Encouraging self-feeding

Your baby will need progressively less help to eat, and may well prefer to spoon soft foods up for himself. If more purée seems to go on the floor or his lap than in his mouth, you could use a two-spoon system: give him a spoon to hold so that he can make his own attempts at self-feeding, and use another spoon yourself to get some of the food to his mouth.

Experimentation

The more you allow your baby to experiment, the quicker he will learn to feed himself. It may be a messy procedure, but you should not discourage his

attempts, or worry that his table manners are less than perfect. He will be quick to pick up any anxieties on your part and could soon turn mealtimes into a battleground. Allow him to explore the feel of the food and take his time over eating it.

"Your baby can now manage food with a lumpier texture and he'll pick out some of the pieces himself to pop in his mouth."

Remember
• Offer finger foods as part of your baby's meals to give him chewing practice and encourage him to feed independently.

• Do not offer your baby nuts, raw or lightly cooked eggs, soft or unpasteurized cheeses or shellfish.

Finger foods

Finger foods are excellent for teaching self-feeding and should begin to play a useful part in your baby's diet; he will enjoy the freedom of movement they give him, and will appreciate the fact that he can eat this kind of food without adult intervention. Let him try steamed or raw vegetable sticks with a cold dip, or a favourite purée with bread sticks as finger foods. Remember that finger foods should be firm

"When he is teething, finger foods may be more appealing for your baby than eating from a spoon."

enough for your baby to pick up, yet tender enough for him to chew and swallow easily. Just because your baby has teeth, it doesn't mean that he instinctively knows how to use them for chewing: young babies are quite likely to bite off a piece of food, try to swallow it whole and choke, so they must not be left unsupervised even for a moment when eating.

Ideal finger foods

• **vegetables** such as carrot or cucumber sticks, cauliflower or green beans – to begin with it is better to lightly steam vegetables or cook them in a little boiling water for a few minutes so that they are still a little crunchy but not completely hard; once your baby becomes more proficient at chewing, start giving him raw vegetables

• **fruit** such as banana chunks or apple or pear slices – introduce soft fruit such as banana or kiwi fruit slices to begin with if your baby finds it difficult to chew (some babies are allergic to kiwi fruit, so watch carefully for any adverse reaction the first time you give him this fruit)

• **dried fruit** such as apricots, figs or apple pieces

• **fingers of toast, rice cakes, rusks or bread sticks**

• **mini sandwiches** with soft fillings, such as mashed banana, cream cheese or flaked tuna

• **Cheddar cheese sticks, cheese slices or mini cheeses**

• **dry cereals**

• **cooked pasta shapes**

• **small pieces of chicken or turkey**

• **mini meatballs or chicken balls**

BRUSHING YOUR BABY'S TEETH

Start brushing your baby's teeth as soon as they appear – at least twice a day, in the morning and at bedtime. Make toothbrushing fun, perhaps by giving your baby his own toothbrush to hold while you brush your teeth. Bend down and show him what you are doing and encourage him to copy you. Of course, he won't manage a proper clean, but it will give him the right idea.

For most children a mild-tasting fluoride toothpaste (varieties for children have a slightly lower fluoride content) and a good diet are sufficient to protect teeth. Too much fluoride is not good for your child and can result in discoloured teeth. All you need is a pea-sized amount of toothpaste and a soft brush to apply it with. Encourage your child to spit out the toothpaste rather than swallow it.

Teething

During the three months leading up to your baby's first birthday, he may cut several teeth, so it is still important to offer textured foods that will encourage him to chew. Vegetable finger foods cooled in the fridge are especially soothing to chew on if your baby is teething. Chilled, peeled cucumber sticks are ideal. Semi-frozen banana chunks are also good for relieving sore gums. Keep a teething ring in the fridge for him to bite on when he's not hungry.

Opinions differ as to how far teething affects babies' well-being, but it is probable that it does cause some distress, and even makes them fussier than usual about their food. For a few days before each tooth breaks through the gum, you may notice a hard, whitish bump under the surface. Your baby might dribble, so put a little petroleum jelly around his mouth and chin to help prevent them becoming dry and red. If his gums are particularly tender, he may reject being fed from a spoon. If this is the case, offer him finger foods to eat instead.

Preventing tooth decay

Children run a greater risk of tooth decay than adults because teeth are more vulnerable to acid when they are newly formed. In addition, during the first year or two after birth, the immune mechanism in the mouth is not fully developed.

To limit the possibility of tooth decay, never give your baby bottles filled with anything but milk or water. If your baby drinks fruit juice from a bottle, his teeth and gums will be in contact with damaging sugary and acidic fluids for prolonged periods of time. Always dilute fruit juice and give it to your baby only at mealtimes in a cup or beaker. Milk itself contains a form of sugar that would be corrosive if the teeth were never cleaned, so be sure to brush your baby's teeth at bedtime. After brushing your baby's teeth at night, avoid giving him any sweet drinks or more food. At night there is not enough saliva in the mouth to wash away harmful acid, so restrict night-time drinks to water.

Remember

• There is no such thing as a "healthy" sugar. Honey, brown sugar, fruit sugars and sucrose all rot teeth.

• As soon as teeth appear, buy a mild toothpaste designed for children and brush your baby's teeth morning and night.

• It is best to give your child sweet things to eat with meals, as the flow of saliva is greater when eating. Saliva helps neutralize acid in the mouth. Diluted juice with meals is fine but it is best to give him water or milk between meals.

• Encourage your baby to drink from a cup or beaker, and offer only water, diluted juice or him usual milk.

• Try to dispense with bottles, apart from perhaps a bottle at bedtime, by the time your baby is one year old.

• When teething, it can be soothing for your baby to chew on a clean, wet washcloth that has been placed in the freezer for 30 minutes.

• Rubbing a sugar-free teething gel on to the gums may help ease pain, as these gels contain a local anaesthetic. Alternatively, you could give your baby infant paracetamol or try homeopathic teething granules.

A varied menu

Towards the end of your baby's first year, solid food will replace much of her milk diet. It is important to introduce lots of different textures and flavours at this stage while your baby is so receptive to new foods. Offer some food mashed, some whole, some grated and some diced: it's surprising what a few teeth and strong gums can manage. Finger foods that allow your baby to feed herself will become an increasingly important part of her daily diet, and will accustom her to independent eating and many new textures.

1 Cheesy pasta stars
Tiny stars or other soup pasta shapes make an ideal introduction to pasta. Here they are combined with a tomato sauce enriched with grated Cheddar and sweetened with carrot. (See page 64 for recipe.)

2 Quick chicken couscous
Couscous, which is made from crushed semolina, has a mild taste and soft texture that is perfect for babies. It is also quick to cook and combines well with a variety of vegetables and even fruit. (See page 66 for recipe.)

3 Assorted dips
These colourful savoury and sweet purées are served with toast, cheese shapes, fruit pieces or raw vegetable sticks, which may be chilled to soothe gums made sore by teething. (See pages 62–63 for recipes.)

1 ripe **avocado**, halved and stoned

60g (2oz) **soft cream cheese**

1 tbsp snipped **chives**

1 ripe **tomato**, skinned, deseeded and chopped

Steamed vegetable shapes

vegetables such as sweet potato, carrot, potato or parsnip, washed and peeled

Creamy avocado dip & vegetable fingers

↻ Preparation: 10 minutes; cooking: 8 minutes   ✄ Makes 4 portions

✎ Provides folate, potassium and vitamins A, C and E

An avocado has the highest protein content of any fruit, and babies like its mild creaminess. This dip also makes a good sandwich filling if mixed with grated cheese or chopped watercress.

▶ Cut the vegetables into sticks or shapes, place in a steamer and cook until tender, about 8 minutes.

▶ Scoop out the avocado flesh. Mash until smooth and mix with the remaining ingredients. (For adults you can add lemon juice, seasoning, chopped coriander and maybe a little finely chopped chilli.)

1 small **red pepper**, halved and deseeded

½ tbsp **vegetable oil**

1 **shallot**, finely chopped

1 ripe **tomato**, skinned, deseeded and chopped

200g (7oz) **soft cream cheese**

Raw vegetable shapes

vegetables such as carrot, celery, cucumber, pepper and kohlrabi, washed and peeled

TIP If your baby finds raw vegetables too hard, offer steamed cauliflower or root vegetables. Reduce the steaming time progressively.

Red pepper dip & vegetable fingers

↻ Preparation: 10 minutes; cooking: 10 minutes   ✄ Makes 4 portions

✎ Provides beta-carotene and vitamins A, B12 and C   ❄ Suitable for freezing

The vegetables for this dip should be cut into pieces small enough to be easily grasped, but not so tiny that they could be swallowed whole. You can also offer toast, pitta fingers or mild cheese shapes.

▶ To make the dip, roast the red pepper, then peel and roughly chop.
▶ Meanwhile, warm the oil in a small frying pan, add the shallot and sauté until softened but not coloured. Combine the red pepper with the shallot, tomato and cream cheese, and blend together to make a smooth cream.

▶ Cut the raw vegetables into strips, or make novelty shapes using miniature biscuit cutters.

250g (8oz) **swede**, peeled and chopped

125g (4oz) **parsnips**, peeled and chopped

250ml (8fl oz) **milk**

30g (1oz) grated **Cheddar cheese**

Easy mashed vegetable duo

↻ Preparation: 10 minutes; cooking: 22 minutes   ✄ Makes 4 portions

✎ Provides calcium, fibre, folate, potassium, protein and vitamins A, B12 and C

This recipe makes both a good smooth purée and a slightly coarser-textured dish, as preferred.

▶ Place the vegetables in a saucepan with the milk. Bring to the boil, cover and simmer for 20 minutes, or until soft.

▶ Remove the pan from the heat and stir in the cheese until melted. Mash to the desired consistency.

Fruity baby muesli

⏲ Preparation: 10 minutes, plus 2–12 hours soaking   ✂ Makes 2 portions
🍴 Provides fibre, iron, magnesium, B vitamins (except for B12), vitamin C and zinc

Oats raise blood sugar levels relatively slowly, so oat-based breakfast cereals provide a more sustained energy boost than other cereals.

▶ Put the oats and wheatgerm in a bowl with the dried apricot and sultanas. Pour over the grape juice. Leave to soak for at least 2 hours or overnight.

▶ Add the apple and grapes to the soaked cereal and blend. (Once your baby has mastered the art of chewing, there is no need to blend this muesli.)

30g (1oz) **rolled oats**

30g (1oz) **toasted wheat**

1 **dried apricot** or **pear**, chopped

1 tbsp **sultanas**

150ml (5fl oz) **white grape juice** or **apple juice**

½ **red apple**, peeled and grated

3 **grapes**, halved and deseeded

Apple & date porridge

⏲ Preparation: 2 minutes; cooking: 12 minutes   ✂ Makes 2 portions
🍴 Provides calcium, fibre and B vitamins including folate

▶ Put the apple and dates in a pan with the water and cook over a medium heat for 5 minutes.

▶ Meanwhile, heat the milk in a pan, stir in the oats, bring to the boil and simmer, stirring constantly, for 3–4 minutes, or until thickened. Mix with the fruit, then blend to the desired consistency.

1 **sweet eating apple**, peeled, cored and chopped

45g (1½oz) **dates**

4 tbsp **water**

150ml (5fl oz) **milk**

15g (½oz) **rolled oats**

Exotic fruit salad

⏲ Preparation: 10 minutes   ✂ Makes 4 portions
🍴 Provides beta-carotene, fibre, folate and vitamin C

If you can't find perfectly ripe, sweet exotic fruits, substitute peaches or strawberries.

▶ Finely chop all the fruit and simply combine with the orange juice.

½ **mango**, peeled and stoned

½ **papaya**, peeled and stoned

1 **kiwi fruit**, peeled

2 **lychees**, peeled and stoned

juice of 1 large **orange**

Raspberry, pear & peach purée

⏲ Preparation: 5 minutes; cooking: 5 minutes   ✂ Makes 4 portions
🍴 Provides fibre, folate and vitamin C

This is very much a summer purée to be made when raspberries and peaches are ripe and sweet. It is also good mixed with baby rice or mashed banana.

▶ Place the fruit in a saucepan and simmer gently for about 5 minutes. Cool slightly, press through a sieve and mix with the yogurt.

125g (4oz) **raspberries**

2 ripe **pears**, peeled, cored and chopped

1 **peach**, peeled and chopped

2 tbsp **Greek yogurt**

Butternut squash with alphabet pasta

300g (10oz) **butternut squash**, peeled and cubed

2–3 tbsp **alphabet soup pasta**

30g (1oz) **butter**

½ tbsp chopped **fresh sage**

1 tbsp freshly grated **Parmesan cheese** (optional)

⟳ Preparation: 5 minutes; cooking: 20 minutes　⚷ Makes 4 portions
✐ Provides beta-carotene and folate　❄ Suitable for freezing

▶ Put the squash in a steamer and cook until tender, about 15 minutes. Blend to a purée with 4–5 tablespoons of water from the bottom of the steamer.

▶ Meanwhile, cook the pasta in boiling, lightly salted water according to the instructions on the packet, then drain.

▶ Melt the butter in a pan, add the sage and cook gently for 1 minute.

▶ Mix the sage, butter and Parmesan cheese, if using, with the squash and pasta.

Cheesy pasta stars

125g (4oz) **carrots**, peeled and sliced

200ml (7fl oz) **boiling water**

30g (1oz) **butter**

200g (7oz) **tomatoes**, skinned, deseeded and chopped

45g (1½oz) grated **Cheddar cheese**

2 tbsp **soup pasta stars (stelline)**

⟳ Preparation: 10 minutes; cooking: 25 minutes　⚷ Makes 4 portions
✐ Provides beta-carotene, calcium, folate, protein and vitamins B12 and C
❄ Suitable for freezing

Tiny pasta stelline make a good introduction to pasta. The sweet taste of the carrots in this sauce is usually very appealing to babies.

▶ Place the carrots in a small pan, cover with the boiling water and cook until tender, 15–20 minutes.

▶ Warm the butter in a separate pan, add the tomatoes and sauté until mushy. Remove from the heat and stir in the cheese until melted.

▶ Meanwhile, cook the pasta in boiling, lightly salted water according to the instructions on the packet, then drain.

▶ Mix together the cooked carrots with their cooking liquid and the cheese and tomato sauce. Blend to a purée then combine with the pasta stars.

Tomato & tuna pasta sauce

1 tbsp **olive oil**

1 small **onion**, peeled and finely chopped

1 **garlic clove**, peeled and crushed

400g (14oz) **canned chopped tomatoes**

1 tbsp **tomato purée**

½ tsp **balsamic vinegar**

½ tsp **caster sugar**

¼ tsp **dried mixed herbs**

100g (3½oz) **canned tuna in oil**

2 tbsp **soft cream cheese** or **mascarpone cheese**

⟳ Preparation: 5 minutes; cooking 20 minutes　⚷ Makes 4 portions　✐ Provides beta-carotene, potassium, protein and vitamins A, B12, C, D and E　❄ Suitable for freezing

An excellent store cupboard standby, this dish always goes down well.

▶ Heat the oil in a saucepan, add the onion and garlic and sauté for about 5 minutes until softened.

▶ Add the remaining ingredients, except the tuna and cream cheese or mascarpone cheese, and cook uncovered over a medium heat for about 12 minutes.

▶ Drain and flake the tuna, add to the sauce and heat through.

▶ Then stir in the cream cheese or mascarpone cheese until melted into the sauce.

Fillet of fish mornay with vegetables

Preparation: 10 minutes; cooking: 35 minutes   Makes 8 portions

Provides beta-carotene, calcium, protein, B vitamins including folate and vitamin C

Suitable for freezing

This tasty combination of white fish and vegetables in a mild cheese sauce is generally very popular with babies.

▶ Melt the butter in a saucepan, add the leeks and sauté for 2–3 minutes. Add the carrots, cover with water and cook for 10 minutes. Add the broccoli and cook for 5 minutes. Stir in the peas and simmer for a further 5 minutes, or until the vegetables are tender (adding a little more water if necessary).

▶ Meanwhile, put the fish in a pan with the milk, peppercorns, bay leaf and parsley. Simmer for 5 minutes, or until the fish is cooked. Set aside, reserving the cooking liquid. Discard the flavourings.

▶ To prepare the sauce, melt the butter in a pan, stir in the flour and cook for 1 minute. Gradually whisk in the fish cooking liquid, bring to the boil and cook, stirring until the sauce has thickened. Remove from the heat, add the cheese and stir until melted.

▶ Drain the vegetables and mix with the flaked fish and cheese sauce. Blend to a purée of the desired consistency for young babies. Provided the vegetables are tender, this can be mashed or chopped for older babies who are starting to chew.

15g (½oz) **butter**

60g (2oz) **leeks**, washed and finely sliced

125g (4oz) **carrots**, peeled and chopped

60g (2oz) **broccoli**, cut into small florets

45g (1½oz) **fresh** or **frozen peas**

150g (5oz) **cod, hake, plaice** or **haddock fillets**, skinned

150ml (5fl oz) **milk**

3 **peppercorns**

1 **bay leaf**

1 sprig of **parsley**

Sauce

20g (¾oz) **butter**

1 tbsp **plain flour**

45g (1½oz) grated **Cheddar** or **Edam cheese**

Flaked cod with tomatoes & courgettes

150g (5oz) **cod fillet**, skinned

100ml (3½fl oz) **milk**

30g (1oz) **butter**

1 **shallot**, peeled and chopped

90g (3oz) **courgettes**, chopped

375g (12oz) **tomatoes**, skinned, deseeded and chopped

60g (2oz) grated **Cheddar cheese**

TIP *The cod can be microwaved on a high setting for 3 minutes.*

Preparation: 10 minutes; cooking: 20 minutes   Makes 4 portions   Provides beta-carotene, calcium, potassium, protein, B vitamins including folate and vitamin C   Suitable for freezing

▶ Place the fish in a saucepan, cover with the milk and poach gently for about 6 minutes.

▶ Meanwhile, melt the butter in a pan, add the shallot and cook slowly until softened. Add the courgettes and sauté for 5 minutes. Add the tomatoes and sauté for 5 minutes more, or until mushy. Remove the pan from the heat and stir in the cheese until melted.

▶ Flake the fish carefully with a fork, checking for and removing bones, and stir it into the tomato and courgette sauce. For babies who don't yet like lumpy food, blend the final mixture until it reaches a smoother consistency.

California chicken

45g (1½oz) boneless, skinless **chicken breast**, cooked

1 **tomato**, skinned, deseeded and chopped

30g (1oz) **avocado**

2 tbsp mild, full-fat **natural yogurt**

1½ tbsp grated **Cheddar cheese**

Preparation: 10 minutes   Makes 1 portion   Provides calcium, protein, B vitamins including folate, vitamins A, C and E and zinc

Use these ingredients to make yourself a salad or sandwich at the same time as a quick and easy meal for your baby. You can substitute Edam for Cheddar cheese.

▶ Chop the chicken, then combine it with the remaining ingredients. Blend or chop the mixture to the desired consistency. If your baby prefers, you could leave out the cheese.

Quick chicken couscous

20g (¾oz) **butter**

60g (2oz) **leeks**, white part only, washed and finely chopped

60g (2oz) boneless, skinless **chicken breast**, diced

30g (1oz) **parsnips**, peeled and diced

30g (1oz) **carrots**, peeled and diced

250ml (8½fl oz) unsalted **chicken stock** (see page 52)

100g (3½oz) **couscous**

Preparation: 10 minutes; cooking: 20 minutes   Makes 4 portions   Provides beta-carotene, folate, iron and protein

If you prefer, replace the chicken with extra seasonal vegetables.

▶ Warm the butter in a pan, add the leeks and sauté for 5 minutes, or until softened. Add the chicken and sauté until just cooked through.

▶ Meanwhile, place the parsnips and carrots in a steamer, or in a saucepan with boiling water to cover, and cook until tender, about 10 minutes.

▶ Bring the stock to the boil in a pan. Stir in the couscous, remove the pan from the heat, cover and leave for 5 minutes, or until the stock has been absorbed. Fluff with a fork and stir in the chicken and vegetables. Add extra stock or water if necessary.

Fruity chicken with carrots

⟳ Preparation: 10 minutes; cooking: 22 minutes ⚙ Makes 4 portions
🥄 Provides beta-carotene, niacin, protein and vitamin B6 ❄ Suitable for freezing

Apple blends well with chicken to produce a lovely flavour in this quick-to-prepare dish. Well-cooked rice makes a good accompaniment.

▶ Heat the butter in a pan, add the onion and sauté for 3–4 minutes. Add the chicken and sauté until it turns opaque. Add the carrots and cook for 2 minutes, then stir in the chopped apple and pour over the chicken stock.

▶ Bring the mixture to the boil, then cover and cook over a medium heat for about 15 minutes. Chop or purée to the desired consistency.

15g (½oz) **butter**

30g (1oz) **onion**, peeled and finely chopped

75g (2½oz) boneless, skinless **chicken breast**, chopped

125g (4oz) **carrots**, peeled and sliced

½ **dessert apple**, peeled, cored and chopped

300ml (10fl oz) unsalted **chicken stock** (see page 52)

Creamy chicken & broccoli

⟳ Preparation: 5 minutes; cooking: 15 minutes ⚙ Makes 4 portions
🥄 Provides calcium, protein, B vitamins including folate and niacin and vitamins A and C
❄ Suitable for freezing

You could add some small cooked soup pasta, such as stelline, to this recipe to make it more substantial.

▶ To prepare the cheese sauce, melt the butter in a saucepan, stir in the flour and cook for 1 minute. Gradually whisk in the milk, bring to the boil and cook until the sauce has thickened. Remove from the heat, add the cheese and stir until melted.

▶ Meanwhile, steam or microwave the broccoli until tender. Combine the cheese sauce, chicken and broccoli, then roughly chop up the mixture in a blender or by hand.

90g (3oz) **broccoli**, cut into small florets

125g (4oz) boneless, skinless **chicken breast**, cooked and chopped

Mild cheese sauce

30g (1oz) **butter**

2 tbsp **plain flour**

300ml (10fl oz) **milk**

60g (2oz) grated **Edam** or **other mild cheese**

TIP If your baby isn't keen on cheese, make a white sauce flavoured with a pinch of nutmeg.

Baby's bolognese

⟳ Preparation: 10 minutes; cooking: 35 minutes ⚙ Makes 6 portions
🥄 Provides beta-carotene, iron, protein, B vitamins including folate and zinc
❄ Suitable for freezing: sauce only

▶ Warm the oil in a pan, add the onion, garlic and celery and sauté for 3–4 minutes. Add the grated carrots and cook for 2 minutes.

▶ Add the minced beef and stir until browned. Stir in the tomato purée, the fresh and sunblush tomatoes and stock. Bring the mixture to the boil, reduce the heat, cover and cook for about 10 minutes. At this stage, you can chop the meat in a food processor for just a few seconds to give it a slightly softer texture.

▶ Cook the spaghetti in boiling, lightly salted water according to the instructions on the packet. Drain and chop into small pieces. Babies can find the chewy texture of red meat off-putting, so transfer the bolognese sauce to a blender and chop for a few seconds before combining it with the pasta.

1 tbsp **vegetable oil**

½ small **onion**, peeled and finely chopped

1 small **garlic clove**, crushed

15g (½oz) **celery**, finely chopped

30g (1oz) **carrots**, peeled and grated

125g (4oz) lean **minced beef**

½ tsp **tomato purée**

2 **tomatoes**, skinned, deseeded and chopped

1 tbsp **sunblush (semi-dried) tomatoes**, chopped

90ml (3fl oz) unsalted **chicken stock** (see page 52)

45g (1½oz) **spaghetti**

12 to 18 months

Changing needs

"Establish the habit of eating five portions of fruit and vegetables a day now and you will have set up a healthy eating plan for life."

Your child can now enjoy a full varied diet and including her in family meals should be easier. Accordingly, the recipes in this chapter are designed to appeal to your toddler, but also to suit the tastes of the whole family. Towards the end of the first year babies who have been good eaters can often become difficult and fussy. At about this time growth rate slows down dramatically, resulting in a natural decrease in appetite. In addition, your baby's new-found ability to walk and increased independence means that she may become reluctant to sit at the table for any length of time. Recognizing these changes will help you adapt to her needs.

Balancing a mixed diet

At around 12 months old, your baby may look quite chubby, but once she gets up on her feet, she will slim down. Toddlers are on the go all the time and you will find that your child needs quick, energy-boosting snacks between meals.

In this and the following chapters, there are many suggestions for healthy snacks. Encourage your child to eat a variety of snacks, such as fruit, bites of cheese or homemade cake, so they make up a useful part of her mixed diet.

Children's nutrition
Although your child will be joining in with family meals, the dietary advice that applies to you as an adult will not necessarily be appropriate for her. Young children have different nutritional needs and require more calories than adults to sustain the growth of muscle, tissue and bone that takes place throughout childhood. Advice concerning adult fat and fibre intake, for example, does not apply to the under fives.

While health experts tell us that adults and children over five should derive no more than 35 per cent of their calories from fat, they also agree that we should not limit fat in the diets of children under two years of age. Due to the very fast rate of growth in the first two years of life, fat is needed as it is the most concentrated source of energy. Without enough fat in the diet, a child would need to burn up protein for energy. Fat is also important for healthy development of the brain and nervous system. Unless you have been advised by a doctor to do so, don't give your child reduced-fat products, such as semi-skimmed milk. In fact, your child still needs about 400ml (14fl oz) of milk a day, although now she can come off breast milk or formula and drink full-fat cow's milk.

A high-fibre diet, too, is still not appropriate for your child. Young children have small stomachs: fibre is low-calorie bulky material that fills the stomach without meeting a toddler's high calorific needs, and it can even hinder the absorption of vital nutrients.

Keeping milk in the diet

If your child drinks milk only reluctantly and you are worried that she is not taking the recommended 400ml (14fl oz) of milk per day, you can easily smuggle milk into her meals without her noticing.

Yogurts, fromage frais or pasteurized cheese can be used as equivalents to milk. Alternatively, offer a fruity milkshake or smoothie (see page 112), make a cheese sauce (see page 65) for part of the main meal, mash some potatoes with plenty of milk, or whip a half-set jelly with a tin of evaporated milk for dessert.

Ideal dairy products
- fromage frais or yogurt
- cheese: sliced, grated on pasta or on toast • white sauce in fish pie or macaroni cheese
- milk puddings, such as rice pudding or ground rice
- high-quality dairy ice-cream
- fruity or chocolate smoothies or milkshakes

Rainbow of nutrition
Often, the stronger the colour of a fruit or vegetable, the more nutritious it is. For instance, an orange-fleshed sweet potato contains more nutrients than an ordinary potato. Also, different coloured vegetables provide different nutrients, so try to include green, red, orange, yellow, dark blue or purple fruits and vegetables in your child's diet.

The importance of fruit & vegetables

Health experts recommend we all try to include five portions of fruit or vegetables (not including potatoes) in our diet each day (see page 15). Do not be daunted by this – it is not as difficult as it sounds to incorporate five helpings of fresh fruit or vegetables in your child's daily diet.

Five-a-day eating plan

To incorporate five servings of fruit or vegetables into your child's daily diet, try the following eating plan.
- Serve some fresh or cooked fruit or diluted juice with breakfast.
- Add a serving of vegetables or salad to your child's lunch, and follow the savoury course with a serving of fresh or cooked fruit.
- Provide a serving of vegetables at supper time, followed by fresh fruit or a fruit pudding.

Vegetable rejection

Often children raise strong objections to eating vegetables and only 1 in 5 children in the United States eats enough vegetables. If your toddler is especially resistant to eating vegetables, try some of the following suggestions

for incorporating vegetables into her diet without her even noticing.
- Sometimes children who don't like cooked vegetables do like eating them raw, so try giving carrot, red pepper and cucumber sticks with a tasty dip or find a salad dressing that your child loves and make interesting salads.
- If you do cook vegetables they are much more nutritious and taste better if steamed rather than boiled.
- Chinese-style, stir-fry vegetables with a touch of soy sauce and maybe some noodles or rice are popular with many children.
- Try hiding vegetables by blending them into a tomato pasta sauce or soup as in my pasta sauce with hidden vegetables (see page 78). Make oven-baked chips or mash from sweet potato rather than ordinary potato – sweet potato is more nutritious as it is rich in beta-carotene.
- Frozen vegetables are just as nutritious as fresh, and vegetables such as peas and sweetcorn tend to be popular.
- If, after all your efforts, your child is still a confirmed veggie-hater give her fruit instead as it provides nearly all the vitamins you get in vegetables.

Remember
• You can now introduce cow's milk as your child's usual milk, unless she has special dietary needs.

• Offer plain water as a thirst-quencher, or give well-diluted fruit or vegetable juice (at least five parts water to one part juice).

• If your baby has not already learnt to drink from a cup, try to persuade her off a bottle at this age.

• Encourage your child to eat fruit and vegetables as part of her meals and as between-meals snacks.

Making meals fun

Young children, like adults, prefer to eat in company. If your toddler has cutlery she is able to use, is seated at the correct height and has someone to share the meal with, mealtimes will be an enjoyable occasion for her.

You may find that she will eat things she has previously rejected, just because a sibling or friend who has come to play is eating it. Visiting a friend or relative's house often produces the same effect. The excitement of eating with other children or in different surroundings makes her adventurous enough to try new foods. In addition, when you and your child are with other people at a mealtime you may both be more relaxed about the food you are eating.

"Eating as a family helps your child integrate into family mealtimes."

When you are on your own with her, you are probably more focused on what she is eating. There is a certain amount of unconscious pressure for your child if you are overseeing every mouthful she takes, and meals can become rather an ordeal for her. It is easy for both of you to forget that eating should be fun.

Eating sociably at home
Eating as a family will help your child to integrate into regular mealtimes as well as to learn some of your basic family rules about eating at the table. Even if the whole family cannot sit down together at meals during the week – perhaps because the meal is too late for your young child to join in more than occasionally – do sit down beside her while she eats, or ask an older sibling or friend to join her.

Cooking for the family
By now your toddler should be eating the same meals as the rest of the family. Life is too short to cook a different meal for each member of the family and it is much easier to accustom children to new foods at this early age, when their preferences (and prejudices) are not yet fixed. You can interest your child in food, perhaps by talking to her about its form, taste or feel, or by adding a few presentational touches that will appeal to her.

Don't get over-anxious or angry if your toddler refuses to eat a new dish – it can take a few attempts for new foods to be accepted. Instead, make sure that the pudding on offer is nutritious, so that you can relax in the knowledge that she is still eating a healthy diet, even if it's not in the traditional order. Remember that the "balance" of a diet should be assessed over a period of a few days to a week, rather than within a strict limit of 24 hours.

When your child is unwell

When children are unwell they often lose their appetite. However, it is important to ensure that your child's fluid intake is maintained.

Diarrhoea

Approximately 80 per cent of a new baby is water (adults are around 70 per cent water). Consequently, babies and young children are particularly vulnerable to dehydration during periods of diarrhoea or vomiting. If a child is suffering from either of these problems, offer plenty of fluids. Special salt and sugar powders that are dissolved in water replace lost minerals and can be bought from pharmacies. Well-diluted fruit juices, ice lollipops or well-diluted, flat, caffeine-free soft drinks (take the bubbles out first with ice or a swizzle stick) are suitable for children with diarrhoea. Milk is not suitable, but should soon be gradually reintroduced.

Monitor your child's fluid intake and urine output. Signs of dehydration are:
• less frequent urination
• more concentrated, dark yellow urine
• dry mouth and lips
• sunken eyes
• lethargic behaviour.
Contact your doctor if your child shows these signs or if the diarrhoea persists for more than 24 hours.

Upset tummy

If your child has an upset tummy try the American BRAT diet (see right). Offer small amounts of each of the foods. After 48 hours introduce potatoes, cooked vegetables (especially root vegetables) and a boiled egg. Leave out dairy foods for a while as an inflamed gut can sometimes be aggravated by lactose in dairy foods.

Foods during illness

If your child is off her food but not suffering from diarrhoea or vomiting,

give her liquids that are nutritious – milk, milkshakes (see page 112), fruit smoothies or hot chocolate are good. Children who are reluctant to take fluids are often willing to eat ice lollipops. Give frozen juice bars or make your own from fresh fruit juice, puréed fruit or yogurt (see page 177).

Offer simple, easily digested foods, such as homemade chicken soup (see page 52), steamed fish and mashed potato, scrambled egg on toast or mashed banana. Antibiotics kill the good bacteria in the body as well as the harmful ones. If your child is taking antibiotics, you could give her live yogurt to help maintain the levels of beneficial bacteria in the body.

Constipation

If your child is constipated, give her plenty of water and diluted fruit juices. Cut down on sugary and fatty foods and offer fruit, vegetables and wholegrain cereals, but do not overload the digestive system with fibre as this is not a suitable way to relieve constipation in young children. Natural yogurt, prunes and prune juice are more useful in gently relieving it.

Regression

Don't be surprised if your child reverts to more babyish feeding habits even after she has recovered from being ill. While she is ill, she needs extra reassurance in the form of cuddles and she may want her drinks from a bottle again. Until her appetite returns, the memory of her more babyish comforts may make her want to eat the kinds of things you thought she had grown out of. (In fact, this may be the case throughout her early childhood whenever your child is ill.) Try not to worry, she will soon be back to her old self with a healthy appetite ready to try out new foods again.

Remember
• Keep your child's fluid intake high during illness.

• Recognize that she may revert to slightly babyish feeding habits for a short period of time.

The BRAT diet
• **Bananas** settle an acid stomach and provide potassium to regulate the body's mineral balance.

• **Rice** helps relieve diarrhoea and provides the body with energy and protein.

• **Apples,** especially stewed apples, are a traditional cure for gastroenteritis.

• **Toast** (dry white) helps settle the stomach and provides carbohydrate for energy.

Food for the senses

Your child can now enjoy a full, varied diet and it should be easier to integrate him into family meals. The recipes in this section are designed to appeal to your toddler, but also to suit the tastes of the whole family. During this stage your child needs plenty of freedom to explore his food with his hands. Allowing him to do this will stimulate his interest in food and heighten his enjoyment of mealtimes. The foods on these pages are designed to appeal to the eye, to the senses of smell and touch and, of course, to the taste buds.

1 Raspberry frozen yogurt
Scoops of frosty, frozen yogurt decorated with crisp wafers and chocolate drops make a mouth-watering, and tactile, dessert. (See page 84 for recipe.)

2 Yogurt pancakes
The contrast of sticky maple syrup, ripe, cool and juicy summer fruits and warm pancakes is tempting. (See page 84 for recipe.)

3 Root vegetable chips
The perfect finger food, these colourful and sweet-tasting chips are made from sweet potato, beetroot and parsnip. They make an interesting, crunchy snack and are great for parties and picnics. (See page 76 for recipe.)

4 Chicken sausage snails
A simple dish of chicken sausages and mashed potato becomes, with the help of a little imagination, an eye-catching picture on a plate and an appealing meal. (See page 81 for recipe.)

Bananas with maple syrup

⟳ Preparation: 3 minutes; cooking: 3 minutes   ✂ Makes 1 portion

⚡ Provides calcium, iron, protein, B vitamins including folate and zinc

generous knob of **butter**

1 small **banana**, peeled and sliced

1 tbsp **maple syrup**

1/8 tsp **ground cinnamon**

These make a delicious breakfast or pudding served with a toasted fruit muffin, toasted raisin bread, pancakes or waffles.

▶ Melt the butter in a saucepan. Add the sliced banana and cook, stirring occasionally, for 1 minute.

▶ Add the maple syrup and cinnamon and cook for 1 minute more.

Root vegetable chips

⟳ Preparation: 10 minutes; cooking: 15 minutes   🔥 200°C/400°F/gas 6

✂ Makes 4 portions   ⚡ Provides beta-carotene, fibre, potassium and vitamin E

1 **sweet potato**, scrubbed

1 **parsnip**, peeled

2 **carrots** or 1 **raw beetroot**, peeled

can of **spray oil** for baking or **oil** for deep frying

freshly ground **sea salt** (optional)

TIP You can also make these chips using sliced plantain.

Encourage your child to eat more vegetables by making these crunchy chips. They also make a healthy alternative to packet crisps.

▶ Slice all the vegetables wafer thin by hand or by using a slicing blade in a food processor. Spray some oil onto a couple of large baking sheets and brush to cover the surface. Heat the baking sheets for 5 minutes in the preheated oven.

▶ Place the vegetables onto the baking sheets in a single layer and lightly spray with oil. Cook in the oven for 10–12 minutes, turning halfway through. Transfer to kitchen paper, sprinkle with sea salt, if desired, and serve cold.

▶ Alternatively, deep fry the vegetables in a deep-fat fryer at 190°C (375°F). Add each vegetable separately, and fry until crisp and golden, about 4–5 minutes.

Courgette & tomato frittata

⟳ Preparation: 5 minutes; cooking: 30 minutes   ✂ Makes 8 portions

⚡ Provides calcium, protein, B vitamins including folate and vitamins A and C

2 tbsp **vegetable oil**

1 **onion**, peeled and chopped

175g (6oz) **courgettes**, thinly sliced

salt and freshly ground **black pepper**

2 **tomatoes**, skinned, deseeded and chopped

4 **eggs**

1 tbsp **milk**

2 tbsp freshly grated **Parmesan cheese**

You can make this versatile frittata with a variety of ingredients. Served cold it is perfect for taking on a picnic.

▶ Heat the oil in a 24cm (9½ in) non-stick frying pan. Add the onion and courgettes, season lightly and cook for about 15 minutes. Add the tomatoes and continue to cook for 3–4 minutes.

▶ Beat the eggs with the milk and pepper, and pour over the vegetables. Cook over a medium heat for about 5 minutes, or until the eggs are set underneath. Preheat the grill to high.

▶ Sprinkle the Parmesan over the frittata and cook briefly under the grill until golden (if necessary, wrap the pan handle with foil to prevent burning). Cut into wedges and serve hot or cold.

Variations

▶ Omit the courgettes and tomatoes. Instead, add 125g (4oz) cooked diced ham and 75g (2½ oz) peas to the beaten egg mixture.

▶ Omit the courgettes. Add 1 small diced and sautéed red pepper and 2 cubed boiled potatoes to the egg.

Mini veggie bites

⟳ Preparation: 10 minutes; cooking: 10 minutes   ⚙ Makes 8 rissoles
⚗ Provides beta-carotene, fibre, potassium and vitamin C   ❄ Suitable for freezing

*Encourage your children to enjoy eating vegetables with this tasty recipe –
the easy-to-hold rissoles even taste good served cold.*

100g (4oz) grated **carrot**

100g (4oz) grated **courgette**

100g (4oz) grated **potato**

salt and freshly ground **black pepper**

2 tbsp **plain flour**

vegetable oil for frying

▶ Squeeze out excess moisture from the grated vegetables. The best way to do this is to lay the vegetables on several sheets of kitchen paper and then cover the vegetables with more paper and press down to soak up the excess liquid.
▶ Mix the vegetables in a bowl together with the seasoning and flour and form into 8 round rissoles using your hands.
▶ Heat the oil in a frying pan and fry the rissoles, gently flattening them with a spatula. Sauté for about 5 minutes, turning halfway through.
▶ Drain on kitchen paper. They should be golden and crisp on the outside and fully cooked inside.

Pasta cartwheels with cheese & broccoli

⟳ Preparation: 10 minutes; cooking: 35 minutes   🌡 180°C/350°F/gas 4
⚙ Makes 4 portions   ⚗ Provides calcium, protein, B vitamins including folate, vitamin A and zinc   ❄ Suitable for freezing: sauce only

125g (4oz) **pasta cartwheels**

125g (4oz) **broccoli**, cut into small florets

60g (2oz) **frozen sweetcorn**

Cheese sauce

30g (1oz) **butter**

30g (1oz) **plain flour**

300ml (10fl oz) **milk**

pinch of **nutmeg**

75g (2½oz) grated **Cheddar cheese**

salt and freshly ground **black pepper**

Topping

2 tbsp freshly grated **Parmesan cheese**

1½ tbsp **fresh breadcrumbs**

▶ Cook the pasta in boiling, lightly salted water according to the instructions on the packet. Drain and set aside.
▶ Meanwhile, place the broccoli and sweetcorn in a steamer and cook for 4–5 minutes, or until tender. Cover to keep warm and set aside.
▶ To make the sauce, melt the butter in a small pan. Add the flour to make a paste and stir over a low heat for 1 minute. Gradually whisk in the milk, bring slowly to the boil and cook until thickened, stirring constantly. Remove from the heat, add the nutmeg, stir in the Cheddar cheese until melted, then season.
▶ Stir the vegetables into the sauce then mix with the pasta. Pour the mixture into a greased gratin dish, and scatter over the Parmesan cheese and breadcrumbs. Bake in the preheated oven for about 15 minutes.

Variation

▶ To make macaroni cheese, omit the vegetables and replace the cartwheels with 150g (5oz) of macaroni.

Pasta & sauce with hidden vegetables

⟳ Preparation: 10 minutes; cooking: 30 minutes ✎ Makes 4 portions

✐ Provides beta-carotene, folate, potassium and vitamins C and E

❄ Suitable for freezing: sauce only

2 tbsp **olive oil**

1 small **onion**, peeled and chopped

1 **garlic clove**, peeled and crushed

75g (2½oz) **carrots**, peeled and chopped

75g (2½oz) **courgettes**, chopped

75g (2½oz) **mushrooms**, sliced

400g (14oz) **canned chopped tomatoes**

125ml (4fl oz) **vegetable stock** (see page 47)

¼ tsp **brown sugar**

salt and freshly ground **black pepper**

250g (8oz) **pasta twists (fusilli)**

If your baby is reluctant to eat vegetables, one solution is to resort to disguise. This sauce has lots of vegetables blended into it. Mix it with fun pasta shapes and you are on to a winner! A tablespoon of red pesto makes a nice addition.

▶ Warm the oil in a pan, add the onion and garlic, and sauté for about 3 minutes. Add the carrots, courgettes and mushrooms, and cook for about 15 minutes, or until softened. Add the tomatoes, vegetable stock and brown sugar, season to taste, and simmer for 10 minutes. Blend to a purée.

▶ Meanwhile, cook the pasta in boiling, lightly salted water according to the instructions on the packet. Toss with the sauce, and serve.

Fusilli with quick-and-easy cheese sauce

⟳ Preparation: 5 minutes; cooking: 6 minutes ✎ Makes 4 portions

✐ Provides calcium, protein, B vitamins including folate, vitamin A and zinc

200g (7oz) **pasta twists (fusilli)**

125g (4oz) **frozen peas**

Sauce

150ml (5fl oz) **single cream**

125g (4oz) grated **Gruyère cheese**

This is an easy recipe to make – the cheese is simply melted into the cream to make a tasty sauce. If your child prefers, leave out the peas and add some strips of ham instead.

▶ Cook the fusilli in boiling, lightly salted water according to the instructions on the packet. About 3 minutes before the pasta is done, add the frozen peas.

▶ Meanwhile, place the cream and cheese in a saucepan and cook over a gentle heat until the cheese has melted.

▶ Drain the pasta and peas and toss them with the cheese sauce.

Pasta salad with tuna and sweetcorn

⟳ Preparation: 7 minutes; cooking: 12 minutes ✎ Makes 2 portions

✐ Provides protein, B vitamins and vitamins C, D and E

60g (2oz) **pasta twists (fusilli)**

100g (3½oz) **canned tuna in oil**, drained and flaked

40g (1¼oz) **canned** or cooked **frozen sweetcorn**

3 **cherry tomatoes**, quartered

1 **spring onion**, finely chopped

Dressing

2 tbsp **mayonnaise**

1 tsp **lemon juice**

1 tsp **light olive oil**

If you like you could also add some avocado to this salad.

▶ Cook the pasta in boiling, lightly salted water according to the instructions on the packet.

▶ Mix together the ingredients for the dressing.

▶ Mix the cooked pasta together with the tuna, sweetcorn, tomatoes and spring onion and toss in the dressing.

Orzo with colourful diced vegetables

⏱ Preparation: 10 minutes; cooking: 15 minutes 🥄 Makes 2 portions 🔪 Provides beta-carotene, calcium, folate, protein and vitamins A and C ❄ Suitable for freezing

90g (3oz) **soup pasta (orzo)**

60g (2oz) **carrots**, peeled and diced

60g (2oz) **courgettes**, diced

60g (2oz) **broccoli**, diced

30g (1oz) **butter**

30g (1oz) freshly grated **Cheddar** or **Parmesan cheese**

Orzo is the name given to tiny pasta shapes that resemble barley kernels (you can also find riso or puntalette – "grains of rice"). Its creamy, slightly chewy texture is very appealing to children.

▶ Put the pasta in a saucepan together with the diced vegetables. Pour over enough boiling water to cover the pasta and vegetables generously and cook for about 12 minutes, or until all the vegetables are tender. Drain thoroughly.

▶ Melt the butter in a large pan, stir in the drained pasta and vegetables, then remove from the heat.

▶ Add the grated cheese and toss until the cheese has completely melted.

Bow-tie pasta with ham & peas

⏱ Preparation: 5 minutes; cooking: 15 minutes 🥄 Makes 4 portions 🔪 Provides calcium, protein, B vitamins including folate, vitamin A and zinc ❄ Suitable for freezing: sauce only

150g (5oz) **pasta bows (farfalle)**

1/2 **vegetable stock cube**

Sauce

20g (3/4oz) **butter**

15g (1/2oz) **plain flour**

300ml (10fl oz) **milk**

1/4 tsp **mustard powder**

60g (2oz) **frozen peas**

60g (2oz) grated **mature Cheddar cheese**

60g (2oz) sliced **cooked ham** or **prosciutto**, cut into strips

salt and freshly ground **black pepper**

Bow-tie pasta is a good shape for young children – don't worry if they treat it as finger food: good manners will come in time! This is also successful made with green and white narrow pasta noodles (tagliolini or taglierini).

▶ Cook the pasta in boiling, lightly salted water according to the instructions on the packet.

▶ Meanwhile, make the sauce. Melt the butter in a small pan, stir in the flour to make a paste, then gradually whisk in the milk and mustard. Stir in the peas and cook for 3 minutes.

▶ Remove from the heat and stir in the cheese until melted. Add the ham, heat through, season then toss with the pasta.

Variations

▶ To make a vegetarian version, omit the ham and add 75g (2½oz) sliced button mushrooms sautéed in a little butter until tender.

▶ Alternatively, omit the ham and add steamed small broccoli florets and diced carrots and add to the cheese sauce.

▶ You could also make this using a mixture of grated Cheddar and Gruyère cheeses.

300g (10oz) **salmon fillets**, skinned

300g (10oz) **cod fillets**, skinned

600ml (20fl oz) **milk**

4 **peppercorns**, 1 **bay leaf** and a **parsley stalk**

30g (1oz) **butter**

1 **onion**, peeled and finely chopped

3 tbsp **plain flour**

1/2 tsp **mustard powder**

125g (4oz) **frozen peas**

125g (4oz) **canned** or **frozen sweetcorn**

1 tbsp snipped **chives**

40g (1 1/2 oz) grated **Cheddar cheese**

salt and freshly ground **black pepper**

Mashed potato

1kg (2lb) **potatoes**, peeled and cut into chunks

4 tbsp **milk**

25g (1oz) **butter**

salt and **white pepper**

1 beaten **egg white**

Joy's fish pie

Preparation: 15 minutes; cooking: 50 minutes   180°C/350°F/gas 4
Makes 4 portions   Provides calcium, fibre, omega-3 fats, potassium, protein, B vitamins including folate, vitamins A and D and zinc   Suitable for freezing

A good fish pie with creamy mashed potato is one of those ever-popular nursery foods. You can leave out the peas and sweetcorn if you prefer and add two chopped hard-boiled eggs instead.

► For the mashed potato, boil some lightly salted water, add the potatoes and boil until tender.

► Meanwhile, put the fish in a shallow pan with the milk, peppercorns and herbs. Bring to the boil, then cover and cook for 5 minutes, or until the fish flakes easily. Remove the fish, strain the milk and reserve. Flake the fish with a fork, checking carefully for bones, and set aside.

► Melt the butter in a small pan, add the onion and sauté until softened. Stir in the flour to make a paste and cook for 1 minute. Gradually add the strained milk, stirring until the sauce thickens.

► Mix in the mustard, peas, sweetcorn, chives and Cheddar cheese. Cook for 2 minutes. Season and add the fish. Then spoon the mixture into a suitable ovenproof dish.

► Drain and mash the potatoes. Add milk, butter and seasoning. Spread the potato over the fish, making peaks with a fork. Brush with beaten egg white and cook in the preheated oven for 25 minutes.

700g (1lb 8oz) medium-sized **Maris Piper** or **King Edward potatoes**

300g (10oz) **salmon fillets**, skinned

100g (3 1/2 oz) grated **Gruyère cheese**

2 medium **egg yolks**, lightly beaten

2 tbsp chopped **fresh parsley**

1 small **onion**, peeled and finely chopped

salt and **white pepper**

100ml (3 1/2 fl oz) **vegetable oil**

Rosti salmon cakes

Preparation: 20 minutes; cooking: 40 minutes   Makes 8 fish cakes
Provides calcium, omega-3 fats, potassium, B vitamins and vitamins A, C, D and E
Suitable for freezing

Rosti is the name given to the grated potato cakes popular in Switzerland and Germany. These salmon fish cakes are slightly crispy on the outside and moist inside. They are the best I have ever eaten, and my children love them too.

► Cook half the potatoes in their skins for 20 minutes in lightly salted water over a medium heat. Drain and leave to cool.

► Meanwhile cut the salmon into bite-sized chunks and mix with the grated cheese, egg yolks, parsley and chopped onion and season well. Peel and grate the cooked potatoes and stir into the salmon mixture.

► Peel and grate the uncooked potatoes, squeeze out the excess moisture and season with salt and ground white pepper. Using your hands, shape the salmon mixture into 8 round fish cakes and then press each fish cake into the raw, grated potato until coated on both sides.

► Heat the oil in a large frying pan and cook the fish cakes a few at a time until golden and cooked through (about 4 minutes on each side). Drain any excess oil onto kitchen paper.

Chicken sausage snails

⟳ Preparation: 20 minutes; cooking: 1 hour 10 minutes

✄ Makes 4 portions   ⚡ Provides iron, protein, B vitamins including folate and zinc

❄ Suitable for freezing: chicken sausages only

Using a little imagination you can make succulent homemade chicken sausages into a fun and visually appealing meal.

▶ Put the chicken in a food processor with the onion, parsley, crumbled stock cube, apple and breadcrumbs. Chop for a few seconds then season the mixture lightly.

▶ Form the mixture into four sausages each about 12cm (5in) long. Spread the flour on a plate and use to coat the sausages. Heat the vegetable oil in a frying pan, add the sausages and sauté for about 15 minutes, turning occasionally, or until browned on all sides and cooked through.

▶ Meanwhile, place the potatoes in the bottom of a steamer, cover with lightly salted water and cook until tender. Five minutes before the potatoes are done, put the vegetables for decorating in the top of the steamer and cook until tender. Mash the potatoes with the milk, butter and seasoning.

▶ To assemble, form the potato into four dome shapes using an ice-cream scoop and decorate with a ketchup spiral to create a snail-shell effect (you can use a piping bag with a small nozzle for this, or cut a small hole in the corner of a freezer bag and use that). Put a sausage underneath each dome of potato. Use the steamed carrot sticks and peas to make the snail's feelers, and arrange the cabbage as grass.

Chicken sausages

375g (12oz) boneless, skinless **chicken breast**, cubed

1 medium **onion**, peeled and finely chopped

1 tbsp chopped **fresh parsley**

1 **chicken stock cube** dissolved in 1 tbsp **boiling water**

1 large **apple**, peeled and grated

2 tbsp **fresh breadcrumbs**

salt and freshly ground **black pepper**

plain flour for coating

vegetable oil for frying

Mashed potato

500g (1lb) **potatoes**, peeled and cut into chunks

2 tbsp **milk**

30g (1oz) **butter**

salt and **white pepper**

To decorate

shredded **savoy cabbage**

1 **carrot**, peeled and cut into sticks

16 **frozen peas**

tomato ketchup

Turkey meatballs

500g (1lb) **minced turkey**

1 **onion**, peeled and finely chopped

1 small **apple**, peeled and grated

3 tbsp **fresh breadcrumbs**

1 **egg**, lightly beaten

2 tbsp chopped **fresh sage** or **thyme**

salt and freshly ground **black pepper**

plain flour for coating

2 tbsp **vegetable oil** for frying

Red pepper sauce

1½ tbsp **vegetable oil**

2 **shallots**, peeled and finely chopped

1½ **red peppers**, deseeded and chopped

1 tsp **tomato purée**

3 tbsp chopped **fresh basil**

450ml (15fl oz) **vegetable stock** (see page 47)

salt and freshly ground **black pepper**

TIP *These can be made ahead and frozen, then simply defrosted and reheated in a microwave (just make sure you test the temperature before giving them to your child).*

Turkey balls & pepper sauce

↻ Preparation: 20 minutes; cooking: 40 minutes ⬇ 180°C/350°F/gas 4
♂ Makes 8 portions ⚡ Provides beta-carotene, iron, protein, B vitamins including folate, vitamins C and E and zinc ❄ Suitable for freezing

Served with rice or spaghetti, these little meatballs make a great lunch. If you have time, roast and skin the peppers for the sauce, which can also be made with chicken stock (see page 52).

▶ To make the red pepper sauce, heat the oil in a frying pan, add the shallots and red peppers, and sauté until softened. Stir in the remaining ingredients and season to taste. Bring to the boil and simmer for 15–20 minutes. Blend until smooth.

▶ Mix together all the ingredients for the meatballs, seasoning to taste. Use your hands to form the mixture into about 24 walnut-sized balls. Spread the flour on a plate and use to coat the meatballs. Heat the oil in a frying pan, add the balls and sauté, turning until they are golden all over.

▶ Transfer the meatballs to a casserole, cover with pepper sauce, and cook in the preheated oven for about 20 minutes, or until the meatballs are cooked through and well browned.

Finger picking chicken & potato balls

⏱ Preparation: 10 minutes; cooking: 40 minutes   ⚙ Makes 8 portions
🔪 Provides beta-carotene, folate, potassium, protein and vitamin E
❄ Suitable for freezing

Mashed potato and parsnip give these balls a soft texture and a hint of sweetness, and they are just the right size for picking up and nibbling.

▶ Put the potatoes and parsnips in a pan, cover with water, bring to the boil then simmer, covered, for 12–15 minutes, or until tender.

▶ Meanwhile, heat 1 tablespoon of oil in a frying pan, add the onion and carrot, and sauté for 4–5 minutes. Add the chicken and continue to sauté for about 10 minutes, or until cooked through.

▶ Drain the potatoes and parsnips and mash with half the butter until smooth. Finely chop the chicken, onion and carrot in a food processor and mix with the mashed vegetables.

▶ Form the mixture into 24 walnut-sized balls. Spread the flour on a plate and use to coat them. Heat the remaining oil and butter in a frying pan, add the meatballs and sauté until golden.

125g (4oz) **potatoes**, peeled and chopped

125g (4oz) **parsnips**, peeled and chopped

3 tbsp **vegetable oil**

1/2 small **onion**, peeled and finely chopped

1 **carrot**, peeled and grated

125g (4oz) boneless, skinless **chicken breast**, cut into chunks

large knob of **butter**

plain flour for coating

Shepherd's pie

⏱ Preparation: 5 minutes; cooking: 1 hour 10 minutes   🌡 180°C/350°F/gas 4
⚙ Makes 8 portions   🔪 Provides beta-carotene, iron, potassium, protein, B vitamins including folate, vitamin C and zinc   ❄ Suitable for freezing

If you prefer you can make the shepherd's pie in individual ramekins and decorate with vegetable faces (see page 164).

▶ Warm the oil in a pan, add the onion, red pepper and garlic, and sauté until softened. Add the meat and sauté until browned. If desired, transfer the cooked mixture to a food processor and chop for a few seconds on the pulse setting.

▶ Transfer the meat to a saucepan and add the stock, parsley, yeast extract, tomato purée, Worcestershire sauce and mushrooms. Cook over a medium heat for about 20 minutes.

▶ Meanwhile, boil the potatoes in lightly salted water until tender, then drain and mash with 30g (1oz) of butter and the milk. Season to taste.

▶ Arrange the meat either in one large dish or in individual ramekins, cover with the mashed potato and dot the topping with the remaining butter. Cook in the preheated oven for 20 minutes.

Variation

▶ To make cottage pie, replace the minced lamb with the same quantity of lean minced beef. For the topping, omit the mashed potato and replace it with 1kg (2lb) boiled and mashed swede, or use a combination of mashed swede and potato.

1 1/2 tbsp **vegetable oil**

1 large **onion**, peeled and chopped

1 small **red pepper**, finely chopped

1 **garlic clove**, peeled and crushed

500g (1lb) lean **minced lamb**

300ml (10fl oz) **chicken stock** (see page 52) or **beef stock**

1 tbsp chopped **fresh parsley**

1/2 tsp **yeast extract**

1 tbsp **tomato purée**

1/4 tsp **Worcestershire sauce**

175g (6oz) **mushrooms**, sliced

Mashed potato

1kg (2lb) **potatoes**, peeled and roughly chopped

45g (1 1/2oz) **butter**

4 tbsp **milk**

salt and **white pepper**

TIP To make minced meat more palatable to young children, cook it first and then chop it in a food processor.

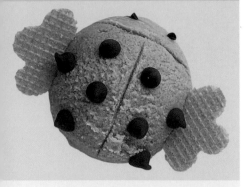

Raspberry frozen yogurt

↻ Preparation: 2 minutes; cooking: 35 minutes, including 20 minutes freezing

⚭ Makes 8 portions   ⚘ Provides calcium, protein and vitamins B12 and C

This frozen yogurt recipe can also be made with a mixture of berries – perhaps strawberries, blackberries and raspberries. A few minutes before you want to eat it, take it from the freezer and allow to soften slightly. Serve by itself or with some fresh raspberries.

250g (8oz) **frozen** or **fresh raspberries**

4 tbsp **caster sugar**

125ml (4fl oz) **water**

300–350ml (10–12fl oz) mild, full-fat **natural yogurt**

6 tbsp **crème fraîche**

2–3 tbsp **icing sugar**

TIP If you don't have an ice-cream maker, place the mixture in a plastic tub and freeze for about 1 hour. Then beat by hand or in a food processor to break up the ice crystals. Freeze again, repeating the beating procedure once or twice during freezing.

▶ Put the raspberries in a saucepan with the sugar and water. Bring to a simmer, then cook for 5 minutes. Purée using a hand-held blender, then strain through a sieve to get rid of the seeds. Leave to cool.

▶ Stir the yogurt and crème fraîche into the raspberry purée and add just enough icing sugar to sweeten. Transfer to an ice-cream maker and freeze for about 20 minutes.

Variation

▶ Mix 375ml (13fl oz) cherry yogurt with 6 tablespoons of crème fraîche. Stir in 200g (7oz) canned stoned black cherries, 100ml (3½fl oz) maple syrup and 45g (1½oz) grated plain chocolate. Transfer to an ice-cream maker, and freeze as described above.

Yogurt pancakes

↻ Preparation: 2 minutes; cooking: 10 minutes   ⚭ Makes 8 portions

⚘ Provides calcium, protein and vitamins B2, B12 and C (served with fruit)

❄ Suitable for freezing (see tip, left)

Mini pancakes are delicious served with fresh fruit and maple syrup. You could also add a few sultanas to a maple syrup-sweetened batter to make sultana pancakes.

1 **egg**, lightly beaten

150ml (5fl oz) mild, full-fat **natural yogurt**

150ml (5fl oz) **milk**

150g (5oz) **self-raising flour**

¼ tsp **salt** or 2 tbsp **maple syrup** (for a sweeter version)

vegetable oil for frying

To accompany

pure **maple syrup**

fresh fruit, such as strawberries, raspberries or sliced peaches

TIP These pancakes can be layered between pieces of waxed or greaseproof paper and then frozen. They can be reheated in a toaster.

▶ Mix together the beaten egg and the yogurt, then stir in the milk, flour and salt or maple syrup. Mix until you have a smooth batter.

▶ Heat a little oil in a frying pan until sizzling hot. Drop heaped tablespoons of batter into the pan, leaving plenty of space around each one, and flatten slightly with a palette knife. They should spread to about 6cm (2½ in) across. Cook for 1–2 minutes until lightly browned, then turn and cook for a further 1–2 minutes until browned on the other side and set in the centre.

▶ Drizzle the maple syrup over the pancakes and serve scattered with fruit.

Raisin toast fingers

↻ Preparation: 10 minutes ✂ Makes 1 portion ✐ Provides magnesium and potassium

Simple to prepare, this filling snack or dessert is an appealing mix of sweet and savoury tastes.

▶ Toast the raisin bread and spread with peanut butter or cream cheese.

▶ Arrange the sliced banana on top and cut into fingers, squares or triangles.

1 slice **raisin bread**

½ tbsp **smooth peanut butter** or **cream cheese**

½ small **banana**, peeled and sliced

Jelly boats

↻ Preparation: 5 minutes; cooking: 10 minutes plus 1 hour 45 minutes setting
✂ Makes 8 portions ✐ Provides vitamin C if using added fruit

Of all the foods I make for parties, these ingeniously simple jellies are perhaps the most popular.

▶ Squeeze the juice from the orange halves (keep it to make into a drink) without breaking the skins. Carefully scrape out the membrane and discard.

▶ Make the jelly according to packet instructions, reducing the amount of water specified by a quarter if using fruit. Divide the fruit, if using, between the orange halves then fill with jelly and refrigerate until set.

▶ Take a wet knife and cut each orange half in half again. Thread a cocktail stick down the centre of each rice paper triangle, then set the sail in the jelly.

Variation

▶ Choose three contrastingly coloured jellies and set each layer separately in a tall glass. Set the first layer of jelly in the fridge with the glass propped at an angle so that the jelly sets diagonally. Do the same with the second layer of jelly. Then, pour in the last layer of jelly and set with the glass standing upright.

2 large **oranges**, halved

1 x 135g (4½oz) **packet fruit jelly**, such as strawberry or orange

1 small can **mandarin orange segments** (optional)

1 small punnet **fresh raspberries** (optional)

To decorate

8 small **rice paper** triangles

8 **cocktail sticks**

NOTE *These jelly boats use cocktail sticks. For young children, place the boats on each child's plate then remove the cocktail sticks before they begin to eat.*

18 months to 2 years

The active toddler

Food tastes are decided early in life, so you should aim to establish a varied, healthy diet for your child while he is still receptive to new foods and before peer pressure and TV advertising take their toll. However, despite your best efforts, your plans may be derailed by a period of faddy or erratic eating and you may have to use a little ingenuity to stimulate his appetite. This chapter is full of ideas for healthy "fast foods" and easy ways to prepare some all-time favourite children's recipes to tempt even the most reluctant child.

"Once your child knows that he can get your full, undivided attention by not eating something or playing with his food, that is exactly what he will do. Remove the food rather than create an issue out of his behaviour."

Busy bodies

As your child nears his second birthday, his growth rate slows down substantially. At the same time, his levels of activity are on the increase because he has greater physical competence and probably a busier, more active daily schedule. As a result, your rounded baby will become a slimmed-down, active toddler, losing much of his "puppy fat".

Although he has high energy requirements, his small stomach will probably cope best with light meals interspersed with "top-up" snacks. Remember that toddlers are not conditioned into eating by the clock, and, quite sensibly, will tend to want to eat only when they are truly hungry.

By this age they will be fairly vocal in their preferences and you will want to give your child easily prepared food that you can rustle up quickly (see pages 92–93) before his hungry demands become furious outbursts. Of course, you will want to create some structure and routine for family mealtimes, but be flexible. The last thing you want to do is make an issue over "correct" mealtimes, turning your child into a resentful eater. Ninety per cent of children are fussy eaters at some point during their childhood.

Tantrums

Remember that your child is entering the stage of toddler tantrums when the frustrations he encounters can lead him to explode with rage. It is hard for you, too, and you may need to try out a number of ways to encourage his eating (see page 91). Avoid using bribes to get him to eat, however, as you will only encourage difficult behaviour.

GRAZING HABITS

Snacks are an important part of a child's diet and you should try to ensure that there are plenty of healthy and tasty snacks available rather than let your child eat chocolates, biscuits or crisps between meals. Prepare a selection of cut-up fresh fruit or vegetables and leave them in the fridge ready for when your child is hungry.

If you are worried that your child's food intake is low, and that the amounts of food she consumes at mealtimes are miniscule, keep a diary of her total food intake over a period of a few days, perhaps a week. Many children have the habit of "grazing" – taking a little food here and there – and if you add up all these snacks you may find that your child's diet is reasonably substantial and balanced.

Limiting sugary foods

As toddlers are exposed to an increasingly varied diet, they may be quick to acquire a "sweet tooth". Since they are most likely to pick up their eating habits from the immediate family, you may need to be strong-minded yourself if you want your child to have a low sugar intake.

It is not just the amount of sugar we eat that harms our teeth but also the frequency with which we put sugary foods in our mouth: each time we eat sugary foods, the bacteria in dental plaque produce acids that attack tooth enamel and can cause tooth decay. Consequently, a packet of sweets consumed all in one go does less harm than eating the sweets over a prolonged period of time.

Try to confine sugary foods to mealtimes, not only to reduce the frequency of eating sugary foods but also because eating other foods at the same time dilutes the acid and reduces the harmful effects of the sugar. Moreover, at mealtimes there is more saliva in the mouth to wash away acids. Cheese is particularly beneficial

at the end of a meal as it is alkaline and helps to neutralize the harmful acid that causes tooth decay.

Do not let sweets and puddings become synonymous with rewards: try to offer other treats, such as stickers or comics. Consider making a rule that sweets are allowed only at certain times, perhaps once a week.

Sweet drinks

Even pure fruit juices contain fructose (a natural sugar) which can cause tooth decay, so confine diluted fruit juices to mealtimes, when they can also benefit your child by increasing the absorption of iron from food. Read labels carefully; sugar can be disguised under other names such as glucose, maltose or dextrose. Some individual cartons of fruit juice contain as much as six teaspoons of sugar. Diet soft drinks are no kinder to teeth as they too contain acids that attack tooth enamel. Sweet drinks at bedtime are not a good idea, as saliva won't wash away the acid during the night and you'll destroy any good work done by toothpaste.

"Top up" foods
For a quick spurt of energy:
- bowl of cornflakes
- pieces of fruit, fresh or dried
- yogurt with honey

For a steady stream of energy:
- raw vegetables with dips
- bread with ham, tuna or cheese
- jacket potato with filling
- baked beans on toast
- salad with hard-boiled egg
- oatcakes with cheese
- freshly made fruit milkshakes

Remember
- The stickier the food, the more likely it is to cause tooth decay. Even seemingly healthy foods, such as raisins or chewy cereal bars, can harm your child's teeth if eaten too often between meals.

- Fruits such as bananas, apples, pears, clementines and grapes make good snacks. They contain slow-release sugars that give your child energy as well as vital vitamins.

Tooth-friendly snacks
- vegetable sticks, such as carrot, cucumber, sweet pepper, celery, on their own or with a dip • cheese • cheese on toast • lightly salted popcorn • toasted seeds • fingers of toast • cream cheese with mini bread sticks • rice cakes, oatcakes • mini sandwiches with Marmite, egg mayonnaise, or cream cheese and cucumber • mini pitta pockets filled with tuna mayonnaise • mini salads, such as mozzarella and tomato, or pasta with tuna and sweetcorn • fresh fruit

The fussy eater

"A fussy diet may be nutritious, if unconventional – no young child ever starves himself! Remember, it is the balance of his diet over several days that really matters."

Refusing food is one of the first ways young children can flex their muscles and assert their drive for independence. It doesn't take them long to realize how easy it is to manipulate you at the dinner table. Indeed, battles at mealtimes are often one of the most stressful aspects of early parenthood. Cajoling a child to eat – whether in the form of bribery or threats – is usually counter-productive.

Keeping calm

However unreasonable your child's eating habits seem to be, try to respond calmly. The aim is to help your child slot into normal family eating, not to force him into co-operation. Don't put pressure on your child to eat the foods you want him to eat. Aim to keep the emotional temperature down: food shouldn't be used as a means to teach a child to do as he is told.

Unfortunately, many children seem to enjoy stretching their parents' patience to the limit: after all, refusing to eat makes them the centre of attention. Refuse to be riled; simply take the rejected meal away but don't offer unhealthy alternatives. Attempting to induce guilt won't work either: telling a child that he has a moral duty to leave a clean plate is unlikely to motivate a two year old into finishing his dinner.

No young child ever starves himself and his fussy diet may well be nutritious, if unconventional. Remember that it is the balance of his diet over several days that really matters.

STRATEGIES TO COPE WITH A FUSSY EATER

• Limit empty calorie snacks, such as crisps or chocolate, and keep a supply of healthy snacks on hand – maybe have a low shelf in the fridge with cut-up fresh fruit and other healthy foods. When children are hungry, they won't wait.

• If your child will not eat vegetables on their own, create recipes that vegetables can be blended into, such as tomato and vegetable sauce for pasta or creamy tomato soup made with carrots and onions. What children cannot see, they cannot pick out. Also, many children who do not like cooked vegetables will eat them raw, such as carrot sticks or sweet pepper with a tasty dip.

• Only buy the foods that you want your child to eat.

• It's important to introduce as many foods as possible at an early age. You could try making a game out of this by blindfolding your child before introducing a new food and asking him to guess what it is.

• Without going to unnecessary lengths, try to make sure your child's food not only tastes good but looks good too. Choose colourful food and arrange it in an interesting pattern on the plate.

• Mealtimes are social occasions, so set a good example by eating with your child as often as possible. You cannot expect your child to realize that mealtimes involve sitting down in one place for some time unless he sees you and the rest of the family doing so. Try to avoid distractions such as watching television at mealtimes.

• Inviting another child over for tea, preferably one with a good appetite, is a good ruse. Invariably, you will find that your child will eat whatever his friend is eating!

• Once a child's palate has become accustomed to the intense sweetness of refined sugary foods it is harder for him to appreciate the more gentle natural sweetness of fruit. So, if you want your child to enjoy fresh fruit, restrict his intake of sugary foods.

• If your child is underweight and not eating well he needs as much energy (calories) as possible. Offer full-fat dairy products, such as cheese, milkshakes or good-quality ice-cream, and avoid using "low-fat" dairy products. Make sure he isn't filling up on drinks, sweets or too much milk.

• Too much food on a plate can be off-putting. Keep portions small and give second helpings if requested. Children tend to find individual portions of food, shepherd's pie in ramekin dishes, for example, much more appealing than a dollop of food on a plate.

• Give your child scope to assert his independence, perhaps by letting him choose two out of the three vegetables offered to him.

• After a period of time, try re-introducing foods that your child once refused.

• Do not give the same recipe to your child over and over again just because you know he likes it. He will probably become bored with it and refuse to eat it after a while.

Faddy eating

Occasionally, children go through periods of eating only a few specific foods. Don't worry too much. Children can thrive on quite a limited range of foods and, except in rare cases, will eventually get bored of a monotonous diet. If, for example, your child wants only peanut butter sandwiches at every meal, make sure the bread is wholemeal and give him a milkshake or glass of milk to accompany the sandwich. At the same time, continue to offer tasty and nutritious alternatives.

Sometimes fads may appear even more irrational: your child might refuse foods that have come into contact with each other on his plate, for instance. In this case, a sectioned plate may provide the solution.

Rejecting specific foods

If your child continually rejects a particular food, you can assume that he really doesn't like it. Try to recognize when your child is being stubborn and when he has a genuine dislike of a particular food.

If vegetables are a problem, there are many ways to disguise them in the diet (see page 71). Meat is another food that is often rejected. A healthy diet need not include meat provided your child's diet includes milk and dairy products, beans and pulses or soya-based products, which will provide adequate quantities of protein, iron and B vitamins (see page 13). However, it is often the texture rather than the taste of meat that children object to. If your child dislikes lumps of meat, try giving him dishes such as spaghetti bolognese (see page 67) or shepherd's pie (see page 83), blending the meat until fairly smooth. Alternatively, make bite-sized meatballs (see page 103) and serve them with ketchup, or mince some meat very finely, moisten with gravy and mix it into a combination of mashed potato and carrot.

Remember

• Avoid empty calories, as in soft drinks or sweets; keep a supply of healthy snacks.

• Offer full-fat milk, yogurts and cheese. Semi-skimmed milk should not be offered as a drink until your child is at least two years old.

• If your child likes to play with his food before eating it, let him, and forget about perfecting table manners for the time being.

• Provide small servings or make individual portions of food: these are less off-putting and allow your child some control over how much food he takes.

• Change the venue of meals occasionally, even a picnic lunch on the floor may work.

Fast food for toddlers

The active toddler's hunger rarely coincides with regular mealtimes. Because she uses up energy so quickly with her new-found independence, light, frequent snacks may best suit her needs. She is also too young to wait patiently for meals, so it is a good idea to be able to offer easy-to-prepare, healthy "fast foods". All the foods shown here are visually appealing and have interesting textures and vibrant flavours – and all can be eaten on the run.

1 Pinwheel sandwiches
The most versatile of fast foods, shaped sandwiches make savoury mouthfuls. Toddlers will adore these sticky spirals of soft brown bread rolled with their favourite fillings. (See page 95 for recipe.)

2 Chunky tomato & cream cheese dip
Children often prefer vegetables raw, especially if cut to form whimsical shapes, and they love dunking them into dips. This ensemble makes a nutritious between-meals snack. (See page 94 for recipe.)

3 Kebabs in pitta pockets
Miniature kebabs can be grilled, taken off the skewers and stuffed into warm pitta bread pockets with some colourful salad leaves. Chicken with tomatoes, and tofu with chunky vegetables are delicious combinations. (See pages 98 and 102 for recipes.)

1

2

3

Scrambled eggs with cheese & tomato

2 **eggs**

1 tbsp **milk** or **single cream**

salt and freshly ground **black pepper**

15g (½oz) **butter**

1 **tomato**, skinned, deseeded and chopped

2 tbsp grated **Gruyère cheese**

Preparation: 2 minutes; cooking: 6 minutes   Makes 2 portions

Provides calcium, iron, protein, B vitamins and vitamins A and E

Scrambled eggs make a quick and nutritious family breakfast. Serve them with a toasted bagel or buttered toast. For a special breakfast or brunch, add strips of smoked salmon.

▶ Beat the eggs with the milk and season lightly. Melt the butter in a saucepan over a low heat, add the chopped tomato and sauté for 1 minute.

▶ Add the egg mixture and heat, stirring continuously with a wooden spoon, until the eggs start to cook. Add the cheese and continue to stir until the eggs are set.

Apple, mango & apricot muesli

45g (1½oz) each chopped **dried mango** and **apricots**

30g (1oz) **sultanas** or **raisins**

125g (4oz) **muesli base**, or 60g (2oz) each of **oat flakes** and **wheat flakes**

30g (1oz) finely chopped **hazelnuts** (optional)

350ml (12fl oz) **apple and mango juice** or plain **apple juice**

½ **red apple**, cored and chopped

extra **fresh fruit**, such as banana or raspberries (optional)

NOTE *This recipe contains nuts. Omit the nuts if there is a family history of nut allergy.*

Preparation: 5 minutes, plus overnight soaking   Makes 4 portions   Provides beta-carotene, fibre, iron, potassium, protein, B vitamins including folate, vitamin A and zinc

Unfortunately, many breakfast cereals designed for children are low in nutrients and high in sugar. I make a healthy, Swiss-style muesli for my family, using a bought muesli base – a mixture of rolled oats, wheat, barley and rye flakes – and fresh fruit. This mix, without the added fresh fruit, can be kept refrigerated for several days.

▶ Soak the dried fruit, muesli base and nuts in the juice overnight or for several hours. In the morning, stir in the apple and your chosen extra fresh fruit and serve with milk, if desired.

Variation

▶ Make a deliciously unusual muesli by substituting grape juice for the apple juice and using chopped dried peaches instead of mango and apricots.

Chunky tomato & cream cheese dip

200g (7oz) **soft cream cheese**

3 tbsp **mayonnaise**

1 tbsp **tomato ketchup**

1 tsp **fresh lemon juice**

¼ tsp **Worcestershire sauce**

¼ tsp **soy sauce**

½ tbsp snipped **chives**

2 **tomatoes**, skinned, deseeded and chopped

TIP *This dip can also be made with low-fat dairy produce, but only for older children.*

Preparation: 10 minutes, plus overnight soaking   Makes 8 portions

Provides vitamins A, B12 and E

Serve this appealing dip with raw and cooked vegetables, bread soldiers or pitta toasts for a tasty and energizing snack.

▶ Simply mix all the ingredients together, blending them thoroughly, and serve.

Variation

▶ To make a cream cheese and chive dip, mix together the same quantities of soft cream cheese and mayonnaise with 3 tablespoons of milk. Mix in 1 teaspoon of Dijon mustard, 2 tablespoons of snipped chives, a pinch of sugar and freshly ground pepper to taste. Blend thoroughly and serve.

Shaped sandwiches

Sandwiches make a quick snack that can be eaten on the run. What's more, you can use all sorts of fillings and types of bread. Try to use foods from each of the main groups – bread, fruit and vegetables, meat and alternatives, dairy products – to make sandwiches that are nutritious alternatives to cooked meals.

Open sandwiches

Cut slices of bread into simple shapes, or into animal shapes using biscuit cutters. Butter and then spread with filling. Try cottage cheese or mashed egg sheep or ducks or Cheddar cheese butterflies; geometric shapes spread with a favourite filling, such as diamond-shaped bread kites spread with mashed avocado, or with thinly sliced ham, turkey or chicken; or bread and cheese squares decorated to look like parcels with red pepper, tomato or chive ribbons.

Double-decker sandwiches

Take three slices of buttered brown or white bread, with the centre slice buttered on both sides. Sandwich together with two complementary but contrasting fillings, such as sliced banana and strawberry jam; grated cheese, shredded lettuce and yeast extract; or egg mayonnaise and tuna mayonnaise. Cut into strips.

Pinwheel sandwiches

Trim the crusts off two thin slices of bread. Overlap the edges slightly and flatten with a rolling pin so that they join together. Butter and spread with a colourful filling and roll up, Swiss-roll-fashion. Cut across into thin rounds. Suggested fillings include peanut butter and jam; cream cheese and mashed avocado; egg mayonnaise; or ham or turkey slices.

Mini pitta bread pockets

Warm a small pitta bread, cut it in half and fill with a savoury mix, such as tuna mayonnaise with salad; grated cheese or shredded chicken or ham with salad; sliced hard-boiled egg with lettuce; or mashed sardines and sliced tomato.

Tortilla wraps

Wraps make a good alternative to sandwiches. Warm small flour tortillas and fill with thin slices of turkey, shredded lettuce and grated cheese with a little salad cream. Try also chicken and salsa or tuna salad.

2 tbsp **vegetable oil**

1 **onion**, peeled and finely chopped

125g (4oz) **carrots**, peeled and diced

1/2 **celery stalk**, finely chopped

30g (1oz) **leeks**, white part only, washed and finely chopped

125g (4oz) **potatoes**, peeled and chopped

60g (2oz) **courgettes**, diced

2 ripe **tomatoes**, skinned, deseeded and chopped

1.5 litres (50fl oz) **chicken stock** (see page 52)

2 tsp **tomato purée**

60g (2oz) **frozen peas**

45g (1½oz) **alphabet pasta**

salt and freshly ground **black pepper**

TIP This soup can also be made with vegetable stock (see page 47).

Alphabet pasta minestrone

↻ Preparation: 10 minutes; cooking: 45 minutes   ⬔ Makes 8 portions
⚕ Provides beta-carotene, fibre, folate, potassium and vitamins C and E
❄ Suitable for freezing

Homemade minestrone makes a nutritious soup for children, and also becomes a satisfying family meal if supplemented by bread and salad. You can add shredded cabbage (about 125g/4oz) to make it even more substantial, if you like. The tiny alphabet pasta shapes appeal to children.

▶ Heat the oil in a large pan, add the onion and sauté for about 5 minutes. Add the carrots, celery and leeks, and sauté until they begin to soften, about 5 minutes. Add the potatoes and courgettes and sauté for 2–3 minutes.
▶ Stir in the chopped tomatoes, stock and tomato purée. Bring to the boil, then cover and simmer for 20 minutes. Add the frozen peas, return the soup to the boil, and cook for 5 minutes.

▶ Stir in the alphabet pasta, return the soup to the boil, then simmer for about 5 minutes. Taste and season lightly.

125g (4oz) **pasta bows (farfalle)**

Sauce

30g (1oz) **butter**

30g (1oz) **leeks**, washed and finely chopped

60g (2oz) **carrots**, peeled and diced

60g (2oz) **courgettes**, diced

60g (2oz) **broccoli**, cut into very small florets

salt and freshly ground **black pepper**

150ml (5fl oz) **single cream**

30g (1oz) freshly grated **Parmesan cheese**

Bow-tie pasta with spring vegetables

↻ Preparation: 10 minutes; cooking: 20 minutes   ⬔ Makes 4 portions
⚕ Provides beta-carotene, calcium, fibre, folate, protein and vitamins A, B12 and C
❄ Suitable for freezing: sauce only

This dish is simple to prepare but never fails to please. You can use other pasta shapes, such as tagliatelle or penne, with the creamy sauce, and you can use other vegetables depending on what your child likes. Try broccoli, sweetcorn and peas.

▶ Cook the pasta in boiling, lightly salted water according to the instructions on the packet.
▶ Meanwhile, melt the butter in a heavy-based saucepan, add the leeks and carrots, and sauté for about 5 minutes. Add the diced courgettes and broccoli and cook for about 7 minutes, or until all the vegetables are tender. Season to taste.

▶ Pour in the cream and cook, stirring, for 1 minute. Remove from the heat and stir in the Parmesan. Toss the pasta with the sauce, and serve.

Pasta twists, broccoli, beansprouts & baby sweetcorn

⏲ Preparation: 5 minutes; cooking: 12 minutes   ⚔ Makes 4 portions
🥄 Provides folate, potassium, protein and vitamins A and C

175g (6oz) **pasta twists (fusilli)**

125g (4oz) **broccoli**, cut into florets

125g (4oz) **baby sweetcorn**, cut into quarters

30g (1oz) **butter**

1/2 tbsp **sunflower oil**

1 **onion**, peeled and finely chopped

1 **garlic clove**, peeled and crushed

175g (6oz) **beansprouts**

1 **chicken stock cube**, dissolved in 100ml (3 1/2 fl oz) **boiling water**

▶ Cook the pasta in boiling, lightly salted water according to the instructions on the packet. Steam the broccoli and baby sweetcorn for 4 minutes, then set aside.
▶ Put the butter and oil in a wok and sauté the onion and garlic for 3 minutes. Add the beansprouts and sauté for 3 minutes more. Add the steamed broccoli and baby sweetcorn and stir-fry for 1 minute.
▶ Stir in the chicken stock, add the cooked, drained pasta and heat through.

Mini pizzas

⏲ Preparation: 10 minutes; cooking: 15 minutes   ⚔ Makes 4 portions
🥄 Provides calcium, protein, B vitamins and vitamin A

2 **muffins**, split in half, or 1 small **baguette**, cut in half

4 tbsp good **tomato sauce** (homemade or bought)

60g (2oz) grated **Cheddar, Gruyère** or **mozzarella cheese**

Topping

15g (1/2 oz) **butter**

1 tbsp chopped **spring onion**

60g (2oz) **courgettes**, thinly sliced

60g (2oz) **mushrooms**, sliced

salt and freshly ground **black pepper**

Adding a selection of colourful vegetables to mini pizzas is a great way to encourage your child to eat more vegetables. For a special occasion, you might like to make an animal-face design as shown below.

▶ To make the topping, warm the butter in a pan, add the spring onion and sauté for 1 minute. Add the courgettes and mushrooms and sauté until just tender, about 4 minutes. Season to taste. Preheat the grill to high.
▶ Lightly toast the muffins or baguette. Divide the tomato sauce between each of the cut sides of muffin or baguette, spread evenly, then scatter with cheese.
▶ Top with cooked vegetables, perhaps making patterns or animal faces, then cook under the grill until the cheese is bubbling and golden.
▶ To create a mouse face (see right, bottom), use steamed courgette pieces for the ears, stuffed olive slices for the eyes, a black olive for the nose, strips of carrot for the whiskers and two sweetcorn kernels for the teeth.

▶ To make a bear face (see right, top), use sliced carrot for the ears, oval shapes cut from a slice of cheese, sliced mushrooms sautéed in a little butter and sliced stoned black olives for the eyes, stoned black olives for the nose and mouth and fine strips of red pepper for whiskers.

Variation

▶ For a non-vegetarian mini pizza, top with diced ham or, if your child prefers, pepperoni in addition to, or instead of, the cooked and raw vegetables.

125g (4oz) **basmati rice**

1½ tbsp **vegetable oil**

1 **onion**, peeled and cut into rings

1 **garlic clove**, peeled and crushed

60g (2oz) **baby sweetcorn**, cut into quarters

60g (2oz) **carrots**, peeled, sliced thinly and cut into shapes with a tiny biscuit cutter

90g (3oz) **broccoli**, cut into small florets

90g (3oz) **beansprouts**

30g (1oz) **red pepper**, cored, deseeded and cut into strips

1 **spring onion**, finely chopped

pinch of **black pepper**

Sweet & sour sauce

175ml (6fl oz) **vegetable stock** (see page 47)

½ tbsp **cornflour** blended with 1 tbsp **cold water**

2 tsp **soft brown sugar**

½ tbsp **soy sauce**

Sweet & sour vegetable stir-fry

⏱ Preparation: 15 minutes; cooking: 15 minutes　🍴 Makes 4 portions

📋 Provides beta-carotene, fibre, folate and vitamins C and E

You can encourage your child to eat vegetables by appealing to her visual senses with this colourful stir-fry. It's important to ensure that the vegetables remain crisp to retain their flavour and nutrients.

▶ Rinse the rice, then cook it in boiling, lightly salted water, according to the instructions on the packet.

▶ For young children, blanch the carrots and broccoli to make them softer to chew.

▶ Heat the oil in a wok or frying pan. Add the onion and garlic and sauté until softened, about 5 minutes. Add the sweetcorn, carrots and broccoli, and stir-fry for a further 3 minutes.

▶ Add the beansprouts, red pepper and spring onion and stir-fry for a further 3 minutes. Season with black pepper.

▶ To make the sauce, blend the vegetable stock with the cornflour paste in a small pan. Mix in the brown sugar and soy sauce. Set over a high heat, bring to the boil and simmer for about 2 minutes, until the sauce is thickened.

▶ Toss the hot vegetables with the sauce, and heat through in the wok. Serve on a bed of fluffy white rice.

275g (9oz) **firm tofu**, cubed

6 **baby sweetcorn**, halved

1 **courgette**, trimmed and sliced into round chunks

8 **cherry tomatoes**

4 **mini pittas**, split in half

salad leaves, to garnish

Marinade

1½ tbsp **soy sauce**

1½ tbsp **runny honey**

1½ tbsp **Chinese plum sauce**

1 tbsp **vegetable oil**

1 **spring onion**, finely chopped

TIP The sweetcorn and courgette may be parboiled before skewering, if preferred.

Sweetcorn, cherry tomato & tofu kebabs

⏱ Preparation: 1 hour 5 minutes, including 1 hour marinating; cooking: 6 minutes

🍴 Makes 4 portions　📋 Provides calcium, fibre, folate, omega-3 fats, protein and vitamins C and E

Tofu (soya bean curd) is a nutritious alternative to meat. Although naturally bland, it is delicious marinated as it soaks up flavours well, and its soft texture appeals to children.

▶ Combine the ingredients for the marinade in a small jug. Put the tofu in a shallow bowl and pour over the marinade. Cover and leave to soak for about 1 hour. While the tofu marinates, soak four wooden skewers in cold water to stop them burning when under the grill. Preheat the grill.

▶ Thread alternate cubes of tofu, sweetcorn, courgette and the tomatoes on the skewers. Brush with some of the marinade. Cook under a hot grill or on the barbecue for about 3 minutes

on each side, basting occasionally, or until the vegetables are tender and the tofu is nicely browned.

▶ Slide the kebabs off the skewers, arrange in the pitta pockets and garnish with salad leaves.

200g (7oz) **sweet potato**, peeled

100g (3¹/₂oz) **butternut squash** or **pumpkin**, peeled

150g (5oz) **potatoes**, peeled

75g (2¹/₂oz) **leeks**, white part only, washed and finely chopped

150g (5oz) **mushrooms**, chopped

2 tbsp chopped **fresh parsley**

125g (4oz) **fresh breadcrumbs**

¹/₂ tbsp **soy sauce**

¹/₂ lightly beaten **egg**

salt and freshly ground **black pepper**

plain flour for coating

vegetable oil for frying

Annabel's vegetable rissoles

⏱ Preparation: 25 minutes; cooking: 10 minutes 🥄 Makes 4 portions

Provides beta-carotene, calcium, fibre, iron, B vitamins and vitamins C and E

❄ Suitable for freezing

TIP This recipe is best made with soft white breadcrumbs, but you can use wholemeal breadcrumbs.

These rissoles are tasty eaten hot or cold and are ideal for a lunchbox or picnic.

▶ Grate the sweet potato, squash and potato. Squeeze out some of the excess moisture from the grated pulp.
▶ In a mixing bowl, combine all the vegetables with the parsley, breadcrumbs, soy sauce and beaten egg. Season to taste.
▶ Form the mixture into about 12 walnut-sized rissoles. Spread the flour out thinly on a plate and use to coat the rissoles lightly.
▶ Heat the oil in a large frying pan, add the rissoles and sauté over a medium heat for 8–10 minutes, turning, until golden on the outside and cooked through.

Vegetarian croquettes

⏱ Preparation: 10 minutes; cooking: 30 minutes 🌡 180°C/350°F/gas 4

🥄 Makes 8 portions Provides beta-carotene, calcium, fibre, folate, protein and vitamins B12 and C ❄ Suitable for freezing

500g (1lb) **potatoes**, peeled and roughly chopped

knob of **butter**

salt and **white pepper**

75g (2¹/₂oz) **broccoli**, cut into small florets

75g (2¹/₂oz) **carrots**, peeled and chopped

45g (1¹/₂oz) **frozen sweetcorn**

60g (2oz) **Cheddar cheese**

60g (2oz) **ready salted crisps**, crushed

▶ Bring a large pan of lightly salted water to the boil, add the potatoes and cook until tender. Drain and mash with the butter and seasoning.
▶ Meanwhile, place the vegetables in a steamer and cook until tender, about 6–7 minutes.
▶ Mix into the mashed potato and season to taste.

▶ Cut the cheese into eight sticks. Use your hands to shape the potato and vegetable mixture around the cheese to form eight sausage-shaped croquettes.
▶ Roll the croquettes in the crushed crisps until well coated and place on a baking tray. Transfer to the preheated oven and bake for 15 minutes.

Salmon starfish

500g (1lb) cold mashed **potatoes**

2 tbsp **tomato ketchup**

1 tsp **Worcestershire sauce**

1 **egg**, lightly beaten

2 tbsp chopped **chives**

375g (12oz) cooked **salmon fillets**, flaked

3 tbsp **fresh breadcrumbs**, plus extra for coating

a little melted **butter**

TIP These fish cakes can be shallow-fried instead of oven-baked.

Preparation: 20 minutes; cooking: 8 minutes   180°C/350°F/gas 4

Makes 8 portions   Provides omega-3 fats, protein, B vitamins including folate and vitamin D   Suitable for freezing

I serve these fish cakes with shredded runner bean "seaweed" and Special tomato sauce (see page 153).

▶ Mash the potatoes with the tomato ketchup, Worcestershire sauce, beaten egg and chives. Mix in the salmon and 3 tablespoons of breadcrumbs. Shape the mixture into flat rissoles.
▶ Use a large star-shaped biscuit cutter to cut eight starfish shapes.

Gently pull out the points of the stars. Coat with breadcrumbs and brush with melted butter.
▶ Set the fishcakes on a lightly greased baking sheet. Transfer to the preheated oven and cook for 4 minutes on each side.

Mini golden fish balls

vegetable oil for shallow frying

knob of **butter**

1 **onion**, peeled and finely chopped

500g (1lb) minced or finely chopped **fish**, such as haddock, bream, whiting, cod or hake

60g (2oz) **carrots**, peeled and finely grated

1 tbsp chopped **fresh parsley**

2 dessertspoons **caster sugar**

½ lightly beaten **egg**

1 tbsp **plain flour**

salt and freshly ground **black pepper**

Preparation: 5 minutes; cooking: 20 minutes   Makes 8 portions
Provides beta-carotene, protein, B vitamins and vitamin E   Suitable for freezing

These fish balls are just the right size for toddlers to pick up. They are not at all fishy and have a slightly sweet taste. My fishmonger prepares a mixture of minced fish, but you could make your own mixture in a food processor.

▶ Heat a tablespoon of vegetable oil and the butter in a small frying pan. Add the onion and sauté for about 5 minutes, or until just softened.
▶ Put the minced fish in a mixing bowl and stir in the onion, carrots, parsley, sugar, beaten egg and flour. Season to taste, then form the mixture

into about 24 balls, each about the size of a large cherry tomato.
▶ Heat a further 3 tablespoons of vegetable oil in the frying pan. Add the fish balls and fry for about 10 minutes, until golden brown all over. Drain on kitchen paper. Serve with ketchup.

Chicken & tomato sauce with rice

⏱ Preparation: 10 minutes; cooking: 30 minutes ✂ Makes 6 portions ⚡ Provides beta-carotene, protein, B vitamins and vitamins C and E ❄ Suitable for freezing

Unlike a real risotto which needs a lot of attention, this tasty and comforting rice dish is easy to make.

▶ Cook the rice in boiling, lightly salted water, according to the instructions on the packet.

▶ Heat the oil in a fairly large saucepan and sauté the onion, garlic and carrot for 7 to 8 minutes. Add the chopped chicken and sauté, stirring occasionally until it is sealed. Add the remaining ingredients apart from the peas and cook covered for 15 minutes. Add the frozen peas and cook for 3 minutes.

▶ Drain the rice when cooked and mix with the chicken and tomato sauce.

200g (7oz) **long grain white rice**

2 tbsp **olive oil**

1 **onion**, peeled and chopped

1 **garlic clove**, peeled and crushed

1 medium **carrot**, peeled and diced

225g (7½oz) **chicken breast fillet**

300g (10oz) **passata**

1 **chicken stock cube** dissolved in 100ml (3½fl oz) **boiling water**

few drops **Worcestershire sauce**

1 tbsp chopped **fresh parsley**

½ tsp **caster sugar**

salt and freshly ground **black pepper**

100g (3½oz) **frozen peas**

Crunchy chicken fingers

⏱ Preparation: 5 minutes; cooking: 13 minutes ✂ Makes 2 portions ⚡ Provides iron, protein, B vitamins including folate and vitamin E ❄ Suitable for freezing: before cooking

Served with a little bowl of ketchup for dunking, these crunchy chicken pieces make a tasty finger food.

▶ Lightly season the flour and put into a plastic bag. Add the chicken pieces and shake until coated.

▶ Dip the chicken fingers in beaten egg then roll them in the cornflakes.

▶ Heat the oil in a frying pan, add the chicken and sauté for about 6 minutes on each side, or until crunchy on the outside and cooked through.

salt and freshly ground **black pepper**

30g (1oz) **plain flour**

1 **chicken breast fillet** (about 150g/5oz), cut into 6 strips

1 small **egg**, lightly beaten

45g (1½oz) **cornflakes**, crushed with a rolling pin

2 tbsp **vegetable oil**

Honey chicken

⏱ Preparation: 1 hour 5 minutes, including 1 hour marinating; cooking: 15 minutes ✂ Makes 2 portions ⚡ Provides beta-carotene, potassium, protein, B vitamins including folate and vitamins C and E

Marinating chicken gives it a lovely flavour. Use any combination of your child's favourite vegetables to make this recipe.

▶ Mix together the ingredients for the marinade and marinate the chicken for 1 hour or, if you prefer, overnight.

▶ Cook the rice in boiling, lightly salted water according to the instructions on the packet, adding the broccoli to the boiling water 5 minutes before the end of the rice cooking time. While the rice boils, heat the sunflower oil in a non-stick saucepan.

▶ Drain the marinade from the chicken, remove the garlic and reserve.

▶ Brown the chicken in the heated oil for about 3 minutes. Add the red pepper and continue to sauté until the chicken and red pepper start to caramelize.

▶ Put the reserved marinade in a small saucepan and bring to the boil. Drain the rice and combine with the chicken, red pepper and the marinade. Season to taste.

1 large **chicken breast fillet** (about 225g/7½oz), cut into thin strips

75g (2½oz) **easy cook** or **basmati rice**

40g (1¼oz) **broccoli**, cut into small florets

1 dessertspoon **sunflower oil**

20g (¾oz) **red pepper**, cut into thin strips

salt and freshly ground **black pepper**

Marinade

1 tbsp **olive oil**

1 tbsp **lemon juice**

1 small **garlic clove**, peeled and sliced

1 tbsp **soy sauce**

1 tbsp **runny honey**

freshly ground **black pepper**

Chicken kebabs with honey & citrus marinade

↻ Preparation: 35 minutes including 30 minutes marinating; cooking: 10 minutes

⚙ Makes 4 portions ⚡ Provides beta-carotene, iron, protein, B vitamins and vitamin C

1 **boneless chicken breast** (about 150g/5oz) and 4 **thighs**, skinned and trimmed, or 2 **chicken breasts**

1/2 **red pepper**, cut into chunks

1/2 small **onion**, peeled and cut into chunks

4 **mini pittas**, split in half

salad leaves, to garnish

Marinade

1 tbsp **soy sauce**

1 tbsp **runny honey**

1 tbsp each freshly squeezed **lemon juice** and **orange juice**

1 tsp **vegetable oil**

TIP *Add 1/2 tablespoon of sesame seeds to the marinade for extra flavour, if liked.*

Use your own choice of vegetables to make up these tasty kebabs, perhaps mushrooms or courgettes.

▶ Combine the marinade ingredients in a bowl. Cut the chicken into small chunks; add to the marinade with the pepper and onion. Cover and leave for at least 30 minutes. While the chicken marinates, soak four wooden skewers in cold water to stop them burning when under the grill.

▶ Preheat the grill to high. Thread alternate pieces of chicken, pepper and onion on to the skewers. Transfer to a hot grill or barbecue and cook for about 5 minutes on each side, or until they are cooked through and nicely browned. Toast the pitta bread.

▶ Slide the kebabs off the skewers, arrange alternate pieces of chicken and vegetable in the pitta bread pockets and garnish with salad leaves.

Chicken bolognese

↻ Preparation: 5 minutes; cooking: 30 minutes ⚙ Makes 8 portions

⚡ Provides beta-carotene, potassium, protein, B vitamins including folate and vitamin E

❄ Suitable for freezing

2 tbsp **vegetable oil**

1 large **shallot**, peeled and finely chopped

1 **garlic clove**, peeled and crushed

1 **leek**, washed, trimmed and sliced

500g (1lb) **minced chicken**

1 **carrot**, peeled and diced

400g (14oz) **canned chopped tomatoes**

125ml (4fl oz) **water**

1 tsp **caster sugar**

2 tsp **tomato ketchup**

2 tsp **fresh thyme leaves**

salt and freshly ground **black pepper**

350g (12oz) **spaghetti** or **tagliatelle**

You can use minced chicken or turkey to make a delicious pasta sauce. This version would make a good cannelloni filling. If you don't have fresh thyme, substitute 1/2 teaspoon of dried thyme.

▶ Warm the vegetable oil in a frying pan, add the shallot and garlic, and sauté over a low heat for 2–3 minutes. Add the leek and sauté for about 3 minutes, until beginning to soften.

▶ Add the chicken, breaking it up with a fork so that it does not stick together, and sauté for about 3 minutes. At this stage you can transfer the cooked chicken to a blender and process for a few seconds so that it has a smoother texture. Add the diced carrot and then stir in the remaining ingredients.

▶ Bring the mixture to the boil and then simmer for about 20 minutes, stirring occasionally, until the vegetables are tender and the chicken is cooked through.

▶ Meanwhile, cook the spaghetti or tagliatelle in boiling, lightly salted water according to the instructions on the packet.

▶ Lightly season the chicken bolognese and serve with the pasta.

Lamb meatballs with a sweet & sour sauce

⏱ Preparation: 20 minutes; cooking: 25 minutes ⚙ Makes 8 portions ✍ Provides iron, protein, B vitamins including folate, vitamin C and zinc ❄ Suitable for freezing

These light and succulent meatballs in a tangy tomato-based sauce are delicious served with rice or pasta. They also make a good finger food served plain with tomato ketchup.

▶ Mix together all the ingredients for the meatballs, seasoning to taste, then form the mixture into about 16 small balls. Spread the flour on a plate and use to coat the meatballs on all sides.
▶ Heat the vegetable oil in a frying pan, then add the meatballs and sauté for 10–15 minutes, turning them occasionally, until browned and almost cooked through.

▶ Meanwhile, mix together all the ingredients for the sauce in a small pan set over a medium-high heat and cook for 4 minutes. Taste and season if necessary.
▶ Pour the sauce over the meatballs in the frying pan and cook over a medium heat for about 10 minutes, or until the sauce has thickened and the meatballs are cooked through.

Meatballs
250g (8oz) **minced lamb**

1 **onion**, peeled and finely chopped

1/2 **red pepper**, finely chopped

1 tbsp finely chopped **fresh parsley**

1 small **apple**, peeled and grated

salt and freshly ground **black pepper**

plain flour for coating

2 tbsp **vegetable oil** for frying

Sweet & sour sauce
400g (14oz) **canned chopped tomatoes**

1 tbsp **malt vinegar**

1 tbsp **brown sugar**

1 tbsp **tomato ketchup**

dash of **Worcestershire sauce**

Couscous with ham & peas

⏱ Preparation: 5 minutes; cooking: 10 minutes ⚙ Makes 4 portions
✍ Provides beta-carotene, potassium and B vitamins including folate

Couscous is a grain made from wheat and is a staple of Middle Eastern cuisine. You can find it in most supermarkets next to the rice section. Very quick and easy to prepare, it combines well with both savoury and sweet foods. This meal can be eaten hot or cold.

▶ Bring the chicken stock to the boil, then pour it over the couscous. Stir with a fork and set aside for about 6 minutes.
▶ Meanwhile, melt the butter in a saucepan and sauté the onion for 2–3 minutes until softened. Add the peas, a generous pinch of sugar and a little salt, and pour over the water. Lower the heat, cover and cook for 3 minutes more.

▶ Fluff up the couscous with a fork, stir in the onion, peas and diced ham, and season to taste.

250ml (8fl oz) **chicken stock** (see page 52)

100g (3 1/2oz) **instant couscous**

15g (1/2oz) **butter**

1/2 small **onion**, peeled and finely chopped

75g (2 1/2oz) **frozen peas**

pinch of **sugar**

pinch of **salt**

50ml (1 3/4fl oz) **water**

30g (1oz) diced **ham**

salt and freshly ground **black pepper**

The fussy eater

The most rapid rate of growth in a child's life is between birth and one year, then, after the first year, a child's growth rate slows down dramatically. This is one of the reasons why toddlers become more exacting food critics with fads such as eating only plain pasta, not eating yogurt with bits in and refusing any dish with visible onions. You will need all your patience at this very trying time. In this chapter I have put together a selection of favourite recipes with that magical ingredient – "child appeal".

1 Chicken chow mein
A lovely combination of tender marinated chicken strips, crisp stir-fried vegetables and Chinese noodles. Even confirmed vegetable haters are often tempted to eat vegetables such as baby sweetcorn and sugar snap peas when they are stir-fried with noodles and soy sauce. (See page 111 for recipe.)

2 Cream of tomato soup
This tasty tomato soup made with fresh tomatoes, carrots and onion is popular with children. Blending vegetables into a soup is a good way to encourage your child to eat more vegetables. (See page 106 for recipe.)

3 Tomato & mascarpone pasta sauce
When all else fails, fussy children can usually be relied upon to eat pasta. This tomato sauce enriched with mascarpone – Italian cream cheese – is quick and easy to prepare. (See page 107 for recipe.)

1

2

3

2 tbsp **vegetable oil**

2 **onions**, peeled and chopped

1 **garlic clove**, peeled and crushed

450g (15oz) **carrots**, peeled

250g (8oz) **sweet potato**, peeled

2 tsp grated **ginger**

1 litre (35fl oz) **chicken stock** (see page 52) or **vegetable stock** (see page 47)

50ml (1¾fl oz) freshly squeezed **orange juice**

salt and freshly ground **black pepper**

100ml (3½fl oz) **coconut cream** or **coconut milk**

chopped fresh **parsley** to garnish

Sweet potato & carrot soup with ginger & orange

⏱ Preparation: 10 minutes; cooking: 30 minutes   🥄 Makes 6 portions

⚡ Provides beta-carotene, folate, potassium and vitamins C and E   ❄ Suitable for freezing

▶ Heat the oil in a large pan and sauté the onions and garlic for about 5 minutes or until softened.

▶ Chop the carrots and sweet potato. Add the grated ginger, carrots and sweet potato and cook for about 5 minutes, stirring occasionally. Add the stock, cover and simmer for about 20 minutes, or until the vegetables are tender.

▶ Blend the soup in a food processor or liquidizer. Stir in the orange juice and season to taste. Then swirl in the coconut cream and garnish with chopped parsley to serve.

---

2 tbsp **olive oil**

1 **onion**, peeled and diced

200g (7oz) **carrots**, peeled and diced

500g (1lb) ripe **plum tomatoes**, skinned and roughly chopped

200g (7oz) **passata**

400ml (14fl oz) **chicken stock** (see page 52) or **vegetable stock** (see page 47)

1 **bay leaf**

sprig of **fresh thyme**

100ml (3½fl oz) **double cream**

salt and freshly ground **black pepper**

Cream of tomato soup

⏱ Preparation: 10 minutes; cooking: 45 minutes   🥄 Makes 5 portions

⚡ Provides beta-carotene, potassium and vitamins A, C and E   ❄ Suitable for freezing

A really good homemade tomato soup is usually a great favourite with children. Pour this one into a thermos flask with a top that doubles as a mug, and take it on outings in cold weather.

▶ Heat the oil in a large saucepan. Sauté the onion and carrots for 5–6 minutes. Stir in the tomatoes, passata, stock, bay leaf and thyme and bring to the simmer. Cover and cook for 35–40 minutes.

▶ Remove the bay leaf and the stalk from the thyme, returning the thyme leaves to the pot. Blend in a food processor until smooth. Stir in the double cream and season with salt and pepper.

125ml (4fl oz) **chicken stock** (see page 52)

1 **bay leaf**

2 skinless, boneless **chicken breasts** (about 300g/10oz)

40g (1¼oz) **butter**

1 **stick celery**, chopped

1 **onion**, peeled and chopped

40g (1¼oz) **plain flour**

300ml (10fl oz) **hot milk**

285g (9oz) **canned sweetcorn**

salt and freshly ground **black pepper**

TIP This tasty and nutritious soup is a meal in itself. Serve with carrot and cucumber sticks and fresh bread.

Cream of chicken soup with sweetcorn

⏱ Preparation: 10 minutes; cooking: 35 minutes   🥄 Makes 6 portions   ⚡ Provides potassium, protein, B vitamins including folate and vitamin C   ❄ Suitable for freezing

▶ Bring the stock and bay leaf to the simmer and place the chicken breasts in the stock. Simmer for 10 minutes. Remove the chicken with a slotted spoon and set aside until cool enough to handle. Reserve the stock and bay leaf.

▶ Melt the butter in a large saucepan and cook the celery and onion for 6–7 minutes. Stir in the flour and cook for 1–2 minutes. Pour in the hot milk and stir until thickened. Add the stock and bay leaf and bring to the simmer.

▶ Tear the cooked chicken into pieces and add to the pan. Simmer for 10–15 minutes, adding the sweetcorn for the last 3 minutes. Season with pepper.

▶ Remove the bay leaf and blend the mixture in a food processor or liquidizer. For a smooth texture, push the mixture through a sieve or purée in a mouli.

Macaroni cheese

⏲ Preparation: 10 minutes; cooking: 12 minutes ⬇ 180°C/350°F/gas 4 🍴 Makes 6 portions 🔪 Provides calcium, protein, B vitamins and vitamin A ❄ Suitable for freezing

When all else fails, most fussy children can be relied upon to eat pasta with grated cheese. Here's a slight variation which should have pretty universal appeal. The crunchy ciabatta topping is optional.

▶ Cook the macaroni until *al dente* (with a slight bite to it). Melt the butter in a saucepan and stir in the flour. Cook for 1–2 minutes, stirring continuously.
▶ Gradually add the milk, bring to the simmer and cook until thickened. Add the cheese and English mustard powder and stir until the cheese has melted. Mix in the macaroni, season to taste and transfer to an ovenproof dish.
▶ Mix the crumbled ciabatta with the olive oil and Parmesan cheese. Scatter over the top of the pasta and bake in the preheated oven for 10 minutes.

225g (8oz) **macaroni**

25g (1oz) **butter**

25g (1oz) **plain flour**

450ml (15fl oz) **milk**

75g (2½oz) grated **Cheddar cheese**

75g (2½oz) grated **Gruyère cheese**

½ tsp **English mustard powder**

salt and freshly ground **black pepper**

50g (1¾oz) **ciabatta loaf crumbs** or **toasted white breadcrumbs**

½ tbsp **olive oil**

2 tbsp freshly grated **Parmesan cheese**

Tomato & mascarpone pasta sauce

⏲ Preparation: 5 minutes; cooking: 20 minutes 🍴 Makes 4 portions 🔪 Provides beta-carotene, potassium and vitamins A, B12 and E ❄ Suitable for freezing

Penne goes well with this lovely, creamy tomato sauce. Some children don't like to see green bits in the sauce, so you can leave out the basil and use 1/4 teaspoon mixed herbs instead.

▶ Heat the olive oil in a saucepan and sauté the onion and garlic for 7–8 minutes. Stir in the passata and sugar, and simmer for 10 minutes with the lid on, stirring occasionally.
▶ Remove from the heat, add the basil and blend in a food processor. Return to the pan and add the mascarpone cheese. Stir until melted and simmer for 1–2 minutes. Season to taste.

1 tbsp **olive oil**

1 **red onion**, peeled and chopped

1 **garlic clove**, peeled and crushed

400g (14oz) **passata**

pinch of **sugar**

2 tbsp torn **basil leaves**

100g (3½oz) **mascarpone cheese**

salt and freshly ground **black pepper**

Spaghetti bolognese

⏲ Preparation: 8 minutes; cooking: 27 minutes 🍴 Makes 6 portions 🔪 Provides beta-carotene, iron, potassium, protein, B vitamins, vitamins C and E and zinc ❄ Suitable for freezing: sauce only

▶ Heat the oil in a saucepan, stir in the onion, garlic and carrot and sauté for 2 minutes. Add the minced beef and cook for about 5 minutes until browned. For a smoother consistency, transfer the sautéed meat and vegetables to a food processor and chop for a few seconds.
▶ Stir in the chopped tomatoes, milk, bay leaf, thyme, salt and pepper. Cover and simmer for 15–20 minutes.
▶ Meanwhile, cook the pasta in boiling, lightly salted water according to the instructions on the packet. Drain and mix with the sauce. If the sauce is too thick you can add a little of the pasta cooking water to thin it out.

1 tbsp **olive oil**

1 **onion**, peeled and chopped

1 **garlic clove**, peeled and crushed

1 medium **carrot**, peeled and grated

300g (10oz) lean **minced beef**

400g (14oz) **canned chopped tomatoes**

125ml (4fl oz) **milk**

1 **bay leaf**

1 tsp **fresh thyme leaves** or ½ tsp **dried thyme**

salt and freshly ground **black pepper**

200g (7oz) **spaghetti**

1 medium **sweet potato,** scrubbed

1 tbsp **oil**

salt

Sweet potato oven wedges

↻ Preparation: 5 minutes; cooking: 40 minutes　　🔻 200°C/400°F/gas 6

✂ Makes 2 portions　　🌿 Provides potassium and vitamins C and E

▶ Cut the sweet potato lengthways into wedges. Place on a baking tray and lightly brush with the oil. Season with a little salt and bake in the preheated oven for 35–40 minutes, turning occasionally until soft inside and golden brown on the outside.

500g (1lb) **courgettes**

salt and freshly ground **black pepper**

75g (2½oz) **plain flour**

40g (1¼oz) **cornflour**

1 tsp **salt**

150ml (5fl oz) **ice-cold water**

vegetable oil for frying

TIP *You can cook other vegetables in this batter – try sweet potato, cauliflower and broccoli.*

Zucchini (courgette) fritters

↻ Preparation: 10 minutes; cooking: 10 minutes　　✂ Makes 4 portions

🌿 Provides fibre, folate, magnesium and potassium

Try these if your child isn't keen on eating vegetables. They are delicious and were very popular with my tasting panel – even confirmed veggie haters.

▶ Wash and dry the courgettes and trim off the ends. Cut them into sticks about 6cm (2½in) long and 1.5cm (½in) wide, and season with a little salt and pepper.
▶ In a bowl, mix together the flour, cornflour, salt and black pepper. Stir in the ice-cold water until the mixture is slightly thicker than the consistency of double cream.
▶ Heat the oil in a deep-fat fryer to 200°C/400°F. Alternatively, use a wok or deep frying pan filled to about 6cm (2½in) with oil. You can tell when the oil is hot enough for frying if a piece of vegetable sizzles as it touches it.
▶ Dip the courgette sticks into the batter and fry them until crispy and golden. Don't fry too many at a time or you will reduce the temperature of the oil. Lift out the basket or remove the zucchini fritters with a slotted spoon. Drain on absorbent paper and serve immediately.

450g (15oz) **carrots,** peeled and thinly sliced

1 small **onion,** peeled and finely chopped

50g (1¾oz) **butter**

2½ tbsp **plain flour**

300ml (10fl oz) **milk**

75g (2½oz) grated **Gruyère cheese**

salt and **white pepper**

1 tbsp chopped **fresh parsley**

65g (2¼oz) **cornflakes,** crushed

Carrots with a crunchy cornflake topping

↻ Preparation: 10 minutes; cooking: 30 minutes　　🔻 180°C/350°F/gas 4

✂ Makes 4 portions　　🌿 Provides beta-carotene, calcium, iron, protein, B vitamins including folate and vitamins A and D

Surprisingly, carrots are more nutritious eaten cooked than raw. This is because the cooking process helps our bodies to absorb the beta-carotene.

▶ Cook the sliced carrots in lightly salted water (or steam) until just tender.
▶ Meanwhile, sauté the chopped onion in half the butter until softened. Remove from the heat, stir in the flour and cook for 1 minute. Gradually whisk in the milk. Return to the heat and stir until thickened and smooth. Take off the heat and stir in the cheese until melted. Season to taste.
▶ Combine the cooked carrots and parsley with the cheese sauce and spoon into a suitable ovenproof dish. Melt the remaining butter and stir in the crushed cornflakes. Arrange the cornflakes over the carrots and cook in the preheated oven for 20 minutes.

Tuna melt

⟳ Preparation: 5 minutes; cooking: 2 minutes ✂ Makes 2 portions
⚡ Provides iron, potassium, protein, B vitamins including folate and vitamins A, D and E

▶ Preheat the grill to high. Mix the flaked tuna, mayonnaise, spring onion and lemon juice. Toast the bread and spread with a little butter or margarine. Divide the tuna filling between the two slices of bread. Cover with the cheese slices.
▶ Place under the grill until the cheese begins to melt and turn golden. Cut each toasted sandwich into squares, fingers or triangles or serve on toasted muffins.

100g (3½oz) **canned tuna in oil,** drained

1½ tbsp **mayonnaise**

1 tbsp **spring onion,** finely sliced

1 tsp **lemon juice**

2 slices **wholemeal bread** or **English muffin,** toasted

butter or **margarine**

2 slices **Emmenthal** or **Gruyère cheese** (about 40g/1¼oz)

Honey & soy salmon skewers

⟳ Preparation: 1 hour 10 minutes, including 1 hour marinating; cooking: 5 minutes
✂ Makes 2 portions ⚡ Provides omega-3 fats, potassium, protein, B vitamins and vitamins D and E

This is a really delicious way to cook salmon and the marinade gives a lovely caramelized, glossy coating. Serve the kebabs with rice.

▶ Mix together the ingredients for the marinade in a shallow dish and stir in the cubes of salmon, making sure they are well coated. Leave to marinate for about 1 hour, turning occasionally. Meanwhile, soak two bamboo skewers in water to stop them burning when under the grill.
▶ Preheat the grill to high. Line a grill pan with foil, thread the cubes of salmon on to the skewers and place on the foil.

Brush the salmon with the marinade and grill for about 5 minutes, basting with the marinade and turning occasionally until golden on the outside but still moist and juicy inside.
▶ Put the remaining marinade in a small pan and heat for a few minutes until reduced. Serve the kebabs with rice and spoon the reduced marinade over the salmon.

150g (5oz) **salmon fillet,** skinned and cut into 2cm (¾in) cubes

Marinade

1 tbsp **runny honey**

1 tbsp **soy sauce**

1 tbsp **light olive oil** or **vegetable oil**

TIP Ensure you remove the cubes of salmon from the skewers before giving them to toddlers.

1 tbsp **olive oil**

1 large **onion**, peeled

1 **garlic clove**, peeled and crushed

1½ slices **white bread**

3 tbsp **milk**

400g (13oz) **chicken breast fillets** or **minced chicken**

1 small **egg**, lightly beaten

4 tbsp **tomato ketchup**

1 tsp **Worcestershire sauce**

2 tbsp chopped **fresh parsley**

½ tbsp **fresh thyme** (optional)

salt and freshly ground **black pepper**

200g (7oz) **canned sweetcorn**

vegetable oil for frying

Diana's chicken & sweetcorn rissoles

⟳ Preparation: 15 minutes; cooking: 10 minutes   ◔ Makes 18 rissoles
⚡ Provides iron, potassium, protein, B vitamins including folate and vitamin C
❄ Suitable for freezing

My friend Diana, who comes from Russia, gave me this recipe. These mini rissoles are popular and easy for little children to eat with their fingers. It's a good idea to make up the mixture and then cook one rissole to test; you can then add extra ketchup, herbs or seasoning, according to taste, before you cook the rest.

▶ Heat the olive oil in a pan and sauté the onion together with the garlic until softened but not golden brown. Soak the bread in the milk.

▶ Place the chicken in a food processor. If using chicken breasts, cut into chunks first then chop for a few seconds. Tear the soaked bread into pieces and add to the chicken together with the beaten egg, tomato ketchup, Worcestershire sauce, parsley, thyme (if using) and salt and pepper. Blend for a few seconds.

▶ Transfer the chicken to a bowl and stir in the sweetcorn. You can put the mixture aside in the fridge at this stage ready for when you want to cook it – leave it there overnight if you wish.

▶ Form the mixture into 18 small round rissoles – it will be quite sticky and it can help to use a wet spoon to shape the mixture. Sauté in vegetable oil until golden and cooked through.

▶ Serve with homemade tomato ketchup (see below).

---

1 small **chicken breast fillet** (about 125g/4oz)

a little **vegetable oil**

Marinade

¾ tbsp **honey**

1 tbsp **lemon juice**

1 tbsp **soy sauce**

1 tsp **light olive oil**

ground **black pepper**

slice of **garlic** (optional)

Tomato ketchup

400g (14oz) **passata**

1 tbsp **balsamic vinegar**

1 tbsp **tomato purée**

1 tbsp **brown sugar**

Tender strips of griddled chicken & homemade tomato ketchup

⟳ Preparation: 32 minutes, including 30 minutes to marinate; cooking: 15 minutes
◔ Makes 2 portions   ⚡ Provides potassium, protein, B vitamins including folate and vitamins C and E   ❄ Suitable for freezing

This is a delicious way to eat chicken and much healthier for your child than chicken nuggets.

▶ In a bowl, mix together all the ingredients for the marinade, add the chicken breast and leave to marinate for about 30 minutes.

▶ Drain the marinade and reserve.

▶ Heat the griddle, brush it with a little oil and cook the chicken for 4–5 minutes on each side or until cooked. (If you don't have a griddle you can heat a little vegetable oil in a saucepan and sauté the chicken breast.)

▶ Meanwhile, strain the marinade, pour it into a small saucepan, bring to the boil and simmer for about 1 minute.

▶ Cut the chicken into strips and serve with the reduced marinade.

▶ To make the tomato ketchup, put all the ingredients into a saucepan. Bring to the boil, then reduce the heat and cook uncovered for about 15 minutes.

Chicken chow mein

Preparation: 10 minutes; cooking: 18 minutes Makes 6 portions Provides beta-carotene, potassium, protein, B vitamins including folate and vitamins C and E

Chow mein means stir-fried noodles. Shiitake mushrooms have a wonderful flavour but can sometimes be difficult to obtain. If you cannot find them, use sliced chestnut mushrooms instead.

► Mix together the ingredients for the marinade and marinate the chicken for 10 minutes. Strain and reserve the marinade. Cook the noodles in boiling, lightly salted water according to the instructions on the packet, then set aside.

► Heat the vegetable oil in a wok or large frying pan and stir-fry the chicken for 5–6 minutes. Remove the chicken and set aside.

► Heat the sesame oil in the wok. Add the garlic and stir-fry for a few seconds. Add the shiitake mushrooms, sugar snap peas, red pepper and baby corn and cook for 4 minutes, stirring occasionally. Add the spring onions, courgette and beansprouts and continue to cook for 4 minutes, stirring occasionally.

► Add the chicken and noodles together with the reserved marinade. Stir-fry for 1–2 minutes or until the noodles are completely heated through.

1 large **chicken breast fillet** (about 225g/7$\frac{1}{2}$oz)

150g (5oz) **fine Chinese egg noodles**

1 tbsp **vegetable oil**

1$\frac{1}{2}$ tbsp **sesame oil**

1 **garlic clove**, peeled and crushed

100g (3$\frac{1}{2}$oz) **shiitake mushrooms**

125g (4oz) **sugar snap peas**

$\frac{1}{2}$ small **red pepper**, cut into thin strips

75g (2$\frac{1}{2}$oz) **baby sweetcorn**, cut into quarters

4 **spring onions**, finely sliced

125g (4oz) **courgettes**

125g (4oz) **beansprouts**

Marinade

2 tbsp **soy sauce**

2 tbsp **sake** (rice wine)

1 tbsp **soft brown sugar**

100g (3½oz) **unsalted butter**

90g (3oz) **granulated sugar**

90g (3oz) **light brown sugar**

1 **egg**

1 tsp **vanilla extract**

125g (4oz) **plain flour**

1 tsp **mixed spice**

½ tsp **baking powder**

¼ tsp **bicarbonate of soda**

¼ tsp **salt**

75g (2½oz) **porridge oats**

175g (6oz) **raisins**

Raisin & oatmeal biscuits

⟳ Preparation: 20 minutes; cooking: 10 minutes   🡇 190°C/375°F/gas 5

◢ Makes 22 biscuits   ✗ Provides fibre, iron and potassium   ❉ Suitable for freezing

▶ Cream together the butter and sugars in an electric mixer or by hand. Beat in the egg and vanilla extract.

▶ Sift together the flour, mixed spice, baking powder, bicarbonate of soda and salt. Add to the mixture and beat until combined. Stir in the oats and raisins.

▶ Lightly grease two baking sheets.

Using your hands, form the dough into about 22 walnut-sized balls. Put them on the baking sheets, widely spaced, and flatten them down a little.

▶ Transfer the biscuits to the preheated oven and bake for about 12 minutes, or until lightly golden all over. Transfer to a wire rack and leave to cool.

60g (2oz) **bran flakes**

300ml (10fl oz) **milk**

125g (4oz) **wholemeal flour**

½ tsp **salt**

1 tbsp **baking powder**

60g (2oz) **butter**

60g (2oz) **caster sugar**

1 **egg**

2 **bananas**, peeled and mashed

90g (3oz) **raisins**

Banana muffins

⟳ Preparation: 15 minutes; cooking: 30 minutes   🡇 180°C/350°F/gas 4

◢ Makes 12 muffins   ✗ Provides fibre, iron and B vitamins including folate

❉ Suitable for freezing

These muffins are full of good natural ingredients. They make superb portable food and can be eaten on the run if there's no time for a proper breakfast.

▶ Soak the bran flakes in the milk for 10 minutes. Sift together the flour, salt and baking powder.

▶ Cream together the butter and sugar, then beat in the egg. Stir in alternate spoonfuls of soaked bran flakes and

flour mixture. Gently fold in the mashed bananas and the raisins.

▶ Line a muffin tray with paper cases and half-fill each case with mixture. Bake in the preheated oven for 30 minutes.

125ml (4fl oz) **coconut milk**

125ml (4fl oz) **pineapple juice**

1 small **banana**, peeled and chopped

1tsp **honey**

Pineapple, coconut & banana smoothie

⟳ Preparation: 3 minutes   ◢ Makes 2 glasses   ✗ Provides potassium and vitamins C and B6

Fruit smoothies and milkshakes make tasty and nutritious drinks.

▶ Place the coconut milk, pineapple juice and chopped banana in a hand-held blender with the honey. Blend together until smooth.

▶ Blend together 350ml (12fl oz) pineapple juice, 90ml (3fl oz) coconut milk, 3 scoops vanilla ice-cream and 150g (5oz) fresh pineapple.

Variations

▶ Add peeled ripe flesh of half a mango or one juicy ripe peach.

Summer berry milkshake

🕑 Preparation: 5 minutes   ⚗ Makes 2 glasses   ⚗ Provides calcium, potassium, protein and vitamins B2, B12 and C (plus other nutrients depending on fruits used)

▶ Blend together the berries and icing sugar and then press through a sieve. Mix together with the yogurt and milk.

200g (7oz) frozen or fresh **summer fruits** or **berries**

2 tbsp **icing sugar**

100ml (3$\frac{1}{2}$fl oz) **raspberry drinking yogurt** or 1 x 150g (5fl oz) carton **mixed berry yogurt**

200ml (7fl oz) **milk**

Frozen yogurt with fresh berries

🕑 Preparation: 20 minutes   ⚗ Makes 4 portions   ⚗ Provides calcium, folate, potassium, protein and vitamins A, B2, B12, C and E

▶ Mix together the yogurt, cream and sugar and freeze and churn the mixture in an ice-cream maker. Alternatively, put into a plastic container and freeze for about 1$\frac{1}{2}$ hours. Remove from the freezer, transfer to a food processor and blend until smooth or simply stir thoroughly to remove ice particles. Freeze for another hour, blend again in the food processor or stir once again and then return to the freezer.

▶ To make the raspberry coulis, purée fresh raspberries, then press through a sieve to remove the seeds and stir in the icing sugar. If using frozen raspberries, heat them in a saucepan until mushy before puréeing them.
▶ Mix the fresh berries with the raspberry coulis and divide between four bowls. Serve scoops of the frozen yogurt on top of the berries and coulis.

500ml (17fl oz) full-fat **natural yogurt**

150ml (5fl oz) **single cream**

115g (3$\frac{3}{4}$oz) **caster sugar**

100g (3$\frac{1}{2}$oz) **strawberries,** hulled and quartered

100g (3$\frac{1}{2}$oz) **blackberries**

100g (3$\frac{1}{2}$oz) **blueberries**

100g (3$\frac{1}{2}$oz) **raspberries**

Raspberry coulis

250g (8oz) **fresh** or **frozen raspberries**

2 tbsp sifted **icing sugar**

2 to 3 years

Mock fried egg: vanilla yogurt with half an apricot on top becomes a simple visual joke.

Savoury dip: a colourful array of vegetable and bread sticks has instant appeal.

Shepherd's pie: make a mini portion in a ramekin and let your child decorate it as she wishes.

Remember

• Don't make your child wait too long for a meal once she has announced she is hungry: she cannot yet wait patiently and may well become irritable.

• Encourage a taste for foods that are not high in sugar. If sugar is kept to a minimum now, she is much less likely to develop a sweet tooth later.

• Leave snacks of sliced fruit or vegetable sticks on a low shelf in the fridge so your child can help herself when hungry.

Early childhood

Children in this age group are often highly appreciative of their food, especially when it has the lively presentation of a party spread. It is surprising just how quiet a group of two to three year olds can be around a table of edible goodies. Others are more erratic and selective. Whatever your child's eating habits, she will enjoy spending time in the kitchen with you, joining in with your cooking activities.

Eating for an active day

Two and three year olds are highly active and often appear, if not thin, at least leggy. Your child will still need frequent small meals to meet her high energy requirements and there may be times when she seems in need of a rapid energy "fix" to stop her becoming over-tired (see page 89). Sugar and carbohydrates from refined sources (such as fizzy drinks or chocolate biscuits) are quickly broken down into glucose and provide an instant "pick-me-up", but fruit or fruit juice are healthier sources of an energy boost. Unrefined carbohydrate foods, such as wholegrain bread and pasta, take longer to break down into glucose, but provide a more sustained energy supply.

Making mealtimes work

By the age of two your child will be able to sit on a secured booster seat at the table with you, and she will be eating very much what the rest of the family eats, though perhaps at different times. It is important, however, to keep her company at mealtimes if she is having her supper before the rest of the family. Leaving her sitting alone at the table, even if you are in the same room, is bound to lead to trouble as she fights for your attention. Aim to

TIPS ON HOW TO HELP CHILDREN WHO ARE OVERWEIGHT

• Adopt a healthier eating pattern as a family rather than cut down on the food offered to your child. Don't buy foods that you don't want your child to eat.

• Give less processed fatty foods and more complex carbohydrates (brown rice, potatoes, wholemeal bread), fruit and vegetables, low-fat dairy foods and fish, chicken or lean meat.

• Try to avoid fried food. Grill, bake or microwave instead and put only a scrape of butter or margarine on bread.

• Encourage your child to eat more vegetables – make stir-fries, vegetable soups, hidden vegetable tomato sauce and give her raw vegetables with a dip.

• Give your child plenty of fresh fruits – add fruits to breakfast cereals, make fruit smoothies and fresh fruit kebabs and give fresh fruit for dessert.

• Encourage the drinking of water rather than juice or fizzy drinks. Semi-skimmed milk can be introduced from two years provided the child is eating a varied diet.

• Cut out between-meal snacks of crisps or chocolate biscuits and give healthy foods such as mini sandwiches or cottage cheese and fruit instead.

encourage her enjoyment of food: try to include her in the family's lunch or evening meal as often as possible. Don't feel obliged to make novelty foods all the time, but do think about giving everyday meals some "child appeal".

Without spending more than a few moments, a simple plate of food can be made to appeal to a child's sense of form and colour; fresh fruit arranged in a pattern will bring a smile to her face and stimulate her interest.

Cooking: a new activity

You can encourage your child's interest in food by involving her in its preparation early on. Children often take great pride in helping to lay the table, knead dough or mix ingredients, and can be fascinated by quite ordinary tasks that adults take for granted: just think how many ways there are to prepare an egg, or how ingredients change shape, texture and colour if heated or frozen. All this is a new experience for your child. Provided you keep her away from sharp knives and electrical equipment, there are plenty of supervised activities she can take part in, from breaking eggs into a bowl to cutting out biscuits with shaped cutters. There are simple recipes in this book that would be ideal for your child to help you make. Try Mini pizzas (page 97), Cheesy bread animals (page 120), Character fairy cakes (page 128), Shortbread cookies (page 131) and Chewy apricot & chocolate cereal bars (page 179).

"Let your child feel free to experiment with rolling dough and cutting out interesting cookie shapes."

Fun foods

By the time your child reaches her second birthday, she should regularly be joining in family meals and continuing to broaden her tastes. This is an excellent time to encourage an active interest in food, perhaps by allowing her to participate in fun, simple cooking activities, or to help choose favourite dishes for a birthday tea with friends. Plan a party tea around a theme, perhaps serving foods with different distinctive shapes, or choosing a colour scheme. Bring out the healthier savoury dishes before you serve the sweet things.

1 Open sandwiches
Daintily cut open sandwiches make easy finger foods for small children. These sandwiches are spread with butter or cream cheese, then topped with rounds of cucumber or tomato, squares of mild cheese or ham, or rosettes of smoked turkey. (See page 95 for recipe.)

2 Heart-shaped chicken nuggets
These chicken and apple patties, with their moist interior and crunchy coating, will be an instant hit with children. (See page 125 for recipe.)

3 Annabel's pasta salad
A dish of multi-coloured pasta with plenty of vegetable chunks and a lively dressing should appeal to both small children and any accompanying parents. (See page 122 for recipe.)

4 Parcel birthday cake
Bold and bright birthday sponge cakes shaped to look like parcels make superb centrepieces. (See page 129 for recipe.)

1 tbsp **olive oil**

1 **garlic clove**, peeled and crushed

1 **onion**, peeled and chopped

75g (2¹/₂oz) **carrots**, peeled and diced

400g (14oz) **canned chopped tomatoes** or 8 **fresh tomatoes**

1 tbsp **tomato purée**

600ml (20fl oz) **vegetable stock** (see page 47)

2 slices **white bread**, shredded

salt and freshly ground **black pepper**

pinch of **sugar**

2 tbsp torn **fresh basil leaves**

Tomato soup

↻ Preparation: 10 minutes; cooking: 26 minutes　🔪 Makes 8 portions
🖊 Provides beta-carotene, folate and potassium　❄ Suitable for freezing

This quick-to-make tomato soup recipe differs from the one on page 106 as it is dairy-free and soothing for children when they are unwell. I prefer to use canned tomatoes as so many fresh tomatoes lack flavour, but if you have ripe, full-flavoured, medium-sized tomatoes you can use them instead.

▶ Warm the olive oil in a large pan over a low heat, add the garlic, onion and carrots, and sauté for 10 minutes.
▶ Add the remaining ingredients except for the basil. Simmer for 10 minutes, stirring occasionally, until all the vegetables are soft.
▶ Stir in the basil and simmer for a further 5 minutes. Liquidize the mixture using a blender.

250g (8oz) **strong plain flour**, plus **plain flour** to dust

pinch of **salt**

¹/₂ sachet (¹/₂ tbsp) **fast action dried yeast**

¹/₂ tsp **honey**

pinch of **cayenne pepper**

1 tsp **mustard powder**

about 150ml (5fl oz) **warm water**

60g (2oz) grated **mature Cheddar cheese**

2 tbsp freshly grated **Parmesan cheese**

To decorate

1 **egg**, beaten

currants

sesame seeds

poppy seeds

grated **Cheddar cheese**

Cheesy bread animals

↻ Preparation: 1 hour 30 minutes, including 1 hour rising; cooking: 20 minutes
🌡 200°C/400°F/gas 6　🔪 Makes 6 bread rolls　🖊 Provides calcium, protein and vitamin B12　❄ Suitable for freezing

Children adore making bread – it's a bit like playing with playdough – and they will have great fun forming this delicious cheesy bread into animal shapes.

▶ Sift the flour and salt into a mixing bowl. Stir in the yeast, honey, cayenne pepper and mustard and just enough of the water to form a soft dough.
▶ Transfer to a floured surface and knead lightly for about 5 minutes to make a smooth, pliable dough. Gradually knead the grated cheeses into the dough (this will produce a slightly streaky effect).
▶ Shape the dough into six animal figures and transfer to a floured baking sheet. Cover them loosely with a tea-towel and leave to rise in a warm place for about 1 hour, or until doubled in size.

▶ Brush with beaten egg and add currants for eyes. Sprinkle the tops with sesame seeds, poppy seeds or grated cheese. Transfer to the preheated oven and bake for 20 minutes, or until golden brown. The underside should sound hollow when tapped. Leave on a wire rack to cool.

Variation
▶ To make cheese and onion bread rolls, add 1 tablespoon of finely chopped spring onion to the dough after adding the grated cheeses.

Mini baked potatoes

⟳ Preparation: 10 minutes; cooking: 45 minutes ⬇ 200°C/400°F/gas 6

✎ Makes 6 portions ✐ Provides folate, protein and vitamin B12 (cranberry & turkey filling); folate, protein and vitamin B12 (tuna & sweetcorn filling); fibre, folate, potassium and protein (barbecue bean filling) ❄ Suitable for freezing: undecorated only

Small baked potatoes look especially attractive when made into little sailing ships decorated with a cheese triangle sail and a red pepper flag. Each of the fillings suggested here is sufficient for three potatoes.

▶ Wash the potatoes, pat dry, prick with a fork, brush with oil and sprinkle with sea salt. Place in the preheated oven and bake for about 40 minutes, or until crispy on the outside and tender inside (test with a skewer). Preheat the grill to high.

▶ Cut the potatoes in half, scoop out the flesh into a bowl and mash thoroughly. Mix the ingredients from your chosen topping with the mashed potato then spoon the mixture back into the skins.

For a simple grated cheese topping, just sprinkle a little over each of the potatoes.

▶ Place the potatoes under the grill (they can be arranged in a muffin tray to keep them upright). Heat for a few minutes, or just until lightly golden on top. If desired, decorate the potatoes as boats, securing the cheese sails and red pepper flags with cocktail sticks.

3 small **baking potatoes**

oil for brushing

sea salt

grated **Cheddar cheese** (optional)

Cranberry & turkey filling

1 tsp **cranberry sauce**

1 tbsp **smooth peanut butter**

1 tsp **milk**

60g (2oz) **turkey**, shredded

Tuna & sweetcorn filling

60g (2oz) cooked **frozen** or **canned sweetcorn**

2 tbsp **mayonnaise**

60g (2oz) **canned tuna**, flaked and drained

1 **spring onion**, finely sliced

freshly ground **black pepper**

1 tbsp grated **Cheddar cheese**

Barbecue bean filling

250g (8oz) **canned barbecue baked beans**, or 250g (8oz) plain **baked beans** seasoned with **Worcestershire sauce**

1 tbsp grated **Cheddar cheese**

To decorate

Cheddar cheese slices, cut into 6 triangles

red pepper slice, cut to make 6 flag shapes

6 **cocktail sticks**

NOTE If decorating, remove the cocktail sticks when serving.

Thousand Island salad dressing

⟳ Preparation: 2 minutes ✎ Makes 4 portions

✐ Provides calcium and vitamins B12 and E

This versatile dressing goes well with a green salad, or sliced tomatoes and avocado. You could add 1 tablespoon of finely chopped parsley to garnish.

▶ Simply blend all the ingredients together, transfer to a clean container

and refrigerate, or whisk thoroughly and use immediately.

6 tbsp **mild, full-fat natural yogurt**

3 tbsp **mayonnaise**

3 tbsp **tomato ketchup**

½ tsp **Worcestershire sauce**

salt and freshly ground **black pepper**

150g (5oz) **pasta bows (farfalle)**

75g (2½oz) **French beans**

100g (3½oz) **canned** or **frozen sweetcorn**

60g (2oz) **carrots**, peeled and grated

4 **cherry tomatoes**, quartered

Dressing

30g (1oz) **onion**, peeled and grated

4 tbsp **vegetable oil**

1 tbsp **white wine vinegar**

2 tbsp **water**

½ tsp chopped **fresh ginger root**

1 tbsp **celery**, chopped

1 tbsp **soy sauce**

1½ tsp **tomato purée**

1 tsp **caster sugar**

salt and freshly ground **black pepper**

Annabel's pasta salad

Preparation: 10 minutes; cooking: 12 minutes ✂ Makes 4 portions ✒ Provides beta-carotene, fibre, folate, protein (especially when tuna or chicken is added) and vitamin E

This salad's delicious dressing is popular with my children as a dip for raw vegetables (I make up a big bottle of it to keep in the fridge). The salad is great for lunchboxes, picnics or as a side dish served warm or cold. Use three-colour pasta if possible.

► Cook the pasta in boiling, lightly salted water according to the instructions on the packet.

► Meanwhile, put the beans in a steamer and cook for 4 minutes. Add the sweetcorn to the steamer and cook for 3–4 minutes, or until tender.

► Combine all the ingredients for the dressing in a blender or food processor, adding only a little salt and pepper, and process until smooth.

► Combine the cooked pasta with the steamed vegetables, grated carrot and cherry tomatoes, and toss with some of the dressing.

Variation

Add 30g (1oz) diced cucumber, 75g (2½oz) diced cold chicken or tuna to this salad, and vary the vegetables, according to taste.

200g (7oz) **penne**

2 tbsp **olive oil**

1 **red onion**, peeled and chopped

4 **plum tomatoes**, quartered, deseeded and roughly chopped

200g (7oz) **canned tuna in oil**, drained

75g (2½oz) **sunblush (semi-dried) tomatoes**, chopped

1 tsp **balsamic vinegar**

100g (3½oz) **canned** or **frozen sweetcorn**

small handful **basil leaves**, torn

salt and freshly ground **black pepper**

Penne with tuna, tomato & sweetcorn

Preparation: 5 minutes; cooking: 10 minutes ✂ Makes 4 portions ✒ Provides fibre, iron, protein, B vitamins and vitamin D

A simple, tasty pasta dish, this can be rustled up using mainly ingredients which you keep in your store cupboard.

► Cook the pasta in boiling, lightly salted water according to the instructions on the packet.

► Heat the olive oil in a frying pan and sauté the onion for about 6 minutes, stirring occasionally until softened.

► Stir in the fresh tomatoes and cook for 2–3 minutes until heated through and beginning to soften.

► Add the tuna, sunblush tomatoes, balsamic vinegar, sweetcorn and basil, season and heat for 1 minute before stirring into the pasta.

Pasta with courgettes, peppers & sausages

↻ Preparation: 10 minutes; cooking: 18 minutes ⚔ Makes 4 portions
📈 Provides beta-carotene, fibre, folate, protein and vitamin B12

1 tbsp **vegetable oil**

1 small **onion**, peeled and sliced

60g (2oz) **red peppers**, cut into diamond shapes

100g (3¹/₂oz) **courgettes**, sliced

300g (10oz) **passata**

¹/₂ **chicken stock cube**, finely crumbled

125g (4oz) **pasta bows (farfalle)**

100g (3¹/₂oz) **sausages**, cooked and sliced

▶ Warm the oil in a frying pan, add the onion and sauté until softened. Add the peppers and cook for 3–4 minutes. Add the courgettes and cook for 3 minutes more.
▶ Pour the passata into the pan then stir in the crumbled stock cube. Bring the mixture to the boil, then cover and simmer for 10 minutes.

▶ Meanwhile, cook the pasta bows in boiling, lightly salted water, according to the instructions on the packet.
▶ Add the sliced sausages to the sauce and cook until just heated through. Drain the pasta, toss it with the sauce and serve at once.

Salmon teriyaki with noodles & beansprouts

↻ Preparation: 5 minutes; cooking: 40 minutes, including 30 minutes for the salmon to marinate ⚔ Makes 4 portions 📈 Provides omega-3 fats, protein, B vitamins and vitamins D and E

2 x 125g (4oz) **salmon fillets**, skinned

100g (3¹/₂oz) **fine egg noodles**

1 tsp **cornflour**

1 tbsp **vegetable oil**

75g (2¹/₂oz) **beansprouts**

2 **spring onions**, thinly sliced

50ml (1³/₄fl oz) **chicken stock** (see page 52)

Marinade

3 tbsp **soy sauce**

2 tbsp **sake** (rice wine)

2 tbsp **caster sugar**

Simple to prepare, this dish is a great favourite with my three children. Oily fish, such as salmon, trout, tuna, sardines and mackerel, contain omega-3 fatty acids which protect against heart disease and strokes. Eating oily fish also helps brain development and research shows that including oily fish in the diet can help children who are dyspraxic or dyslexic.

▶ Put the marinade ingredients in a small saucepan and boil rapidly for 2 minutes until slightly thickened. Allow to cool, then pour over the salmon and leave to marinate for at least 30 minutes.
▶ Cook the noodles in boiling, lightly salted water according to the instructions on the packet and then rinse in cold water. Set aside.
▶ Drain the marinade from the salmon and reserve. Stir a teaspoon of cornflour into the marinade.
▶ Heat half a tablespoon of oil in a small frying pan and sauté the salmon for about 2 minutes on each side until just cooked. Pour away some of the

excess oil from the pan, pour over half the reserved marinade and cook for about 1 minute. Set aside.
▶ Heat the remaining oil in a wok or small frying pan and stir-fry the beansprouts and spring onions for 2 minutes, then stir in the noodles.
▶ Add the chicken stock to the remaining marinade. Pour this over the noodles and beansprouts and cook for 1 minute.
▶ Serve the salmon on top of a bed of noodles and beansprouts.

Chinese noodles with chicken & beansprouts

Preparation: 10 minutes; cooking: 15 minutes   Makes 4 portions

Provides potassium, protein, B vitamins including folate, vitamins C and E and zinc

Don't be afraid to try out new tastes on your child – these noodles flavoured with a mild curry and coconut sauce were very popular with my tasting panel. In fact, young children often like unusual flavours, such as olives or sweet and sour cucumbers, and tend to like mild curries.

▶ Heat the vegetable oil in a wok or frying pan and stir-fry the spring onions, garlic and chopped red chilli for about 2 minutes. Add the chicken and continue to stir-fry for 2 minutes.

▶ Add the curry paste, chicken stock and the coconut milk and cook for 5 minutes over a low heat. Add the sweetcorn and beansprouts and cook for 3–4 minutes. Finally, add the peas, noodles and prawns and cook for about 3 minutes more.

½ tbsp **vegetable oil**

3 **spring onions**, chopped

1 **garlic clove**, peeled and crushed

½ tsp **red chilli**, chopped

1½ **chicken breast fillets** (about 225g/7½oz), cut into strips

1 tsp **Korma curry paste** (or 2 tsp, for more adventurous children)

150ml (5fl oz) **chicken stock** (see page 52)

150ml (5fl oz) **coconut milk**

75g (2½oz) **baby sweetcorn**, cut into quarters

100g (3½oz) **beansprouts**

75g (2½oz) defrosted **frozen peas**

125g (4oz) **Chinese noodles**

100g (3½oz) small **prawns**

Golden turkey fingers

⟳ Preparation: 40 minutes, including 30 minutes marinating; cooking: 10 minutes
⚡ Makes 4 portions ⚕ Provides protein, B vitamins including folate and zinc
❄ Suitable for freezing: uncooked

250g (8oz) **turkey breast fillets**

juice of 1 **lime** or 1/2 **lemon**

1 **shallot,** peeled and sliced

plain flour, for coating

salt and freshly ground **black pepper**

75g (2 1/2 oz) **dry breadcrumbs**

1 1/2 tbsp snipped **chives**

1 **egg,** lightly beaten

vegetable oil for shallow frying

► Cut the turkey into 1cm (1/2 in) strips, removing any skin. Place in a bowl with the lime or lemon juice and shallot. Cover and refrigerate for 30 minutes.
► Spread some flour on a plate and season with salt and pepper. On another plate, mix together the breadcrumbs and chives. Dip the turkey strips first in the seasoned flour, then in the beaten egg and finally in the breadcrumb and chive mixture.
► Heat the oil in a frying pan, add the turkey strips and sauté until golden and cooked through, about 10 minutes.

Heart-shaped chicken nuggets

⟳ Preparation: 25 minutes; cooking: 6 minutes ⚡ Makes 8 portions
⚕ Provides protein and B vitamins ❄ Suitable for freezing

The addition of apple gives these nuggets a delicious, moist flavour. If you don't have a heart-shaped cutter, try another shape, but keep to fairly simple lines.

375g (12oz) **chicken breast fillets,** cut into chunks

1 large **onion,** peeled and diced

2 tbsp chopped **fresh parsley**

1 small **apple,** peeled and grated

45g (1 1/2 oz) **fresh white breadcrumbs**

1 **chicken stock cube,** crumbled

60g (2oz) **dry breadcrumbs**

60g (2oz) **cheese and onion flavour crisps,** finely crushed

vegetable oil for frying

► Put the first six ingredients in a food processor and chop for a few seconds until well combined. Shape the mixture into a flat disc.
► Use a 6cm (2 1/2 in) biscuit cutter to press out heart shapes. Mix together the dry breadcrumbs and crisps on a plate and press the pieces into the coating.
► Heat enough oil for shallow frying in a large frying pan. Add the nuggets and cook for about 6 minutes, turning occasionally, until lightly golden and cooked through.

Caramelized chicken breasts

⟳ Preparation: 5 minutes; cooking: 20 minutes ⚡ Makes 4 portions
⚕ Provides protein, B vitamins including folate and zinc

1 1/2 tbsp **olive oil**

1 **onion,** peeled and thinly sliced

1 small **garlic clove,** peeled and crushed

salt and freshly ground **black pepper**

2 **chicken breast fillets** (about 300g/10oz)

1 tbsp **malt vinegar**

1 1/2 tbsp **tomato ketchup**

1 tbsp **soy sauce**

1/2 tbsp **soft brown sugar**

► Warm 1 tablespoon of the oil in a heavy-based saucepan. Add the onion and garlic and sauté for 10 minutes until soft and lightly golden.
► Remove the onion with a slotted spoon and add the remaining oil. Season the chicken and pan-fry for about 7 minutes on each side.
► When the chicken is nearly cooked add the vinegar, ketchup, soy sauce and brown sugar and cook over a high heat for 1 minute.
► Return the onion to the pan, cover and cook for about 2 minutes. Serve with rice.

300g (10oz) **chicken breast fillets**

1½ tbsp **vegetable oil**

1 small **onion,** peeled and sliced

1 **garlic clove,** peeled and crushed

60g (2oz) **baby sweetcorn,** quartered

60g (2oz) **carrots,** peeled and cut into strips

60g (2oz) **cauliflower,** cut into florets

60g (2oz) **courgettes,** cut into strips

freshly ground **black pepper,** to taste

Marinade

2 tbsp **soy sauce**

2 tbsp **sake** (rice wine)

½ tsp **soft brown sugar**

1 tsp **sesame oil**

1 **spring onion,** finely chopped

TIP For additional flavour, add ½ teaspoon finely chopped fresh root ginger to the marinade.

Teriyaki chicken stir-fry

Preparation: 40 minutes, including 30 minutes marinating; cooking: 15 minutes
Makes 4 portions　Provides beta-carotene, folate and other B vitamins, iron, potassium, protein, vitamins C and E and zinc

▶ Cut the chicken breasts into thin strips. Combine the marinade ingredients in a dish. Add the chicken, and leave to marinate for at least 30 minutes.

▶ Heat the vegetable oil in a lidded wok or large frying pan, add the onion and garlic and stir-fry, uncovered, for 2 minutes.

▶ Strain the marinade from the chicken and set aside. Add the chicken to the wok and stir-fry until it changes colour. Add the baby sweetcorn to the wok with the carrots and cauliflower, stir-fry for 3 minutes, then add the courgettes, and continue to stir-fry for 2 minutes.

▶ Pour in the marinade. Cover the wok and cook for 2 minutes, or until the vegetables are tender and the chicken is cooked through. Season with a little freshly ground black pepper.

Variation

▶ Replace the chicken with 375g (12oz) fillet or rump steak, beaten until tender and cut into strips.

---

4 **chicken breast fillets** (about 800g/20oz), cubed

425g (14oz) **canned lychees**

1 **red pepper,** deseeded and cut into triangles

Marinade

3 tbsp **soy sauce**

3 tbsp **honey**

½ tbsp **lemon juice**

To decorate

8 **cherry tomatoes** or **radishes**

16 **whole cloves**

8 **spring onion fans** (see below)

TIP To make spring onion fans, cut spring onions into 7cm (3in) lengths. Make four slashes at one end of each. Place in iced water until the ends curl.

Chicken caterpillar kebabs

Preparation: 40 minutes, including 30 minutes marinating; cooking: 15 minutes
180°C/350°F/gas 4　Makes 8 portions　Provides beta-carotene, iron, protein, B vitamins, vitamin C and zinc

▶ Mix together the marinade ingredients in a shallow dish. Add the chicken and leave to marinate for at least 30 minutes. While the chicken marinates soak eight bamboo skewers in water to stop them burning.

▶ Thread the chicken on to the skewers, putting half a lychee and a red pepper triangle between each piece of chicken. Arrange on a baking tray and transfer

to the preheated oven. Cook for about 15 minutes, basting with the marinade and turning occasionally, until cooked through.

▶ To decorate, make a face for each caterpillar using a cherry tomato or radish, studded with clove eyes. Attach it to the tip of the skewer, and thread on a spring onion tail.

Annabel's tasty meatballs

⟳ Preparation: 10 minutes; cooking: 15 minutes   ✂ Makes 8 portions
✦ Provides iron, protein, B vitamins and zinc   ❄ Suitable for freezing

*These meatballs are easy to prepare and delicious (the apple keeps them
wonderfully moist). They are good on their own or served with spaghetti
and Special tomato sauce (see page 153).*

▶ In a mixing bowl, combine all the
ingredients except for the flour and
vegetable oil. Use your hands to form the
mixture into about 24 walnut-sized balls.
Spread the flour on a plate and use to
coat the meatballs.

▶ Warm the oil in a frying pan, add the
meatballs and fry over a high heat for
about 3 minutes, until browned on all
sides. Lower the heat a little and fry for
12 minutes, or until cooked through.

500g (1lb) lean **minced beef**

1 **onion**, peeled and finely chopped

1 tbsp chopped **fresh parsley**

1 **chicken stock cube** dissolved in
2 tbsp **hot water**

1 small **apple**, peeled and grated

1/2 tsp **Worcestershire sauce**

pinch of **brown sugar**

salt and freshly ground **black pepper**

plain flour for coating

vegetable oil for frying

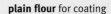

Hungarian goulash

⟳ Preparation: 15 minutes; cooking: 2 hours 20 minutes   ⬇ 150°C/300°F/gas 2
✂ Makes 8 portions   ✦ Provides beta-carotene, iron, potassium, protein, B vitamins
including folate, vitamin C and zinc   ❄ Suitable for freezing

*For young children, chop the meat and vegetables into small pieces or process
in a blender for just a few seconds. Serve with pasta noodles.*

▶ Spread the flour on a plate, season
lightly and use to coat the beef. Warm
the vegetable oil in a flameproof
casserole dish, add the beef and sauté
until browned all over. Remove with
a slotted spoon and set aside.
▶ Add the onions to the casserole and
sauté for 5 minutes. Add the red pepper
and sauté for 3–4 minutes, then add the
mushrooms and cook for 3 minutes.
Sprinkle over the paprika and cook for
about 2 minutes.
▶ Return the sautéed meat to the dish,
pour in the stock and stir in the tomato

purée, tomato ketchup, Worcestershire
sauce and chopped parsley. Cover,
transfer to the preheated oven and cook
for about 2 hours. Check that the meat
is tender. Season to taste and stir in the
sour cream. Set aside and keep warm.
▶ Cook the noodles in boiling, lightly
salted water according to the instructions
on the packet. Drain, arrange a bed of
noodles on each plate and top with a
serving of goulash.

plain flour for coating

salt and freshly ground **black pepper**

500g (1lb) lean **braising steak**,
cut into cubes

2 tbsp **vegetable oil**

2 **onions**, peeled and chopped

1 **red pepper**, deseeded and
chopped

250g (8oz) **mushrooms**, sliced

1 tbsp **paprika**

400ml (14fl oz) **chicken stock** (see
page 52) or **beef stock**

3 tbsp **tomato purée**

1 tbsp **tomato ketchup**

1 tsp **Worcestershire sauce**

2 tbsp chopped **fresh parsley**

6 tbsp **sour cream**

200g (7oz) **pasta noodles**, such
as **tagliatelle**

Sponge cake mixture

125g (4oz) **soft margarine**

125g (4oz) **caster sugar**

2 **eggs**

1 tsp **vanilla extract**

¼ tsp grated **lemon zest** (optional)

125g (4oz) **self-raising flour**

60g (2oz) **raisins** or **sultanas** (optional)

To decorate as pigs

pink **food colouring**

175g (6oz) **ready-to-roll white icing**, plus icing sugar to dust

3 tbsp **apricot jam**, sieved and warmed gently

pink marshmallows

coloured **writing icing**

red **liquorice laces**

To decorate as hedgehogs

Make a spiky hedgehog with chocolate buttercream icing and spikes made from broken flaked chocolate sticks.

To decorate as clowns

Decorate a white-iced cake with yellow grated icing hair, a red icing nose and mouth and black writing icing eyes.

TIP Ready-to-roll icing can sometimes be bought in a range of colours, but it is easy to tint your own icing by kneading in some food paste colouring or a few drops of food colouring, as described in this recipe.

Character fairy cakes

⟳ Preparation: 20 minutes; cooking: 20 minutes, plus decorating time

⬇ 180°C/350°F/gas 4   ✂ Makes 15 cakes   🏃 Provides vitamins A and B12

❄ Suitable for freezing: before decorating

Decorated fairy cakes are great for parties. Here I describe how to make a piggy face, but you could try clowns, spiky chocolate hedgehogs or ladybirds made with red and black icing. Older children will enjoy helping to decorate these.

▶ Cream together the margarine and sugar until pale and fluffy. Beat in the eggs one at a time then add the vanilla extract and lemon zest if using.

▶ Fold in the flour and raisins, if using, and mix until soft and creamy.

▶ Line a bun tray with paper cases and half-fill each case. Transfer to the preheated oven and bake for about 20 minutes. Leave to cool on a wire rack.

▶ Add a few drops of the pink food colouring to the icing and knead until an even colour tone is achieved. Lightly dust a work surface with icing sugar and roll out the icing until it is about 2.5mm (⅛ in) thick.

▶ Use a round pastry cutter or glass to cut out discs of icing slightly larger than the cakes. Brush the cake tops with a little warmed apricot jam and set the icing on top.

▶ Make a pig's snout by attaching a marshmallow, halved across the diameter, to the centre of the cake using jam; draw on nostrils with writing icing and use edible silver balls for the eyes. Add halved marshmallow ears and a short strip of liquorice for the mouth.

Parcel birthday cake

Preparation: 20 minutes; cooking: 1 hour, plus decorating time
180°C/350°F/gas 4 ☑ Makes 20 portions ⚡ Provides vitamins A and B12
❄ Suitable for freezing: undecorated only

▶ Pour the sponge cake mixture into a greased and lined 20cm (8in) square tin and a 23 x 12 x 7cm (9 x 5 x 3in) loaf tin. Transfer to the preheated oven and bake the loaf tin for 45 minutes and the square tin for 1 hour. Turn out and leave to cool on a wire rack.

▶ Divide the loaf cake into the desired number of blocks to form the small parcels. Slice all the cakes across and sandwich the halves together with a layer each of raspberry jam and buttercream.

▶ Choose your colour scheme, then tint the white icing, as described in the previous recipe.

▶ Brush the top and sides of the cake blocks with apricot jam. Lay the icing over the top, either in a single sheet or in strips for a striped effect. Make icing bows in contrasting colours, sticking them down with jam. Decorate further with icing spots or flowers, or leave plain; or you can even add a few marzipan animals.

4 x quantities **sponge cake mixture** (see Character fairy cakes, opposite)

Filling

250g (8oz) **raspberry jam**

1 quantity **buttercream** made with 175g (6oz) **soft butter** beaten with 375g (12oz) **icing sugar**, 1 tbsp **milk** and 1 tsp **vanilla extract**

To decorate

red, blue, green and yellow **food colourings**

1.25kg (2½lb) **ready-to-roll icing** (see Tip, opposite), plus **icing sugar** to dust

8 tbsp **apricot jam**, sieved and warmed gently

45g (1½oz) **butter**

140g (4½oz) **soft brown sugar**

2 **eggs**

175g (6oz) **plain flour**, sifted

¾ tsp **baking powder**

200ml (7fl oz) **boiling water**

140g (4½oz) **stoned dates**, chopped

¾ tsp **bicarbonate of soda**

¾ tsp **vanilla extract**

Butterscotch sauce

100g (3½oz) **soft brown sugar**

65g (2¼oz) **butter**

125ml (4fl oz) **double cream**

TIP *This pudding can be made in advance, kept in the refrigerator and reheated before serving.*

Sticky toffee pudding

Preparation: 10 minutes; cooking: 40 minutes 190°C/375°F/gas 5
Makes 8 portions Provides vitamins A and B12 Suitable for freezing

This is one of those classic sticky nursery puddings that never fails to please children and adults alike.

▶ Cream together the butter and sugar. Beat the eggs into the mixture, then fold in the flour and baking powder.

▶ Pour the boiling water over the dates and add the bicarbonate of soda and vanilla extract. Add this mixture to the batter and blend well.

▶ Butter a 28 x 18cm (11 x 7in) ovenproof dish. Pour the batter into the dish (don't worry that the consistency is very liquid) and bake in the preheated oven for 40 minutes.

▶ Preheat the grill. To make the sauce, put the brown sugar, butter and cream in a pan and heat gently for about 5 minutes. Remove the pudding from the oven, pour over half the sauce and place under the hot grill until it bubbles. Serve the remaining sauce separately.

125g (4oz) **self-raising flour**

2 tbsp **cocoa powder**

125g (4oz) **soft margarine**

125g (4oz) **caster sugar**

2 **eggs**, lightly beaten

grated zest of 1 small **orange**

60g (2oz) **plain chocolate chips**

Chocolate orange mini muffins

Preparation: 20 minutes; cooking: 12 minutes 180°C/350°F/gas 4
Makes 30 mini muffins or 15 medium muffins Provides vitamin A
Suitable for freezing

Mini muffins are just the right size for small children. However, if you prefer to make adult-size portions, bake this quantity of muffin mixture in medium muffin trays to make about 15 cakes.

▶ Sift together the flour and cocoa.
▶ Cream the margarine and caster sugar. Add the eggs to the creamed mixture, a little at a time, together with a tablespoon of the flour mixture.
▶ Mix in the remaining flour and

cocoa until blended. Then stir in the orange zest and chocolate chips.
▶ Line some muffin trays with paper cases and two-thirds fill each of the cases.
▶ Transfer to the preheated oven and cook for 10–12 minutes.

125g (4oz) **butter** (cold)

60g (2oz) **caster sugar**

30g (1oz) **ground almonds**

pinch of **salt**

90g (3oz) **plain flour**, plus extra
to dust

60g (2oz) **cornflour**

glacé icing or **icing sugar**
to decorate (optional)

edible silver balls to decorate
(optional)

Shortbread cookies

Preparation: 15 minutes; cooking: 15 minutes   180°C/350°F/gas 4
Makes 12–15 cookies   Provides vitamin A   Suitable for freezing

▶ Beat together the butter and sugar until fluffy. Add the remaining ingredients and beat until the mixture sticks together and begins to form a ball.
▶ Dust a pastry board with flour, turn out the mixture, and knead gently for 1–2 minutes to form a smooth dough. Roll the dough out until 5mm (¼in) thick. Cut into shapes using biscuit cutters.
▶ Using a palette knife, transfer the shapes to a greased baking sheet. Bake in the preheated oven for 15 minutes, or until lightly golden. Leave to cool on the tray, then lift off. Ice or decorate, as desired.

White chocolate chip cookies

Preparation: 25 minutes; cooking: 14 minutes   180°C/350°F/gas 4
Makes 24 cookies   Suitable for freezing

The perfect recipe for chocolate chip cookies! I like them best with white chocolate but you could use semi-sweet chocolate chips instead.

▶ Combine the butter, shortening and sugars and beat in an electric mixer until the mixture is smooth. Add the egg and vanilla and continue to beat until all ingredients are well blended.
▶ In a mixing bowl stir together the flour, baking powder and salt. Stir the flour mixture into the first mixture, then add the chocolate chips.

▶ Using your hands, shape into walnut-sized balls (about 3cm/1in diameter). Place on greased baking sheets spaced well apart as the cookies will spread, and bake in the preheated oven for about 14 minutes. Let the cookies cool on the sheets, then transfer them to a wire rack. You can store the cookies in an airtight container for up to a week.

50g (1¾oz) **unsalted butter**

50g (1¾oz) **vegetable shortening**

125g (4oz) **soft brown sugar**

100g (3½oz) **granulated sugar**

1 **egg**

1 tsp **vanilla essence**

150g (5oz) **plain flour**

1 tsp **baking powder**

½ tsp **salt**

175g (6oz) **white chocolate**, cut
into small chunks

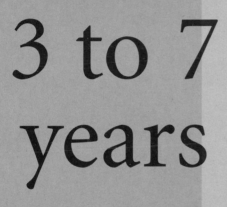

3 to 7 years

Pre-school & beyond

"As your child reaches pre-school age this is a good time to educate him on the basics of good nutrition."

The greatest change in your child's life at this stage of development will probably be starting nursery then moving on to school, and that means eating has to fit into more of a routine. Nursery-age children will need a good breakfast to keep them alert until lunchtime. Then packed lunches may soon become an essential part of your child's diet, too, and they will need to be nutritious and sustaining.

A healthy & varied diet

Between the ages of three and five your child's manual dexterity should greatly improve and he should be able to master all the basic eating skills. He should also have his first full set of teeth. Around this age many children will start noticing commercials that push unhealthy foods. This is a good time to explain the basic principles of nutrition to your child.

If parents offer fresh fruit and vegetables in a defensive or apologetic way, children will begin to reject them. So if you can make these fresh foods seem to be the appealing, tasty foods they really are, then your child will not equate "healthy" with "nasty". Vitamin pills are no substitute for fresh fruit and vegetables in your child's diet.

Breakfasts for brain power

The first meal of the day is the most important as your child will probably have fasted for at least 12 hours and his blood sugar levels will be very low. Your child's brain will also need a kick start first thing in the morning. Although weighing only 4 per cent of your child's total body weight, the brain uses approximately 20 per cent of the body's energy at rest. The brain's energy stores are also very small, so in order to keep it functioning at its best, it needs constant glucose replacement.

Improving blood sugar levels by eating a good breakfast after the night's fast raises blood glucose – "fuel for the brain"– and will help to improve your child's performance. Recent research has shown that children who eat a nutritionally balanced breakfast work faster, make significantly fewer mistakes on tasks requiring sustained attention, demonstrate greater physical endurance and appear less tired to teachers than children who do not.

Breakfast sets the pattern for healthy eating throughout the rest of the day. When children miss breakfast, they often binge on chocolate biscuits or crisps later in the morning. For maximum energy and brain power to last throughout the morning a good breakfast should ideally include food from each of these groups:
- **complex carbohydrate**: wholegrain cereal, bread
- **protein**: dairy products, eggs, nuts and seeds
- **vitamins and minerals**: fruit or fruit juice.

A healthy breakfast need take no longer than 10 minutes to eat from start to finish. By giving your child cereal with milk or peanut butter on toast, a yogurt or some cheese and a glass of fruit juice, you are providing him with a food from each group and an excellent start to the day.

The key role of carbohydrates

Carbohydrates provide the body's main source of energy. Children need plenty of them not only because they are active and use up masses of energy, but also because they are growing. Make sure your child's breakfast includes some unrefined carbohydrates, such as wholemeal bread, wholegrain cereals and fruit. The fibre contained in these foods helps slow down the rate at which sugar is released, giving longer-lasting concentration and sustained energy.

If your child eats predominantly refined carbohydrates at breakfast, such as a bowl of sugary cereal or white bread with chocolate spread, he will have a burst of energy to fuel his activity for a while, but this will be short-lived. When it is gone, his blood-sugar level starts to fall, which can result in poor concentration, erratic learning, disruptive behaviour and fatigue. He would do better with a breakfast of complex carbohydrates such as a bowl of muesli with fruit, or cheese on wholemeal toast.

Top nutritious quick-to-prepare breakfast ideas

- Cheese on toast or sealed toasted sandwiches made in an electric sandwich maker are delicious. Try cheese and tomato or ham and cheese.

- Make a fruit salad using seasonal fruits mixed with some fresh orange juice and a little lemon juice mixed with a little sugar – or mix fresh fruit with fruit yogurt. Different fruits contain different vitamins, so try to include plenty of variety.

- Make French toast: dip bread into beaten egg mixed with 2 tbsp milk and fry in butter until golden.

- Fruity milkshakes or fruit smoothies are a good way to encourage your child to consume more fruit. Try sieved berries sweetened with icing sugar mixed with milk and a little raspberry or strawberry drinking yogurt (you can also use frozen berries).

- Make scrambled eggs extra special by adding ingredients such as chopped fresh tomatoes, grated cheese or ham. Add a minute before the eggs are done.

- Boiled egg with toast soldiers spread with butter and Marmite are popular with most children.

- Dried fruit compôte or stewed fruit, such as apples or rhubarb, with brown sugar are delicious.

- Baked beans on toast make a warm and satisfying breakfast.

- Make toast with peanut butter, honey and banana. Spread slices of toasted granary bread with peanut butter and a little honey and top with sliced bananas.

Remember

• Children are great mimics and will be affected by adults' attitudes to eating. If parents do not eat healthily themselves, or refuse to try new dishes, children are likely to copy their conservative eating habits. If a member of the family is slimming, don't discuss it in front of the children. You need to avoid creating eating anxieties.

• When setting up a healthy eating plan, enlist the help of visitors, grandparents and other carers. If everyone is aware of your food policies, your child will be treated consistently.

• Ensure that your child eats a substantial breakfast, particularly on weekdays if he will be at nursery or pre-school. If he is a very slow eater and you are short of time, give him a sandwich or healthy muffin to eat on the way.

• Iron absorption can be inhibited by the tannin in tea, so it's best to avoid giving tea to children at breakfast.

Good iron-boosting breakfast combinations

• boiled egg with wholewheat toast, yogurt and a glass of orange juice

• bowl of fortified cereal with milk and dried fruit or kiwi fruit

Refined carbohydrates contain less nutrients than complex carbohydrates as many are lost in the processing. For example, white flour contains less zinc than wholemeal flour. Zinc is vital for growth and aids resistance to infection.

Increasing iron in the diet

Iron deficiency is the most common nutritional deficiency, affecting about 25 per cent of young children. Two symptoms are tiredness and lack of concentration, so increasing iron intake could improve your child's schoolwork. Iron is important for transporting oxygen in the blood to all the body's organs, including the brain, so iron is important for good brain function.

Fortified cereals and wholemeal bread are good sources of iron. However, it is difficult for our bodies to absorb iron from a non-meat source – red meat provides the form of iron that is most easily absorbed by the body. To improve the absorption of iron from a plant source, your child will need to consume a vitamin C-rich fruit (such as kiwi fruit or berries) or vitamin C-rich juice (such as orange or cranberry juice) along with the plant source.

Breakfast cereals

Many of the cereals designed to appeal to children contain up to 50 per cent sugar, are high in salt and are so highly processed that, unless they are fortified, they contain very little fibre, vitamins or minerals. Healthy cereals include Shredded Wheat, Weetabix, Granola, muesli and porridge. Even if your child adds sugar, it will be a lot less than the 4–5 teaspoons per bowl you might find in other cereals.

Outside the home

Some time after his third birthday, if not before, your child may be looked after by a childminder or start attending nursery school. If lunch is provided, check that it is well balanced and nutritious. Where a packed lunch is required, try to make it interesting and healthy.

Briefing carers

If you find that your child is always over-hungry when he comes out of pre-school, ask a teacher or carer to monitor what he eats and report back to you. Children are usually quite hungry after a pre-school day and it can be a good time to encourage them to snack healthily. If you bring a nutritious snack, such as a banana or a cheese and tomato sandwich, when you collect your child, you will usually find that he will eat it eagerly.

If you have a policy of no sweets or chocolates between meals, then let carers and relatives know so that you can be consistent with your rules. You might suggest other treats, such as exotic fruits or homemade biscuits.

It may not be a good idea to ban sweets altogether, because there is a danger of making them into an even more desirable "forbidden fruit". It is probably easier to limit sweets to certain specific times, such as after meals or at weekends. If you keep to your rule, your child will soon stop asking for them at any other time.

Fast food

Many "fast foods" are high in saturated fat, salt or sugar relative to their nutrient content. To encourage your children to eat a nutritious diet, make healthy versions of their fast food favourites, such as Mini pizzas (page 97), Crunchy chicken fingers (page 101), Oven-baked chips (page 163) and tempting Ice lollies (page 177).

Tasty & nutritious packed lunches

When your child brings his lunch to school, he carries a little piece of home with him. Whenever I make packed lunches for my three children it is a challenge to come up with something new to entice them to eat healthy food and bring smiles to their faces after a long morning at school. Simple touches can make all the difference: try drawing a face on your child's banana with a felt pen and decorating it with stickers, or cutting sandwiches into interesting shapes using cookie cutters.

If you want to boost your child's brainpower and concentration at school, you need to make sure that his lunchbox contains a variety of foods from the following groups:

• a source of protein for growth and alertness throughout the day
• complex carbohydrates for slow-release energy
• calcium for growing bones

"You don't have to give your child a sandwich for lunch; try tortilla wraps or pitta pockets, chicken drumsticks or pots of pasta or rice salad."

"Young children like miniature portions, such as individual wrapped cheeses, tiny boxes of raisins and mini muffins."

• vitamins and minerals from fruit and vegetables
• a little fat for staying power
• water, pure fruit juice or a fruit smoothie.

So, a typical healthy lunchbox might include a wholemeal sandwich or pitta bread pocket with tuna, chicken, egg, cheese or peanut butter; a pot of yogurt or yogurt drink; a piece of fruit or some dried fruit and a treat like a small chocolate bar, cookies, mini muffin or crisps.

Lunchbox combinations
There are a huge number of options for creating a healthy packed lunch for your child. Here are some healthy but tasty suggestions for each nutrient. Choose from each category to create a well-balanced lunch for your child.

• **Protein** Choose lean meats, such as turkey slices, chicken skewers and roast beef, for his sandwich. Fish, such as tuna, is also a good source of protein: try making a tuna pasta salad. Boiled eggs wrapped in clingfilm and individually wrapped mini cheeses are also popular sources of protein.

• **Carbohydrates** Choose complex carbohydrates such as wholegrain bread, pasta, new potatoes or basmati rice. These release calories slowly and help to keep up energy levels and concentration. Refined carbohydrates provide more short-lived energy. Sandwiches don't have to be made using sliced bread. Try tortilla wraps, pitta bread, bagels or mini baguettes; for example, toast an English muffin or bagel, spread with a little marinara sauce, top with some grated Swiss, Cheddar or mozzarella cheese and place under the grill until the cheese has melted. Wrap in foil. Alternatively, try making little pots of pasta or rice salad.

• **Calcium** After he has reached the age of one and your child has been weaned, switch to full-fat cows' milk. He should be drinking 400ml (14fl oz) of milk a day or the equivalent in dairy products. One pot of yogurt and 30g (1oz) of hard cheese provide the same amount of calcium as 200ml (7fl oz) of milk. Until the age of two, your child needs full-fat milk because it provides necessary calories and vitamin A. Children under five shouldn't have a low-fat diet, so choose whole milk products, such as full-fat yogurt, rather than low-fat versions.

Supermarkets are full of bio-yogurts and drinks containing friendly bacteria known as probiotics. These are packaged in small plastic bottles that are an ideal size for lunchboxes. Probiotics can help prevent food poisoning and other digestive system infections.

Dried figs, seeds and nuts also provide moderate amounts of calcium. Canned sardines are a rich source.

• **Vitamins and minerals** Always include some fresh fruit in your child's lunchbox; dried fruit, such as dried apricots or raisins, are good, too. Raw vegetables with an accompanying dip are usually popular with children, or you can prepare salad kebabs with cherry tomatoes, cucumber, sweet pepper and cheese.

Include a vitamin C-rich drink, such as orange juice, or a vitamin C-rich fruit such as kiwi fruit, to help boost iron absorption. Choose unsweetened pure fruit juice or make a fruit smoothie. Don't give vitamin-enriched fruit juice drinks: many contain a lot of water and sugar or artificial sweeteners.

Preserving lunchbox contents

• In hot weather keep the contents of your child's lunchbox cool by including a small ice-pack. Alternatively, place a carton or plastic container of juice in the lunchbox and freeze

overnight. By lunchtime the juice will have defrosted.

• Wrap sandwiches in cling film or silver foil to keep them fresh.

• To prevent sandwiches from getting squashed by bottles of juice, pack them in a rigid plastic container.

• To avoid soggy sandwiches, make sure you dry the ingredients before you put them in the sandwich. For example, if you wash lettuce, dry it before putting it into the sandwich. A layer of dry lettuce between filling and bread can also help stop sandwiches becoming soggy. If you are going on a picnic, some of the wet ingredients can be packed separately and can be added to the sandwich just before eating.

Hot food at lunch

When the weather gets colder it's a good idea to include something hot in your child's lunchbox. A wide-mouthed mini thermos flask is ideal for serving up a delicious cup of homemade or good-quality bought soup.

Remember

If your child suffers from a nut allergy or any other serious food allergy it is important that you inform the school. Sometimes children swap items of food with their friends and many schools have a policy of asking parents not to include any foods containing peanuts in school lunchboxes.

Ruses

• It's sometimes good to get children to make their own sandwiches for their lunchbox. They are more likely to eat them if they have chosen the bread and the filling.

• Start a cookie cutter collection – sandwiches cut into funny shapes will appeal to your child.

MORE IDEAS FOR LUNCHBOXES & PICNICS

Sandwich fillings

• Bacon, lettuce and tomato

• Sliced turkey with lettuce, mayonnaise and cranberry sauce

• Sliced turkey with Swiss cheese, tomato, cucumber and alfalfa sprouts mixed with salad cream or mayonnaise

• Chopped pineapple, slivers of ham or turkey and honey mustard

• Roast beef, lettuce, pickled cucumber, tomato and a little mild horseradish or mustard

• Shredded chicken, chopped tomato, chopped hard-boiled egg, snipped chives, lettuce and mayonnaise

• Tuna, sweetcorn, finely chopped spring onion and mayonnaise

• Prawns with lettuce and mayonnaise mixed with a little tomato ketchup

• Cream cheese and smoked salmon

• Chopped hard-boiled egg mashed with a little mayonnaise, snipped chives or cress, salt and freshly ground pepper

• Sliced Swiss cheese, cherry tomatoes and shredded lettuce

• Cream cheese and cucumber

• Grated cheese and carrot with a little mayonnaise

• Tomato, mozzarella, avocado and French dressing

• Hummus, grated carrot and sliced cucumber

• Peanut butter and sliced banana with a little honey

• Peanut butter and strawberry jam or cranberry sauce

• Peanut butter and raisins

Snack ideas

• A bag of bite-sized carrots, cucumber sticks and cherry tomatoes with a small container of hummus or sour cream and chive dip

• Dried fruit such as apricots, figs, mangoes, apples, raisins

• Thin slices of ham or turkey wrapped around cheese sticks

• Very small vegetables and fruits, such as baby carrots, cherry tomatoes, clementines, small bananas

• Popcorn, provided it is not covered in salt or sugar

• Rice cakes

• Miniature cheeses

• Nuts, for example, honey-roasted cashew nuts for over fives, provided there is no nut allergy in the family

• Probiotic mini yogurt drinks

• Squeeze-and-eat sachets of fromage frais

Healthy snacks

Young children expend a lot of energy running around, their stomachs are small and it is often difficult for them to eat enough at mealtimes to keep them going all day. Also, many young children just don't have the patience to sit down and eat a proper meal. Snacks are therefore a very important part of their diet and if you encourage your child to eat healthy snacks in preference to chocolate biscuits and crisps, it is likely that these habits will continue later in life and your child will enjoy a much healthier diet.

1 Fruit skewers
Children should eat five portions of fruit and vegetables each day, and this is a fun way of encouraging your child to eat more fruit. (See page 147 for recipe.) You can also make skewers using a mixture of fresh and dried fruit.

2 Turkey pasta salad
This dish is a delicious combination of moist turkey, sweetcorn, cherry tomatoes and pasta, tossed in a dressing flavoured with soy sauce, honey and lemon. (See page 145 for recipe.) Keep salads like this in the fridge for your child to snack on when he is hungry.

3 Cherry tomato & mozzarella salad
Quick and easy to put together, this is an attractive salad of sweet cherry tomatoes with mini balls of mozzarella cheese and fresh basil. (See page 144 for recipe.)

1

2

3

1 tbsp **sunflower oil**

60g (2oz) **pumpkin seeds**

60g (2oz) **sunflower seeds**

1 tbsp **honey**

1 tbsp **soy sauce**

TIP Toasted pumpkin seeds make a nutritious snack food and are full of valuable vitamins and minerals.

Toasted seeds with honey & soy sauce

↻ Preparation: 2 minutes; cooking: 3 minutes   ⚡ Makes 4 portions   ⚡ Provides iron, magnesium, omega-3 fatty acids, potassium, protein, B vitamins, vitamin E and zinc

These make a delicious nibble any time of the day and can also be sprinkled over salads. You can mix the toasted seeds with raisins if you like.

▶ Heat the oil in a non-stick frying pan and cook the seeds, stirring for about 2 minutes until lightly browned.

▶ Remove from the heat, add the honey and soy sauce, return to the heat for 1 minute, then leave to cool.

---

1 **English muffin**

generous knob of **butter**

2 **eggs**

2 tbsp **single cream**

salt and freshly ground **black pepper**

butter for spreading

Muffins with creamy scrambled eggs

↻ Preparation: 5 minutes; cooking: 5 minutes   ⚡ Makes 1 portion

⚡ Provides calcium, protein, B vitamins including folate and vitamins A and D

If you like, you could top these muffins with grilled tomato halves or perhaps add some snipped chives to the scrambled eggs.

▶ Preheat the grill to high. Split the muffin in half and toast until golden. Meanwhile, melt the butter in a pan over a gentle heat. Whisk the eggs with the cream and season with salt and pepper.

▶ Swirl the melted butter in the pan and pour in the eggs. Leave for a few seconds, then stir with a wooden spoon until the eggs are just beginning to set.

▶ Spread the split muffin with butter and pile the scrambled eggs on top.

Variation

▶ To make a delicious tuna topping instead of scrambled eggs, flake a small tin of tuna into a bowl, and stir in 2 tablespoons of tomato ketchup, 3 tablespoons of crème fraîche and two chopped spring onions. Top the toasted muffin with the tuna mixture, sprinkle with Cheddar cheese and return to the grill for 2–3 minutes until golden and bubbling.

200g (7oz) **canned tuna in oil**

3 tbsp **mayonnaise**

2 tsp **white wine vinegar**

4 **spring onions,** chopped

salt and freshly ground **black pepper**

a few drops of **Tabasco sauce**

2 **eggs,** hard-boiled

1 large or 2 small **tomatoes,** deseeded and chopped

a handful of **salad cress**

2 **pitta breads**

Pitta pockets with tuna, egg & tomato

↻ Preparation: 8 minutes; cooking: 10 minutes   ⚡ Makes 2 portions

⚡ Provides beta-carotene, magnesium, potassium, protein, B vitamins including folate and vitamins A, D and E

Stuffed pitta pockets with a nutritious filling make a good snack or light lunch. This tuna mix is delicious.

▶ Drain the oil from the tin of tuna and, in a bowl, mix flaked tuna together with the mayonnaise, white wine vinegar, spring onions, salt and pepper and Tabasco sauce.

▶ Peel and roughly chop the hard-boiled eggs and add to the tuna mix with the tomato and salad cress, stirring well.

▶ Cut the pitta breads in half to give four pitta pockets. Toast the bread and divide the mixture between them.

1 tbsp **vegetable oil**

1 small **onion,** sliced

1/2 small **red pepper,** sliced

1 large **chicken** or **turkey breast fillet** (about 225g/7 1/2 oz)

1/2 tsp **dried oregano**

1/2 tsp **mild chilli powder**

salt and freshly ground **black pepper**

1/2 **iceberg lettuce**

2 tbsp **mayonnaise**

4 **mini flour tortillas**

2 tbsp grated **Cheddar cheese**

Chicken wraps

⏱ Preparation: 8 minutes; cooking: 10 minutes ⚒ Makes 4 rolls 🔪 Provides beta-carotene, potassium, protein, B vitamins including folate and vitamins A, C and E

▶ Heat the vegetable oil in a frying pan. Fry the onion and red pepper for 4–5 minutes until softened.

▶ Cut the chicken into thin strips and add to the pan with the oregano and chilli powder. Fry for 3–4 minutes until cooked. Season with salt and pepper.

▶ Finely shred the lettuce and mix with the mayonnaise.

▶ Heat the tortilla according to the instructions on the packet. Divide the lettuce between the four tortillas, sprinkle over the Cheddar cheese, then add the chicken mixture on top. Roll up.

Ham & cheese sandwich

⏱ Preparation: 4 minutes ⚒ Makes 1 portion 🔪 Provides calcium, iron, potassium, protein, B vitamins, including folate and vitamin A

40g (1 1/4 oz) wafer-thin slices of **ham**

2 tbsp grated **Cheddar cheese**

a handful of shredded **lettuce**

1 1/2 tsp **mayonnaise**

2 slices **bread**

a little **butter** or **margarine**

▶ Cut the ham into strips and mix together with the grated cheese, lettuce and mayonnaise. Spread each slice of bread thinly with butter.

▶ Arrange the filling on top of one of the slices and top with the remaining slice.

▶ Remove the crusts and cut the sandwich into four squares, or cut horizontally into three fingers.

Variation

▶ To make a toasted version, preheat the grill, then mix 25g (1oz) wafer-thin slices of ham, cut into pieces with 25g (1oz) grated Cheddar cheese and 1 teaspoon of mayonnaise. Toast and butter a slice of granary bread and arrange the cheese and ham on top. Place under the grill until the cheese has melted.

Cherry tomato & mozzarella salad

150g (5oz) small **cherry tomatoes**, cut in half

150g (5oz) **mozzarella**, diced

4 **fresh basil leaves**, torn into pieces (optional)

Dressing

1½ tbsp **light olive oil**

1 tsp **soy sauce**

1 tsp **balsamic vinegar**

pinch of **sugar**

salt and freshly ground **black pepper**

⟳ Preparation: 5 minutes　　⚔ Makes 2–3 portions　　⚗ Provides calcium, potassium, protein, B vitamins including folate and vitamins A and E

Mini balls of mozzarella, called mozzarelline, can be substituted for regular mozzarella. These create a very attractive dish. If you are taking this salad on a picnic, pack the dressing in a small plastic container and mix with the tomatoes and cheese when you're ready to eat.

▶ Mix together the cherry tomatoes and diced mozzarella.
▶ To make the dressing, simply whisk together all the ingredients.

▶ Toss the tomatoes and mozzarella in the dressing and then add the fresh basil, if using.

Summer pasta salad

150g (5oz) **pasta bows (farfalle)**

150g (5oz) **canned sweetcorn**

16 **cherry tomatoes**, cut in half

4 **spring onions**, finely sliced

150g (5oz) ball **mozzarella**, cut into small cubes

½ **cucumber**, peeled, quartered, deseeded and cut into small chunks

Dressing

3 tbsp **light olive oil**

1 tbsp **honey**

1 tbsp **soy sauce**

1 tbsp **red wine vinegar**

freshly ground **black pepper**

⟳ Preparation: 8 minutes; cooking: 12 minutes　　⚔ Makes 4 portions　　⚗ Provides beta-carotene, calcium, folate, potassium, protein and vitamins A, B12, C and E

Light and energizing, this delicious, healthy pasta salad is a favourite with adults as well as children of all ages.

▶ Cook the pasta in boiling, lightly salted water according to the instructions on the packet. Drain and refresh under cold water.
▶ To make the dressing simply whisk together all the ingredients.

▶ Place the pasta in a large serving bowl. Add all the remaining ingredients and pour over the dressing. Toss the salad in the dressing and serve immediately.

Chicken caesar salad

40g (1¼oz) **pasta shapes**

1 tbsp **vegetable oil**

1 **chicken breast fillet** (about 150g/5oz), cut into bite-sized pieces

2 tbsp freshly grated **Parmesan cheese**

1 **baby gem lettuce** or ½ **Cos lettuce** or **Romaine lettuce**, cut into pieces

Dressing

2 tbsp **mayonnaise**

1 tsp **lemon juice**

½ **garlic clove**, peeled and crushed

⅛ tsp **Dijon mustard**

few drops **Worcestershire sauce**

few drops **Tabasco sauce**

⟳ Preparation: 6 minutes; cooking: 4 minutes　　⚔ Makes 1 portion　　⚗ Provides beta-carotene, potassium, protein, B vitamins including folate and vitamins C and E

This is a classic recipe and deservedly so. To save time, use ready-cooked chicken breast.

▶ Cook the pasta in boiling, lightly salted water according to the instructions on the packet.
▶ Meanwhile, heat the oil in a pan, add the chicken and fry for 3–4 minutes until cooked through. Leave to cool.
▶ Mix together all the dressing

ingredients with 1 tbsp of the grated Parmesan cheese.
▶ Combine the lettuce, drained pasta and chicken and toss with most of the dressing (there will probably be a little too much).
▶ Scatter over the remaining Parmesan.

Pasta salad with prawns

⏱ Preparation: 5 minutes; cooking: 12 minutes   ✂ Makes 1–2 portions   🍴 Provides
beta-carotene, potassium, protein, B vitamins including folate, vitamins C and E and zinc

Prawns are the perfect ingredient for a pasta salad. Avocados really add to the flavour, but if your child doesn't like them, simply leave them out.

► Cook the pasta in boiling, lightly salted water according to the instructions on the packet. Put the prawns, avocado, cherry tomatoes and shredded lettuce into a bowl together with the drained, cooked pasta.

► Mix together the mayonnaise, tomato ketchup, Worcestershire sauce and lemon juice, if using, and toss the salad with this dressing.

100g (3½oz) **pasta shapes**

100g (3½oz) **cooked prawns**

½ small **avocado**, peeled and chopped

4 **cherry tomatoes**, quartered

½ **gem lettuce**, shredded

Dressing

3 tbsp **mayonnaise**

1 tbsp **tomato ketchup**

dash of **Worcestershire sauce**

squeeze of **lemon juice** (optional)

Turkey pasta salad

⏱ Preparation: 10 minutes; cooking: 10 minutes   ✂ Makes 2 portions   🍴 Provides
beta-carotene, potassium, protein, B vitamins including folate and vitamins C and E

Turkey pasta salad is a definite hit with my children and an ideal candidate for including in your child's lunchbox. Select lovely moist slices of turkey at the delicatessen counter of the supermarket.

► Cook the pasta in boiling, lightly salted water according to the instructions on the packet. Meanwhile, whisk together all the ingredients for the dressing.

► Put the chopped turkey, avocado (if using), sweetcorn, tomatoes and spring onions into a bowl together with the drained pasta and toss with the dressing.

50g (1¾oz) **pasta shapes**

100g (3½oz) **turkey** or **chicken breast fillet**, cooked and chopped

½ small **avocado**, peeled and chopped (optional)

100g (3½oz) **canned** or **frozen sweetcorn**

2 **tomatoes**, skinned, deseeded and chopped or 6 **cherry tomatoes**

2 **spring onions**, thinly sliced

Dressing

3 tbsp **light olive oil**

1 tbsp **runny honey**

1 tbsp **soy sauce**

1½ tbsp freshly squeezed **lemon juice**

Shakes

Many of the fruit juices marketed for children are full of sugar and water and often contain less than 10 per cent juice. If you are ready to compromise on nutrition because of their convenience, you should consider that in just a few short minutes, you can make your own delicious and nutritious shakes using fresh or frozen fruit, yogurt, milk or ice-cream.

Fruity cranberry shake

Defrost 150g (5oz) frozen summer fruits, such as strawberries, raspberries, blueberries, blackberries and cherries, purée and push through a sieve.

Blend together the puréed fruit with a 125g (4oz) carton of strawberry yogurt, 150ml (5fl oz) cranberry juice and one chopped banana. Serves two.

Cookies & cream shake

Place six chocolate Oreo cookies, broken into pieces, 300ml (10fl oz) milk and two scoops of vanilla ice-cream in a

blender and process until smooth. Serves two.

---

juice of 1 large **orange** (about 150ml/5fl oz)

150ml (5fl oz) **apple juice**

1 small **banana**, peeled

2 large or 4 small **strawberries**, hulled

Energy-boosting smoothie

⌚ Preparation: 3 minutes   ✂ Makes 2 glasses   🥄 Provides folate, potassium and vitamins B6 and C

Fruit smoothies provide instant energy and are quick and easy to prepare. Experiment with various combinations of fruits to suit your child's taste.

▶ Simply blend all the ingredients together and serve. You could also add

a ripe peach or half a small, ripe mango to this smoothie.

15g (1/2oz) **butter**

2 ripe **peaches**, stoned and chopped but not peeled

2 **plums**, stoned and chopped

3 **strawberries**, hulled and quartered

1 1/2 tbsp **soft brown sugar**

60g (2oz) **raspberries**

60g (2oz) **blueberries**

1 tbsp **rose water** or **water**

Peach & berry compôte

⌚ Preparation: 5 minutes; cooking: 5 minutes   ✂ Makes 2 portions
🥄 Provides beta-carotene, fibre, folate, potassium and vitamin C

You can use peaches, nectarines and any berries, or even stoned and halved cherries, to make this delicious fruit compôte.

▶ Melt the butter and sauté the peaches and plums for 2 minutes. Add the strawberries, sprinkle over the sugar

and cook for 2 minutes more. Stir in the raspberries, blueberries and water and heat through for 1 minute.

Fruit salad

⏲ Preparation: 5 minutes 🔪 Makes 2 portions 🖌 Provides beta-carotene, fibre, potassium and vitamins C and E

The citrus juice and choice of fruit make this a lovely, refreshing fruit salad. If you like you could add a little fresh chopped mint for even greater "zing".

▶ Mix together the orange, lemon or lime juice and honey and pour over the prepared fruits. If using, sprinkle the mint over the top to decorate.

juice of 1 **orange** (about 100ml/3½fl oz)

1 tbsp **lime** or **lemon juice**

1 tbsp **runny honey**

2 **kiwi fruit,** peeled and chopped

2 ripe **peaches,** peeled, stoned and chopped

6 **strawberries,** hulled

½ small **mango,** peeled, stoned and chopped

8 **grapes**

chopped **fresh mint** (optional)

Fruit skewers

⏲ Preparation: 5 minutes 🔪 Makes 2 portions
🖌 Provides beta-carotene, fibre, potassium and vitamins C and E

A good way of encouraging your child to eat more fruit is to thread chunks of different fruits on to skewers – use either bamboo skewers or thin straws. Your child will delight in pulling off the fruit one by one.

▶ Take a chunk of each of your chosen fruits and thread them, one at a time, on to each skewer, to provide a colourful and tasty mix. Push the skewers in half an upturned melon and serve.

Use any combination of the following fruits

seedless grapes

chunks of **pineapple**

slices of **kiwi fruit**

strawberries

chunks of **mango**

chunks of **plum**

dried fruits, such as **apricots** or **figs**

½ **melon** made into melon balls (optional)

TIPS With these brownies, always err on the side of underdone rather than overdone. They will firm up as they cool down.

TIPS Although they are wonderful warm, brownies don't cut well until they are completely cool.

185g (6¹/₂oz) **unsalted butter**

185g (6¹/₂oz) good quality **dark chocolate,** broken into squares

3 large **eggs**

275g (9oz) **golden caster sugar**

40g (1¹/₄oz) **cocoa powder**

85g (3oz) **plain flour**

50g (1³/₄oz) **white chocolate,** chopped

50g (1³/₄oz) **milk chocolate,** chopped

My favourite brownies

⟳ Preparation: 15 minutes; cooking: 35–40 minutes   🔥 180°C/350°F/gas 4
🥄 Makes 16 squares   ✍ Provides vitamins A, B12 and D

My son Nicholas likes to make these himself. They are irresistible to all the family and disappear in no time.

▶ Grease and line a 20cm (8in) square baking tin. Cut the butter into pieces and place in a heatproof bowl together with the dark chocolate.

▶ Sit the bowl on top of a pan of simmering water (the base of the bowl should not touch the water) and stir until the butter and chocolate are melted. Alternatively, melt the chocolate and butter in a microwave on a high setting for about 2 minutes, stirring halfway through. Set aside to cool.

▶ Break the eggs into a large bowl, add the sugar and whisk for about 3–5 minutes until pale and creamy and roughly double the original volume.

▶ Gently fold in the cooled chocolate mixture, then sift the cocoa and flour into the chocolate/egg mixture and fold in. When folding in, take care not to over-mix, or the brownie will become heavy. Stir in the white and milk chocolate chunks.

▶ Pour the mixture into the prepared tin and bake in the preheated oven for about 35 minutes. If the mixture is very liquid in the centre when you remove it from the oven, cook for a few minutes longer until fudgy in the middle. Take care not to overcook. The mixture will firm up as it cools.

▶ Leave until completely cool before cutting into squares.

Summer berry muffins

⏱ Preparation: 15 minutes; cooking: 25 minutes   🌡 200°C/400°F/gas 6

🍴 Makes 8 large muffins   🌿 Provides vitamins A and E

White chocolate and a mixture of tempting berries complement each other beautifully in these delicious, easy-to-prepare muffins.

▶ Line a muffin tray with 8 paper muffin cases. In a large bowl, combine the flour, soft brown sugar, salt and baking powder and set aside.

▶ In a separate bowl, whisk together the vegetable oil, egg, vanilla essence and milk. Add the mixed dry ingredients and stir until blended. Gently fold in the berries and white chocolate.

▶ Spoon the mixture into the muffin cases and sprinkle with demerara sugar.

▶ Bake for about 25 minutes until risen and just firm. Allow to cool a little, then transfer to a wire cooling rack.

185g (6½oz) **plain flour**

150g (5oz) **soft brown sugar**

½ teaspoon **salt**

2 tsp **baking powder**

80ml (2½fl oz) **vegetable oil**

1 **egg**

1 tsp **vanilla essence**

80ml (2½fl oz) **full-fat milk**

100g (3½oz) **fresh raspberries**

75g (2½oz) **blueberries**

65g (2oz) **white chocolate chips**

1 tbsp **demerara sugar**

White chocolate & cranberry cookies

⏱ Preparation: 30 minutes; cooking: 10 minutes   🌡 190°C/375°F/gas 5

🍴 Makes 35 cookies   🌿 Provides vitamins A and D   ❄ Suitable for freezing

Delicious, chewy white chocolate and cranberry cookies are very easy to make. They should be quite soft when you take them out of the oven, so that when they cool down they are crisp on the outside but moist inside.

▶ Beat the butter together with the sugars. With a fork, beat the egg together with the vanilla essence and add this to the butter mixture.

▶ In a bowl, mix together the flour, baking powder and salt. Add this to the butter and egg mixture and blend. Mix in the white chocolate and cranberries.

▶ To make the cookies, line four baking sheets with non-stick baking paper. Using your hands, form the dough into walnut-sized balls and arrange on the baking sheets, spaced well apart.

▶ Bake in the preheated oven for 10 minutes. Allow to cool for a few minutes and then transfer to a wire rack.

100g (3½oz) softened **unsalted butter**

100g (3½oz) **golden caster sugar**

100g (3½oz) **light muscovado sugar**

1 **egg**

1 tsp **vanilla essence**

175g (6oz) **plain flour**

½ tsp **baking powder**

½ tsp **salt**

150g (5 oz) **white chocolate,** cut into small chunks

75g (2½oz) **dried sweetened cranberries**

Chocolate chip, raisin & sunflower seed cookies

⏱ Preparation: 15 minutes; cooking: 12–14 minutes   🌡 180°C/350°F/gas 4

🍴 Makes 14 biscuits   🌿 Provides fibre, iron, potassium, protein and vitamin E

❄ Suitable for freezing

Packed full of nutrients, these cookies provide sustained energy.

▶ Cream together the butter and sugar until light and fluffy. Beat in the egg and vanilla essence. Stir in the remaining ingredients until combined.

▶ Using a tablespoon, spoon the mixture on to two non-stick or lined baking sheets, leaving enough space between the biscuits for the dough to spread.

▶ Bake for 12–14 minutes until golden in the preheated oven. Cool on a wire rack.

75g (2½oz) **unsalted butter**

75g (2½oz) **golden caster sugar**

1 small **egg**, beaten

1 tsp **vanilla essence**

85g (3oz) **raisins**

25g (1oz) **plain** or **milk chocolate chips**

40g (1¼oz) **sunflower seeds**

50g (1¾oz) **plain flour**

½tsp **bicarbonate of soda**

½ tsp **salt**

40g (1¼oz) **porridge oats**

Family meals

They say that families that eat together, stay together, and this section is all about finding recipes with that magical ingredient "child appeal", so you can make one meal to suit everyone in the family. It's a shame that so many children live on a very limited "junk food" diet when there are so many other wonderful foods they would enjoy eating if only they were given the chance. Encourage your child to eat a varied diet and try some of these recipes, many of which are my family's favourites. I've done the hard work already as every one of my recipes is tested on a panel of children and without their seal of approval the dishes would not feature in this book.

1 Sleeping cannelloni
Make humourous decorative additions to this Italian classic for instant appeal. The stuffed cannelloni tubes have the usual "blanket" of cheese sauce, but with mushroom faces, grated cheese hair with green pepper bows and black olive boots. (See page 156 for recipe.)

2 Beef tacos
Crispy corn tacos stuffed with minced beef or chicken strips, beans and salad are always popular with children. The filling in these tacos has a hint of chilli and coriander to give it a little kick. (See page 173 for recipe.)

3 Paella
Give supper a Spanish flavour with this festive one-pot meal of chicken, sausages, prawns and vibrant yellow rice. A colourful dish packed with goodness. (See page 166 for recipe.)

1

3

30g (1oz) **butter**

1 medium **onion**, peeled and chopped

1 **garlic clove**, peeled and crushed

1 **leek**, washed and thinly sliced

350g (12oz) **potatoes**, peeled and cut into chunks

1 **bay leaf**

1 sprig of **thyme** (optional)

1.5 litres (50fl oz) unsalted **chicken stock** (see page 52) or **vegetable stock** (see page 47)

salt and freshly ground **black pepper**

60g (2oz) **orzo**

60g (2oz) **watercress**

Leek, potato & watercress soup with orzo

↻ Preparation: 10 minutes; cooking: 27 minutes   🍴 Makes 6 portions

🥄 Provides beta-carotene, folate, potassium and vitamins A, B6, C and E

❄ Suitable for freezing

The combination of leek and potato makes a classic soup that has always been very popular. The addition of watercress gives it a particularly special flavour and a wonderful freshness to balance the earthy flavour of the vegetables. Orzo is a tiny pasta shape that looks like grains of rice. Like other small and unusual pasta shapes, it goes down very well with children.

▶ Melt the butter in a large pan and sauté the onion and garlic for 5 minutes. Add the leek and continue to cook for 2 minutes. Add the potatoes, bay leaf and thyme, if using, pour over the stock and season to taste. Bring to the boil and then simmer, covered, for 15 minutes.

▶ Meanwhile, cook the orzo in boiling, lightly salted water according to the instructions on the packet. Add the watercress to the soup. Cook for 5 minutes longer. Remove the bay leaf and thyme and liquidize the soup. Stir in the orzo, heat through and adjust the seasoning.

---

1 large **chicken** plus **giblets**

12 **carrots**, peeled and cut in half

1 large **red onion**, peeled and cut into pieces

1 **leek,** white part only, washed and cut into pieces

2 **celery sticks** and **leaves,** cut into pieces

Maldon sea salt

white pepper

3 or 4 sachets **bouquet garni**

4 **bay leaves**

4 **chicken stock cubes**

1 tsp **sugar**

7 litres (245fl oz) **water**

vermicelli (thin pasta)

Old-fashioned chicken soup

↻ Preparation: 20 minutes; cooking: 3 hours 20 minutes   🍴 Makes 15–20 portions

🥄 Provides beta-carotene, potassium, protein, B vitamins and vitamin C

❄ Suitable for freezing

I make large quantities of this nutritious soup, which I divide into smaller batches and freeze. Then, when I want to give my children chicken soup, I simply reheat a batch and add some cooked vermicelli for extra substance.

▶ Cut the chicken into about eight pieces, clean well and put into a very large pan with the giblets. Cover with water and boil for 20 minutes. Skim off the scum from the surface with a slotted spoon.

▶ Add the rest of the ingredients (apart from the vermicelli), cover and simmer over a low heat for about 3 hours.

▶ Remove the bay leaves and bouquet garni. Allow to cool, and then leave in the fridge overnight.

▶ The next day, skim off the layer of fat on the surface of the mixture and strain the soup through a sieve into another bowl. Take the chicken meat off the bones and tear it into pieces.

▶ Place some of the shredded chicken and a few of the carrots into the bowl of soup. Freeze in batches.

▶ When you want to use the soup, cook some vermicelli, if using, in boiling, lightly salted water, according to the instructions on the packet, and reheat a batch of the soup. Add the cooked pasta to the soup and serve.

TIP When all else fails, pasta is a great stand-by for children. It's a good idea to keep tasty homemade pasta sauces in the freezer.

Sloppy Joe sauce

⟳ Preparation: 5 minutes; cooking: 40 minutes　🍴 Makes 4 portions　⚡ Provides beta-carotene, iron, potassium, B vitamins, vitamins C and E and zinc　❄ Suitable for freezing

A good source of iron for your child, this tasty meat sauce is very versatile: it can be served on a toasted hamburger bun or as a sauce for pasta or rice.

▶ Heat the oil in a frying pan and sauté the onion and garlic for about 5 minutes or until softened.
▶ Add the minced beef and sauté until browned, stirring occasionally. After it has browned, I like to chop the meat in a food processor for a few seconds to make it less lumpy and softer to chew.
▶ Return the beef to the pan and stir in the remaining ingredients. Simmer over a low heat for about 30 minutes or until the sauce is thick.

1 tbsp **olive oil**

1 small **onion**, peeled and finely chopped

1 **garlic clove**, peeled and crushed

225g (8fl oz) lean **minced beef**

400g (14oz) **canned chopped tomatoes**

1 tsp **red wine vinegar**

1 tsp **brown sugar**

1/2 tsp **salt**

1/2 tsp **Worcestershire sauce**

1/2 tbsp **tomato ketchup**

Special tomato sauce

⟳ Preparation: 5 minutes; cooking: 12 minutes　🍴 Makes 4 portions　⚡ Provides beta-carotene, calcium, protein and vitamins B12 and E　❄ Suitable for freezing

Try this full-flavoured tomato sauce as a base for pizza topping, or add a few mini meatballs or a small tin of tuna to make a simple pasta sauce.

▶ Heat the oil in a frying pan over a low heat, add the garlic and sauté for 30 seconds. Stir in the tomatoes and break them up with a spoon. Add the remaining ingredients except the basil and Parmesan cheese. Season, then simmer gently for 10 minutes.
▶ Stir in the basil and Parmesan, and cook just until the cheese has melted.

1 tsp **olive oil**

1 **garlic clove**, peeled and crushed

400g (14oz) **canned tomatoes**

2 tbsp **red pesto**

1/4 tsp **mild chilli powder**

1 tsp **balsamic vinegar**

1 tsp **caster sugar**

salt and freshly ground **black pepper**

1 tbsp **fresh basil**, shredded

2 tbsp freshly grated **Parmesan cheese**

Pasta twists with courgettes

1 tbsp **olive oil**

1 small **onion**, peeled and sliced

1 **garlic clove**, peeled and chopped

100g (3$^1/_2$oz) **courgettes**, sliced

75g (2$^1/_2$oz) small **button mushrooms**, sliced

300g (10oz) **passata**

1 tsp **vegetable stock powder** dissolved in 50ml (1$^3/_4$fl oz) **boiling water**

$^1/_2$ tsp **balsamic vinegar**

$^1/_2$ tsp **sugar**

salt and freshly ground **black pepper**

200g (7oz) **pasta twists (fusilli)**

30g (1oz) freshly grated **Parmesan cheese**

Preparation: 10 minutes; cooking: 25 minutes   Makes 4 portions

Provides calcium, fibre, folate, potassium and protein   Suitable for freezing

Another quick recipe that will encourage children to enjoy eating vegetables. Vary the vegetables according to seasonal availability.

▶ Heat the oil in a pan, add the onion and garlic, sauté for 2 minutes. Add the courgettes and button mushrooms, and sauté for 5 minutes. Stir in the passata, vegetable stock, vinegar and sugar, and season to taste. Simmer, uncovered, for 15 minutes.

▶ Meanwhile, cook the pasta in boiling, lightly salted water according to the instructions on the packet.

▶ Remove the sauce from the heat and toss with the drained pasta. Serve with some freshly grated Parmesan.

Creamy chicken with penne

100g (3$^1/_2$oz) **penne**

1 tbsp **olive oil**

1 **shallot**, peeled and chopped or 30g (1oz) **onion**, peeled and chopped

1 **garlic clove**, peeled and crushed

1 **chicken breast fillet** (about 150g/5oz), cut into thin strips

2 ripe **plum tomatoes**, skinned, deseeded and chopped

25g (3$/_4$oz) **sunblush (semi-dried) tomatoes**, chopped

100ml (3$^1/_2$fl oz) **chicken stock** (see page 52)

$^1/_2$ tsp **lemon juice**

50ml (1$^3/_4$fl oz) **double cream**

2$^1/_2$ tbsp freshly grated **Parmesan cheese**

1 tbsp **fresh basil** (optional)

salt and freshly ground **black pepper**

Preparation: 5 minutes; cooking: 12 minutes   Makes 2 portions

Provides calcium, potassium, protein and B vitamins

▶ Cook the penne in boiling, lightly salted water according to the instructions on the packet.

▶ Meanwhile, heat the oil in a frying pan and sauté the shallot and garlic for about 2 minutes.

▶ Add the chicken and continue to cook until sealed, turning occasionally. Add the tomatoes and sunblush tomatoes, and cook for 2 minutes.

▶ Add the stock and lemon juice and cook for 6–7 minutes on a low heat. Stir in the cream and Parmesan and heat through. Stir in the fresh basil and season with salt and black pepper.

▶ Drain the penne and mix thoroughly with the sauce.

Fussy eater's pasta

85g (3oz) **pasta twists (fusilli)**

a little **salt**

30g (1oz) **butter**

4 tbsp freshly grated **Parmesan cheese**

Preparation: 3 minutes; cooking: 11–12 minutes   Makes 1 portion

Provides calcium, protein, vitamins A, B2 and B12 and zinc

When all else fails most children will eat this very simple pasta dish. Serve with a side portion of carrot, sweet pepper, cucumber sticks and cherry tomatoes.

▶ Cook the pasta in boiling, lightly salted water according to the instructions on the packet.

▶ Melt the butter. Drain the pasta shapes and toss in the melted butter and freshly grated Parmesan cheese.

Tagliolini with cheese & Parma ham

Preparation: 5 minutes; cooking: 5 minutes   Makes 4 portions

Provides calcium, potassium, protein and B vitamins

This is a version of a very famous pasta dish that is served in Harry's Bar in Venice. There they make it with very thin, fresh green tagliolini, and it tastes absolutely wonderful.

► Melt the butter in a saucepan, add the flour and cook for 1 minute, stirring occasionally.

► Gradually whisk in the milk. Bring to the boil, stirring continuously until thickened and smooth. Remove from the heat and stir in half the cheese. Season to taste, then stir in the Parma ham.

► Cook the tagliolini in boiling, lightly salted water according to the instructions on the packet. Drain and mix with the cheese sauce. Preheat the grill.

► Transfer the pasta to an ovenproof dish and sprinkle over the remaining Parmesan cheese. Place under the grill for a few minutes until the top is golden and bubbling.

25g (³/₄oz) **butter**

25g (³/₄oz) **plain flour**

450ml (15fl oz) **milk**

50g (1³/₄oz) freshly grated **Parmesan cheese**

salt and freshly ground **black pepper**

70g (2¹/₂oz) **Parma ham**, thinly sliced and cut into strips

500g (17oz) **tagliolini**

Marina's bow-tie stir-fry

Preparation: 35 minutes, including 30 minutes marinating; cooking: 15 minutes   Makes 4 portions   Provides potassium, protein and B vitamins including folate

Stir-fries are great because, as everything is cooked in the same pan, they are quick and easy to make. This is a lovely combination of chicken, vegetables and pasta with a tasty sauce.

► Marinate the chicken in the soy sauce and sugar for about 30 minutes.

► Cook the pasta in boiling, lightly salted water according to the instructions on the packet.

► Heat the vegetable and sesame oils in a wok, add the onion and stir-fry for 3 minutes. Add the marinated chicken and stir-fry for 3 minutes. Add the courgette, peas and beansprouts and stir-fry for 4 minutes. Add the pasta, stirring for 1 minute.

► Put the soy sauce, oyster sauce, apricot jam and chicken stock in a small saucepan and stir over a gentle heat for about 1 minute. Stir the cornflour and water paste into the sauce. Bring to the boil and then heat, stirring for 1 minute.

► Pour the sauce over the chicken, and stir-fry until heated through. Season to taste.

1 **chicken breast fillet** (about 150g/5oz), cut into strips

100g (3¹/₂oz) **pasta bows (farfalle)**

1 tbsp **vegetable oil**

1 tbsp **sesame oil**

1 **onion**, peeled and thinly sliced

150g (5oz) **courgette**, cut into matchsticks

75g (2¹/₂oz) **frozen peas**

100g (3¹/₂oz) **beansprouts**

salt and freshly ground **black pepper**

Marinade

1 tbsp **soy sauce**

¹/₂ tbsp **brown sugar**

Sauce

1 tbsp **soy sauce**

1 tbsp **oyster sauce**

1 tbsp **apricot** or **plum jam**

150ml (5fl oz) **chicken stock** (see page 52)

¹/₂ tbsp **cornflour** mixed with 1 tbsp **cold water**

250g (8oz) **frozen leaf spinach**

30g (1oz) **butter**

1 **onion**, peeled and finely chopped

1 small **garlic clove**, peeled and crushed

125g (4oz) **mushrooms**, sliced

1 tbsp **plain flour**

90ml (3fl oz) **milk**

2 tbsp thick **single cream**

salt and freshly ground **black pepper**

8 **no-precook cannelloni tubes**

Cheese sauce

30g (1oz) **butter**

30g (1oz) **plain flour**

450ml (15fl oz) **milk**

60g (2oz) each grated **Gruyère** and **Cheddar cheese**

½ tsp **mustard powder**

salt and freshly ground **black pepper**

To decorate

passata or **Special tomato sauce** (see page 153)

8 sautéed **button mushrooms**

8 **black olives**

tiny **green pepper** bows and squares

red pepper strips

handful of grated **Cheddar cheese**

Sleeping cannelloni

Preparation: 35 minutes; cooking: 45 minutes   180°C/350°F/gas 4

Makes 8 portions   Provides beta-carotene, calcium, iron, potassium, protein, B vitamins including folate and zinc   Suitable for freezing: undecorated

▶ Place the spinach in a pan without water, cover, set over a low heat and cook gently for 5 minutes, or according to the instructions on the packet. Squeeze out any excess water.

▶ Warm the butter in a pan, add the onion and garlic and sauté until softened. Add the mushrooms and cook for 5 minutes. Stir in the flour and cook for 1 minute. Add the cooked spinach, stir in the milk and cook for 2 minutes. Remove the pan from the heat, stir in the cream and season to taste.

▶ Lightly grease a 25 x 20cm (10 x 8in) ovenproof dish. Use a teaspoon to push the stuffing into the cannelloni tubes, then arrange them in the dish next to one another in a single layer.

▶ To make the cheese sauce, melt the butter in a pan over a low heat, add the flour and stir to make a paste. Cook gently for 2 minutes, then whisk in the milk and cook, stirring, until thickened. Remove from the heat, stir in the cheeses until melted, add the mustard powder and season to taste.

▶ Pour the sauce over the cannelloni, transfer to the preheated oven and bake for 30 minutes.

▶ Decorate to make the dish look like four matchstick bodies sleeping under a sheet and blanket with their heads appearing at one end and their feet at the other. Spread a narrow band of tomato sauce from one side of the dish to the other near the top of the cannelloni tubes to create a turned-down red sheet. Arrange the eight olives in pairs at the bottom of each tube to indicate the feet. Use the mushrooms to make the heads; make three slits in each for two eyes and a mouth, then position at the top of each cannelloni tube. Push the squares of green pepper in each eye slit and the strips of red pepper in each mouth slit. Arrange the grated cheese around each head for the hair and place green pepper bows in it.

6 sheets **no-precook** or **fresh lasagne**

4 tbsp freshly grated **Parmesan cheese**

Tomato sauce

2 tbsp **olive oil**

1 large **onion**, peeled and chopped

1 **garlic clove**, peeled and crushed

1 tbsp **balsamic vinegar**

2 x 400g (14oz) **canned chopped tomatoes**

4 tbsp **sunblush (semi-dried) tomatoes**, chopped

2 tbsp **tomato purée**

1 **bay leaf**

Spinach and ricotta filling

500g (17oz) fresh **spinach**, carefully washed and tough stalks removed

2 tbsp **olive oil**

250g (8oz) **ricotta cheese**

2 tbsp freshly grated **Parmesan cheese**

salt and freshly ground **black pepper**

Cheese sauce

30g (1oz) **butter**

30g (1oz) **plain flour**

450ml (15fl oz) **milk**

75g (2½oz) grated **Cheddar cheese**

salt and freshly ground **black pepper**

Cheese, tomato & spinach lasagne

Preparation: 15 minutes; cooking: 45 minutes   180°C/350°F/gas 4

Makes 6 portions   Provides beta-carotene, calcium, potassium, protein, B vitamins including folate and vitamins A, C and E   Suitable for freezing

▶ For the tomato sauce, heat the olive oil and sauté the onion and garlic for 3–4 minutes. Add the balsamic vinegar and cook for about 30 seconds. Stir in the canned chopped tomatoes, sunblush tomatoes, tomato purée and bay leaf. Bring to the boil and simmer for 10 minutes. Remove and discard the bay leaf. Set aside.

▶ Meanwhile, sauté the spinach in the olive oil until wilted, then drain and roughly chop. Mix with the ricotta cheese, stir in 2 tablespoons of freshly grated Parmesan cheese and season with a little salt and pepper. Set aside.

▶ For the cheese sauce, melt the butter and stir in the flour and cook for about 1 minute. Gradually stir in the milk and cook for about 2 minutes until thickened. Stir in the Cheddar cheese until melted and season to taste.

▶ If using fresh lasagne, cook it in boiling, lightly salted water first, according to the instructions on the packet.

▶ To assemble the lasagne, spoon a third of the tomato sauce on the base of a fairly deep ovenproof lasagne dish (about 18cm sq) and cover with a layer of the spinach and ricotta mixture. Cover with 2 sheets of lasagne, followed by a layer of the cheese sauce, then a layer of tomato sauce. Repeat each layer twice, finishing off with a layer of the cheese sauce.

▶ Sprinkle over the Parmesan cheese and bake in the preheated oven for 30 minutes.

9 sheets **no-precook lasagne**

30g (1oz) freshly grated **Parmesan cheese**

Meat sauce

1 tbsp **olive oil**

1 **onion**, peeled and finely chopped

1 **carrot**, peeled and finely chopped

1 **celery stalk**, finely chopped

1 **garlic clove**, peeled and crushed

500g (17oz) lean **minced beef**

280ml (9$\frac{1}{2}$fl oz) **beef stock**

200g (7oz) **canned chopped tomatoes**

1 tbsp **tomato purée**

2 sprigs **thyme**

2 **bay leaves**

1 tbsp chopped **fresh parsley**

salt and freshly ground **black pepper**

White sauce

40g (1$\frac{1}{4}$oz) **butter**

40g (1$\frac{1}{4}$oz) **plain flour**

450ml (15fl oz) **milk**

pinch of freshly ground **nutmeg**

60g (2oz) grated **Gruyère cheese**

salt and freshly ground **black pepper**

Beef lasagne

Preparation: 15 minutes; cooking: 1 hour 5 minutes   180°C/350°F/gas 4

Makes 6 portions   Provides iron, potassium, B vitamins, vitamins C, E, and zinc

Suitable for freezing

Lasagne is often a favourite dish with children, and the sauce for this recipe can also be used as a tasty meat sauce with pasta.

▶ To make the meat sauce, heat the olive oil in a saucepan, add the onion, carrot and celery and sauté over a low heat for 3–4 minutes. Add the garlic and minced beef and cook until the meat is browned all over.

▶ Transfer the mixture to a food processor and chop for a few seconds to give it a smoother texture.

▶ Return the mixture to the pan, add the stock, bring to the boil, then simmer for 3–4 minutes. Stir in the canned chopped tomatoes, tomato purée, thyme, bay leaves, parsley, salt and pepper. Bring to the boil, then reduce the heat and simmer, covered, for 20 minutes.

▶ Remove the lid and cook for a further 5 minutes, stirring occasionally until most of the liquid has evaporated.

▶ Adjust the seasoning if necessary, remove and discard the thyme and bay leaves, take off the heat and set aside to cool slightly.

▶ To make the white sauce, melt the butter in a saucepan and stir in the flour. Cook over a medium heat for 1 minute, stirring all the time, then gradually whisk in the milk. Bring to the boil, add the nutmeg and simmer for 2 minutes. Remove from the heat, stir in the Gruyère cheese until melted and season to taste.

▶ Cover the bottom of a large lasagne dish with a couple of tablespoons of each sauce. Cover with three sheets of lasagne. Spoon over half the meat sauce and cover with a third of the white sauce. Cover with three more sheets of lasagne. Now cover with the remaining meat sauce and another third of the white sauce. Cover with the last three sheets of lasagne and finish off by spooning over the remaining white sauce and then sprinkling over the Parmesan cheese.

▶ Bake in the preheated oven for about 30 minutes, until golden and bubbling.

1tbs **olive oil**

1 **onion**, peeled and finely chopped

1 **garlic clove**, peeled and crushed

1 small **red pepper**, deseeded and diced

400g (14oz) lean **minced beef** or **lamb**

1 tbsp **red pesto**

1 tbsp **tomato purée**

125ml (4fl oz) **chicken stock** (see page 52)

1 tbsp **fresh oregano** or $\frac{1}{2}$ tbsp **dried oregano**

1 tbsp chopped **fresh parsley**

salt and freshly ground **black pepper**

Pasta twirls with a meat sauce

Preparation: 8 minutes; cooking: 28 minutes   Makes 4 portions   Provides iron, potassium, B vitamins, vitamins C, E, and zinc   Suitable for freezing

▶ Heat the olive oil in a large pan and sauté the onion, garlic and red pepper for about 5 minutes, until softened. Add the meat and cook until browned. At this stage, chop the meat in a food processor to give it a softer texture if preferred.

▶ Return the meat to the pan and stir in the tomatoes, red pesto, tomato purée, chicken stock and herbs and season to taste. Cover and cook over a medium heat for 20 minutes.

▶ Meanwhile, cook the pasta in boiling, lightly salted water according to the instructions on the packet. Mix the pasta with the sauce and serve.

Variation

▶ Spoon the pasta and sauce into a 20cm sq ovenproof dish, cover with half the white sauce used for Beef lasagne (see above), sprinkle with 2 tablespoons grated Parmesan and grill for a few minutes.

175g (6oz) **butternut squash**, peeled and cut into small cubes

1 tbsp **olive oil**

generous knob of **butter**

1 **onion**, peeled and finely chopped

1 **garlic clove**, peeled and crushed

175g (6oz) **risotto rice**

600ml (20fl oz) hot **vegetable stock** (see page 47) or **chicken stock** (see page 52)

8 **sage leaves**, torn into small pieces

3 tbsp freshly grated **Parmesan cheese**

salt and freshly ground **black pepper**

Butternut squash risotto

Preparation: 10 minutes; cooking: 30 minutes   Makes 4 portions
Provides beta-carotene, calcium, potassium and vitamins B2, B12 and E

Risottos are easy to make and this one has a lovely blend of flavours. To make a good risotto, you need a heavy-based pan that will allow even, slow cooking: a large, fairly deep frying pan is ideal. Add the stock gradually for perfect results and stir continuously! If reheating, stir in a little extra stock first.

▶ Steam the squash for 5 minutes.

▶ Heat the olive oil and butter in a heavy-based pan and sauté the onion and garlic over a low heat until soft but not coloured.

▶ Add the rice and stir until well coated. Cook over a medium heat for about 25 minutes, adding the stock one ladleful at a time, allowing the rice to absorb each ladleful of liquid well before adding the next.

▶ About 10 minutes before the end of the cooking time, add the squash and sage. Continue to add the stock until it is all used up.

▶ Stir in the Parmesan cheese and season to taste. The risotto should be thick and creamy, and the texture of the rice should be soft on the outside but firm in the centre.

150g (5oz) **basmati rice**

2 tbsp **vegetable oil**

1 **onion**, peeled and chopped

1 **carrot**, peeled and sliced

100g (3½oz) **broccoli**, cut into small florets

100g (3½oz) **cauliflower**, cut into small florets

1 small **garlic clove**, peeled and crushed

1 tbsp **tomato purée**

1 tbsp **medium curry paste**

400ml (14fl oz) **canned coconut milk**

75g (2½oz) **baby sweetcorn**, cut into bite-sized pieces

50g (1¾oz) **frozen peas**

Curried vegetables with rice

Preparation: 15 minutes; cooking: 25 minutes   Makes 4 portions

Provides beta-carotene, fibre, folate, potassium and vitamins C and E

Suitable for freezing

It's important to encourage young children to be a little adventurous. The flavour of mild curry and coconut makes these vegetables really tasty.

▶ Cook the rice in boiling, lightly salted water according to the instructions on the packet.

▶ Meanwhile, heat the oil in a large saucepan and sauté the onion and carrot for 3 minutes to soften. Add the broccoli and cauliflower and cook for 5 minutes.

▶ Stir in the garlic, tomato purée and curry paste and stir for 1 minute.

▶ Stir in the coconut milk and simmer for 10 minutes.

▶ Add the baby corn and cook for a further 3 minutes. Finally, add the peas and cook for 2 to 3 minutes.

▶ Serve on a bed of the cooked rice.

½ tbsp **vegetable oil**

½ **onion**, peeled and very finely chopped

½ **garlic clove**, peeled and crushed

¼ tsp each **curry powder, ground ginger** and **ground cumin**

75g (2½oz) **button mushrooms**, finely chopped

90g (3oz) **cauliflower**, cut into very small florets

1 **carrot**, peeled and very finely chopped

2 tsp **caster sugar**

3 tsp mild **natural yogurt**

salt and freshly ground **black pepper**

1 packet **filo pastry sheets**

60g (2oz) **butter**, melted

TIP When handling filo pastry, keep the piece you are not working with covered with a damp tea towel to prevent it from drying out and becoming brittle.

Mildly spiced vegetable samosas

Preparation: 35 minutes; cooking: 35 minutes   180°C/350°F/gas 4

Makes 8 portions   Provides beta-carotene and potassium

Suitable for freezing: uncooked

▶ Heat the oil in a frying pan, add the onion and garlic and sauté for 2–3 minutes. Stir in the spices and sauté for 1 minute. Add the vegetables and cook for 5 minutes, stirring occasionally. Stir in the sugar and yogurt. Season and cook for 3–4 minutes.

▶ Lay the filo pastry out flat and cover with a damp tea towel. Place one sheet of pastry on the work surface and brush with melted butter. Fold the pastry in half lengthways and brush again with butter.

▶ Place a tablespoon of filling on one end of the strip, leaving a 2.5cm (1in) border around it. Fold over the corner to make a triangle, then keep folding the parcel over on itself, along the length of the pastry. Seal the flap left at the end with melted butter. Repeat with the remaining pastry and filling.

▶ Place the samosas on a lightly greased baking sheet and brush with more butter. Bake in the preheated oven for 20–25 minutes, or until crisp.

Mini bean & veggie enchiladas

Preparation: 10 minutes; cooking: 15 minutes   Microwave on high or conventional oven at 180°C/350°F/gas 4   Makes 4 portions   Provides calcium, fibre, folate, iron and protein

Small flour tortillas (soft Mexican flatbreads) can be bought and filled with a variety of ingredients. Kidney beans are a good source of protein.

► Heat the oil in a frying pan, add the onion, garlic and chilli if using, and cook gently for 3 minutes.
► Roughly chop the kidney beans. Add the beans to the frying pan with the sweetcorn and chopped tomatoes. Season to taste and cook over a medium heat for 5 minutes. Sprinkle with parsley. Preheat the grill to high.
► Divide the filling among the tortillas, roll them up and top with cheese. Heat through in a microwave for 1–2 minutes, or in a conventional oven for 6 minutes, then grill until golden and bubbly.

Variation

► Replace the beans with two chicken breasts, cut into strips, seasoned and fried. Replace the sweetcorn and tomatoes with half a small red pepper, chopped and sautéed. Heat the enchiladas through then dress with a spoonful each of salsa and sour cream.

1 tbsp **vegetable oil**

$1/2$ **onion,** peeled and chopped

1 small **garlic clove,** peeled and crushed

$1/4$ **red chilli,** finely chopped (optional)

200g (7oz) **canned red kidney beans** or **refried beans**

125g (4oz) **canned** or **frozen sweetcorn,** cooked

200g (7oz) **canned chopped tomatoes,** drained

salt and freshly ground **black pepper**

1 tbsp chopped **fresh parsley**

4 **mini flour tortillas**

45g (1$1/2$oz) grated **Cheddar cheese**

Vegetable stir-fry with prawns in sweet and sour sauce

Preparation: 15 minutes; cooking: 20 minutes   Makes 2 portions   Provides beta-carotene, potassium, protein, B vitamins including folate, vitamins C and E and zinc

► Cook the rice in boiling, lightly salted water according to the instructions on the packet.
► Heat the vegetable oil in a wok and stir-fry the mushrooms, sweetcorn and red pepper for 2 to 3 minutes. Add the sake or water, prawns and spring onions, and cook for 2–3 minutes.
► Mix together all the sauce ingredients and add to the pan along with the spinach leaves. Cook for 2 to 3 minutes until thickened slightly.
► Serve on a bed of the cooked rice.

100g (3$1/2$oz) **basmati** or **long-grain rice**

1 tbsp **vegetable oil**

75g (2$1/2$oz) **chestnut mushrooms,** quartered

75g (2$1/2$oz) **baby sweetcorn,** halved lengthways

$1/2$ **red pepper,** thinly sliced

1 tbsp **sake** (rice wine) or **water**

100g (3$1/2$oz) **cooked king prawns**

2 **spring onions,** sliced

75g (2$1/2$oz) **baby spinach leaves**

Sauce

75ml (2$3/4$fl oz) **chicken stock** (see page 52) or **vegetable stock** (see page 47)

2 tsp **soy sauce**

1 tsp **sesame oil**

1 tbsp **rice wine vinegar**

1 tbsp **tomato purée**

1 tbsp **brown sugar**

Sticky salmon

2 x 150g (5oz) skinned **salmon fillets**, cut into about 4cm cubes

Marinade

1½ tbsp **soy sauce**

2 tbsp **tomato ketchup**

1 tbsp **white wine vinegar**

1 tsp **sweet chilli sauce**

2 tbsp **dark brown sugar**

↻ Preparation: 1 hour 5 minutes, including 1 hour marinating; cooking: 6 minutes
🔥 200°C/400°F/gas 6   ⚬ Makes 2 portions   ⚘ Provides magnesium, omega-3 fatty acids, potassium, protein, B vitamins, vitamins D and E and zinc

Salmon is an excellent food for children as it is quick to cook and a good source of essential fatty acids which are important for brain function, thus the saying "fish is good for the brain". The flavour of the marinade is very moreish. It's funny how the simplest and easiest recipes can very often be the best.

▶ Place all the ingredients for the marinade in a small saucepan and stir over a gentle heat until the sugar has dissolved completely.

▶ Remove from the heat, pour into an ovenproof dish and leave to cool. Add the salmon fillets and turn to coat them in the marinade. Leave to marinate for at least 1 hour.

▶ Cook the salmon fillets in the preheated oven for 20 minutes, basting occasionally until cooked through. Serve with boiled white rice with a dash of soy sauce, or with the noodles and beansprouts mixture used in the recipe for salmon teriyaki on page 123.

Trout with almonds

25g (1oz) **flaked almonds**

½ tbsp **plain flour**

salt and freshly ground **black pepper**

15g (½oz) **butter**

a little **vegetable oil**

2 small **trout fillets**, skin on

squeeze of **lemon juice**

1 tbsp chopped **fresh parsley**

↻ Preparation: 5 minutes; cooking: 15 minutes   ⚬ Makes 2 portions
⚘ Provides calcium, magnesium, omega-3 fatty acids, potassium, protein, B vitamins and vitamins D and E

You can use rainbow trout for this recipe, but if you want to make it for a special meal, such as a birthday dinner, use pink salmon trout, which is a very tasty fish. This dish is quick to prepare, so is perfect for quick evening meals if your child has friends over after school. The toasted almond flakes are highly nutritious and add a wonderful flavour.

▶ Toast the almond flakes on a baking tray in the oven for 5–6 minutes, or in a dry frying pan for a few minutes until golden. Ensure you move them around the pan as they can burn very quickly. Set aside.

▶ Dust the skin side of the trout fillets with flour and season both sides with salt and pepper.

▶ Heat half the butter together with a drizzle of vegetable oil. Place the trout, skin-side down, in the pan and cook for about 5 minutes until the skin is golden and the fish is cooked through. Remove the trout and place on a serving dish.

▶ Add the remaining butter to the frying pan along with the lemon juice, parsley and toasted almonds. Cook for about 1 minute and spoon over the fish. Serve with mashed potato with carrot (see page 165) and peas or broccoli.

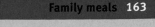

350g (12oz) small to medium **potatoes**, scrubbed

1½ tbsp **olive oil**

freshly ground **sea salt** and **black pepper**

Schwartz-Season-All seasoning (optional)

60g **plain flour**, to coat

100g (3½oz) **cornflakes**

250g (8oz) **plaice fillets** or **cod fillets**, cut into about 16 goujons

1 **egg**, lightly beaten

vegetable oil for frying

TIP The fish can be fried in advance and then reheated in the oven. It can also be baked on a greased baking tray for 10–12 minutes rather than fried.

Fish & oven-baked chips

Preparation: 5 minutes; cooking: 35 minutes   200°C/400°F/gas 6   Makes 4 portions
Provides potassium, protein, B vitamins including folate and vitamins C and E

If you are making these for a special children's tea, why not wrap a portion in greaseproof paper and serve them in a cone made from a rolled-up comic?

▶ Halve the potatoes lengthways, then cut into wedges. Toss in a bowl together with the oil, a little Schwartz seasoning (if using) and salt and pepper, until well coated.

▶ Transfer the potatoes to a roasting tin and bake in the preheated oven for approximately 30 minutes, turning occasionally, until crisp on the outside but tender inside.

▶ Meanwhile, spread the flour on to a plate and season with salt and pepper. Crush the cornflakes by putting them in a plastic bag and smashing them with a rolling pin, then pour on to a plate.

▶ Dip each goujon of plaice first in the seasoned flour, then in the egg, then roll in the crushed cornflakes.

▶ Heat the vegetable oil in a frying pan, add the goujons in batches and fry for 2 to 3 minutes, turning halfway through.

2 tbsp **vegetable oil**

1 medium **onion**, peeled and finely chopped

100g (3½oz) **leeks**, washed and sliced

375g (12oz) **potatoes**, peeled and cut into chunks

1½ tbsp **milk**

30g (1oz) **butter**

salt and freshly ground **black pepper**

200g (7oz) **minced chicken** or **turkey**

½ stick **celery**, chopped

1 small **carrot**, grated

2 tbsp **tomato ketchup**

75ml (2½fl oz) boiling **chicken stock** (see page 52)

½ tsp **fresh thyme** or pinch of **dried thyme**

an extra knob of **butter**

To decorate

1 **leek**, washed and sliced

2 **baby sweetcorn**, halved

1 **tomato**, sliced

1 **carrot**

6 **frozen peas**

basil leaves

Mini chicken & potato pie

↻ Preparation: 15 minutes; cooking: 25 minutes   ⚟ Makes 3 mini pies
⚶ Provides beta-carotene, potassium, protein, B vitamins including folate and vitamins A, C and E   ❄ Suitable for freezing

Children like individual portions, so I make this recipe in three small ramekins, and decorate each pie with vegetables to make humorous faces. These "funny face" pies were very popular with a tasting panel of young consumers!

▶ Heat the oil in a pan and sauté the onion and leeks for 5 minutes to soften.
▶ Meanwhile, cook the potatoes in a pan of lightly salted water until tender, then mash together with the milk and butter. Season to taste.
▶ Add the minced chicken, celery and grated carrot to the onion and leeks and cook for about 7 minutes. Transfer to a food processor and chop for a few seconds to give the mixture a smooth texture, if desired. Return to the pan, add the ketchup, boiling stock and herbs, cover and cook for about 5 minutes.

▶ Preheat the grill. Divide the chicken mixture between three 10cm (4in) ramekin dishes and top with the mashed potato. Dot the tops with a little butter and place under the grill until golden.
▶ Decorate each with vegetables to create a funny face of your design. You could use sliced leeks and peas for the eyes, halved baby sweetcorn for the nose, two thin slices of tomato to make the mouth, carrot strips for the hair and runner beans for a distinctive moustache. You could also add a bow-tie made out of basil leaves, if you choose.

Chicken with gravy & mashed potato with carrot

⏱ Preparation: 10 minutes; cooking: 30 minutes   ✂ Makes 4 portions   ⚡ Provides beta-carotene, potassium, protein, B vitamins including folate and vitamins C and E

Creamy mashed potato and carrot is the perfect partner for succulent griddled chicken and both are made all the more delicious by the gravy.

▶ For the gravy, heat 1 tablespoon of the vegetable oil in a saucepan and cook the onion for 7–8 minutes until beginning to turn golden. Stir in the sugar and water, increase the heat and cook for about 1 minute until the water has evaporated.

▶ Stir in the beef stock, cornflour mixed with water, Worcestershire sauce and tomato purée. Season with salt and pepper. Stir for 2–3 minutes until thickened, then set aside.

▶ For the mashed potato and carrot, put the vegetables into a pan of lightly salted water. Bring to the boil, then cook for 20 minutes or until tender. Drain and mash together with the butter, salt and pepper and enough milk to give the mash a creamy consistency.

▶ Cover the chicken breasts with clingfilm and bash with a mallet so they are not too thick. Season with salt and pepper.

▶ Heat the griddle, brush with the remainder of the vegetable oil and cook the chicken for about 3 minutes on each side, or until cooked through. Alternatively, heat the oil in a frying pan and fry on each side for approximately 4 minutes, or until lightly golden and cooked all the way through.

▶ Serve with domes of mash, using an ice-cream scoop.

4 **chicken breast fillets** (about 600g/20oz)

Gravy

2 tbsp **vegetable oil**

1 **onion**, peeled and thinly sliced

1 tsp **caster sugar**

1 tbsp **water**

200ml (7fl oz) **beef stock**

1 tsp **cornflour** mixed with 1 tbsp **water**

few drops of **Worcestershire sauce**

1 tsp **tomato purée**

salt and freshly ground **black pepper**

Mashed potato and carrot

450g (15oz) **potatoes**, peeled and cut into chunks

1 large **carrot**, peeled and thinly sliced

25g (1oz) **butter**

salt and **white pepper**

a little **milk**

TIP The gravy, mashed potato and carrot can be prepared in advance, so at mealtime, just cook the chicken.

Sticky barbecue drumsticks

⏱ Preparation: 45 minutes, including 30 minutes marinating; cooking: 20 minutes
✂ Makes 4 portions   ⚡ Provides protein and B vitamins   ❄ Suitable for freezing

Barbecued drumsticks are excellent whether eaten hot off the grill or cold from the lunchbox. Wrap the ends of the drumsticks in foil so that they can be eaten with the fingers without getting messy.

▶ To make the marinade, heat the oil in a frying pan, add the onion and sauté until soft. Stir in the sugar and cook gently for 1–2 minutes. Add the remaining ingredients and simmer for 5 minutes.

▶ Pour the mixture into a glass or ceramic bowl and allow to cool. Add the drumsticks and marinate for at least 30 minutes and up to 12 hours in the fridge.

▶ Preheat the grill to a high heat. Transfer the drumsticks to a baking dish, baste well with the marinade and place under the grill. Cook for 20 minutes, turning halfway through and basting again with the marinade.

▶ Check the drumsticks are cooked through, wrap the ends in foil, and serve hot or cold.

4 large **chicken drumsticks**, scored with a knife (remove the skin first if preferred)

Marinade

1/2 tbsp **vegetable oil**

1 small **onion**, peeled and chopped

75g (2½oz) **dark muscovado sugar**

juice of 1/2 **lemon**

1/2 tbsp **Worcestershire sauce**

4 tbsp **tomato ketchup**

1 tbsp **white wine vinegar**

Southern fried chicken

2 **Frenched (part-boned) chicken breasts** (about 300g/10oz)

50g (3½oz) **plain flour**

1 tsp **salt** and a little freshly ground **black pepper**

1 **egg,** lightly beaten

60g **fresh breadcrumbs**

vegetable oil for frying

Marinade

pinch of **cayenne pepper**

150ml (5fl oz) **buttermilk**

Gravy

1 small **onion,** peeled and chopped

1 tsp **plain flour**

1 tsp **tomato purée**

½ tsp **Worcestershire sauce**

300ml (10fl oz) **chicken stock** (see page 52)

⏱ Preparation: 10 minutes, plus several hours marinating; cooking: 15 minutes

🍽 Makes 2 portions   🥄 Provides potassium, protein, B vitamins and vitamins A and D

Marinating the chicken in buttermilk gives it a lovely flavour and makes it wonderfully tender.

▶ To make the marinade, mix the cayenne pepper into the buttermilk.

▶ Place the chicken breasts in the marinade and leave in the fridge for several hours. Either marinate the chicken overnight and cook for lunch the next day or set in the marinade in the morning and cook that evening.

▶ In a shallow bowl, mix together the flour and the salt and pepper. Shake off the excess buttermilk from the chicken breasts and coat with the seasoned flour. Dip into the beaten egg, then coat with the breadcrumbs.

▶ Either deep fry or shallow fry in at least 1cm (½in) of oil in a frying pan for about 10 minutes or until golden brown and cooked through.

▶ To make a gravy, pour off the oil and sauté the chopped onion until softened. Add the flour, cook for 30 seconds, then stir in the chicken stock with the tomato purée and Worcestershire sauce. Bring to the boil, then simmer for a few minutes. Serve with oven-baked potatoes or sweet potato wedges (see page 108).

Paella

1 tbsp **sunflower oil**

1 **garlic clove,** peeled and crushed

1 **onion,** peeled and chopped

2 small **chicken breast fillets** (about 250g/8oz), cut into chunks

1 **red pepper,** deseeded and diced

300g (10oz) **long-grain rice**

1 tsp **turmeric**

1 tsp **mild chilli powder**

750ml (25fl oz) **chicken stock** (see page 52)

1 **bay leaf**

100g (3½oz) **frozen peas**

2 **pork sausages,** grilled and sliced on the diagonal

100g (3½oz) small **cooked, peeled prawns**

salt and freshly ground **black pepper**

⏱ Preparation: 10 minutes; cooking: 25 minutes   🍽 Makes 8 portions

🥄 Provides beta-carotene, magnesium, potassium, protein, B vitamins, vitamin E and zinc   ❄ Suitable for freezing

Paella is a great all-in-one dish that's easy to cook and full of flavour. Whereas the traditional Spanish paella contains a mixture of seafood, including mussels, my child-friendly version is made with chicken, sausages and prawns. The turmeric gives the rice a rich yellow tint.

▶ Heat the oil in a deep, heavy-based frying pan, add the garlic and onion and sauté for 3 minutes. Add the chicken and sauté until sealed on all sides.

▶ Add the red pepper and cook, stirring, for 1 minute. Rinse the rice, then stir it in with the turmeric and chilli powder. Sauté for 1 minute, stirring the mixture constantly.

▶ Pour in the stock, add the bay leaf, stir well, then leave to simmer for 15 minutes, covered, until all the liquid is absorbed by the rice.

▶ Add the peas, sausages and prawns to the pan and simmer, covered, for a further 4–5 minutes. Season, remove the bay leaf and serve.

Enchiladas with turkey & tomato sauce

◷ Preparation: 10 minutes; cooking: 45 minutes   🔥 180°C/350°F/gas 4

🔪 Makes 8 enchiladas   ⚡ Provides beta-carotene, calcium, potassium, protein, B vitamins including folate and vitamins A, C and E   ❄ Suitable for freezing

This is a fabulous recipe, which has become a firm family favourite. It's great for dinner parties, too, and can be made in advance. These enchiladas are tortilla wraps (which you can buy in the supermarket) filled with a delicious minced turkey mixture and then covered with tomato sauce and grated cheese and baked in the oven. Highly recommended!

▶ To make the sauce, heat the olive oil in a medium saucepan and sauté the onion and garlic for 5 minutes until softened. Stir in the passata and oregano then season with salt and pepper. Cover and leave to simmer for 10 minutes.

▶ For the turkey filling, heat the olive oil in a large frying pan or wok, stir in the garlic, onion, pepper and courgette. Cook for 5 minutes, then add the turkey, stirring occasionally. Season with salt and pepper. After 7–8 minutes the turkey should be completely cooked through. Stir in half of the cheese until melted.

▶ Divide the mixture between the mini tortillas and roll up each one to form a cigar shape. Place the rolled tortillas in an ovenproof dish and spoon over the tomato sauce. Sprinkle with the remaining cheese. Bake in the preheated oven for 15–20 minutes until golden.

8 **flour tortillas,** about 19cm (7½in) diameter

Sauce

2 tbsp **olive oil**

1 **onion,** peeled and chopped

1 **garlic clove,** peeled and crushed

400g (14oz) **passata**

1 tsp **fresh oregano**

salt and freshly ground **black pepper**

Turkey filling

1 tbsp **olive oil**

1 **garlic clove,** peeled and crushed

1 **red onion,** peeled and chopped

1 **red pepper,** deseeded and diced

1 small **courgette,** diced

350g (12oz) **minced turkey**

salt and freshly ground **black pepper**

200g (7oz) grated **Cheddar cheese**

1 tbsp **vegetable oil**

1 small **onion**, peeled and chopped

1 **garlic clove**, peeled and crushed

2 **chicken breasts** (about 300g/10oz), skinned and cut into chunks

75g (2½oz) **button mushrooms**, cut into quarters

1 tbsp mild **Korma curry paste**

1 tsp **tomato purée**

200ml (7fl oz) **evaporated milk**

1 **eating apple**, peeled, cored and diced

2 tbsp **sultanas**

salt and freshly ground **black pepper**

1 tsp **lemon juice**

Mild chicken curry with apple

Preparation: 10 minutes; cooking: 25 minutes   Makes 4 portions
Provides beta-carotene, iron, potassium, protein and B vitamins including folate
Suitable for freezing

If your child prefers, you could leave out the mushrooms from this recipe and add some frozen peas about 5 minutes before the end of the cooking time.

▶ Heat the vegetable oil in a medium saucepan. Add the onion and garlic and cook for 5 minutes until softened. Stir in the chicken and the mushrooms and cook for 3–4 minutes until the chicken has turned opaque.
▶ Stir in the curry paste and tomato purée and continue to cook, stirring for about 6 minutes. Stir in the evaporated milk, apple and sultanas and cook for 10 minutes, stirring occasionally.
▶ Season with salt and pepper and stir in the lemon juice.

---

2 **chicken breast fillets** (about 300g/10oz), cut into chunks

Marinade

2 tbsp **yellow bean sauce**

2 tbsp **soy sauce**

2 tbsp **peanut butter**

1 tbsp **rice wine vinegar**

2 tbsp **honey**

NOTE Remove the skewers before serving to young children.

TIP Try threading vegetables, such as pieces of onion or pepper, on to the skewers, alternating with the chicken, to get some extra vegetables into your child's diet.

Chicken satay

Preparation: 35 minutes, including 30 minutes marinating; cooking: 10 minutes
Makes 3 portions   Provides iron, potassium, protein, B vitamins and zinc

Here are two delicious ways to make chicken satay. They should be a great hit with any child who likes peanut butter.

▶ Preheat the grill to high.
▶ Mix all the marinade ingredients with the chicken in a glass or ceramic bowl. Leave to marinate for at least 30 minutes. While the chicken marinates, soak four bamboo skewers in water to prevent them from getting scorched when under the grill.
▶ Thread the chicken on to the skewers and cook under the preheated grill for 8–10 minutes until cooked through, turning and basting occasionally with the marinade.

Variation

▶ Sandwich two chicken breasts between two pieces of cling film then bash them out until they are quite thin, using a rolling pin or a mallet. Remove the cling film and cut each breast into six strips. Make a marinade by mixing 4 tablespoons peanut butter, 5 tablespoons coconut milk, 2 tablespoons lime juice, ½ teaspoon sweet chilli sauce, 2 teaspoons soy sauce, 2 teaspoons honey and 1 teaspoon vegetable oil. Marinate the chicken in the fridge for at least 30 minutes. Meanwhile, soak six bamboo skewers to prevent them from getting scorched when under the grill. Remove the chicken from the marinade and thread on to the skewers in a snake pattern. Reserve the marinade. Cook under a medium-hot grill for 8 to 10 minutes, turning halfway through. Alternatively, cook them first on a griddle, then finish off under the grill. You can make a tasty dipping sauce for the chicken satay using the reserved marinade. Put in a saucepan, bring to the boil and stir in 50ml (1¾fl oz) boiling water. Cook, stirring, for 1 minute over a medium heat.

2 **chicken breast fillets** (about 300g/10oz), cut in half

Marinade

2 tbsp **mango chutney**

1 tbsp **dark brown sugar**

juice of $1/2$ **lime**

1 tsp **soy sauce**

freshly ground **black pepper**

Spinach and mango salad

100g ($3^1/2$oz) **baby spinach**, carefully washed

$1/2$ large **mango**, peeled and chopped

40g ($1^1/4$oz) **dried cranberries**

$1^1/2$ tbsp **toasted pine nuts** (optional)

Dressing

3 tbsp **vegetable oil**

1 tbsp **balsamic vinegar**

1 tsp **sugar**

salt and freshly ground **black pepper**

Sticky mango chicken

↻ Preparation: 1 hour, including 1 hour marinating; cooking: 9 minutes
⚥ Makes 2–4 portions   ⚡ Provides beta-carotene, fibre, iron, magnesium, potassium, protein, B vitamins including folate and vitamins C and E

The spinach and mango salad that accompanies this dish is one of my favourite salads. I love the combination of baby spinach, fresh mango and dried cranberries. If I am making it for older children I add toasted pine nuts.

▶ Mix together the mango chutney, sugar, lime juice, soy sauce and pepper. Pour this over the chicken and leave to marinade for at least 1 hour, turning occasionally. Preheat the grill to medium-high.

▶ Drain the marinade from the chicken and reserve. Place the chicken on a baking tray. Grill for about 6 minutes and then spoon over a little of the marinade and continue to cook for about 3 minutes or until the chicken is turning golden and cooked through.

▶ Meanwhile, mix together all the ingredients for the salad dressing.

▶ In a bowl, combine the spinach, mango, cranberries and pine nuts, if using, reserving some for sprinkling. Toss with the dressing. Serve the chicken on a bed of the salad. Sprinkle toasted pine nuts on top, if using.

175g (6oz) **basmati rice**, rinsed in cold water then drained

4 tbsp **vegetable oil**

1 small **onion**, peeled and finely chopped

60g (2oz) **red pepper**, deseeded and finely chopped

salt and freshly ground **black pepper**

1 beaten **egg**

60g (2oz) **frozen peas**

60g (2oz) **frozen sweetcorn**

1 large **spring onion**, sliced

1 **chicken breast fillet** (about 150g/5oz), cut into thin strips

125g (4oz) **cooked prawns** (optional)

1 tbsp light **soy sauce**

Egg-fried rice with chicken & prawns

🕐 Preparation: 10 minutes; cooking: 30 minutes ✎ Makes 4 portions
✐ Provides beta-carotene, protein, B vitamins including folate, vitamin C and zinc
❄ Suitable for freezing

Egg-fried rice with vegetables and chicken is an appealing, simple meal. Your child may be keen to practise eating with chopsticks; this will be slow going at first, so provide a fork as well.

▶ Cook the rice in boiling, lightly salted water according to the instructions on the packet.
▶ Heat half the oil in a large frying pan or wok, add the onion and sauté for 2 minutes. Add the red pepper and cook for 7–8 minutes.
▶ Season the beaten egg with a little pepper, pour it into the pan, tipping the pan to spread it evenly, and cook until set. Remove from the heat and break the egg up into small pieces with a wooden spatula.
▶ Return the pan to the heat, add the peas and sweetcorn, and cook until tender. Remove the egg/vegetable

mixture from the pan, and set aside. Add the remaining oil and sauté the spring onion for 1 minute. Add the shredded chicken and sauté for 3–4 minutes, or until cooked, then season.
▶ Add the cooked rice and prawns, if using, and toss the rice over a high heat for 2 minutes. Return the egg/vegetable mixture to the pan, add the soy sauce and toss together until heated through.

150g (5 oz) **dried rice noodles**

3 tbsp **oil**

2 **chicken breast fillets** (about 300g/10oz), cut into very thin strips

1 or 2 **garlic cloves**, peeled and crushed

150g (5oz) **beansprouts**

5 **spring onions**, cut into 2cm (3/4in) pieces on a diagonal

2 **eggs**, beaten

3 tbsp **brown sugar**

1½ tbsp **lemon** or **lime juice**

2 tbsp **soy sauce**

3 tsp **sweet chilli sauce**

2 tbsp **oyster sauce**

Paad Thai noodles with chicken

🕐 Preparation: 15 minutes; cooking: 15 minutes ✎ Makes 4 portions
✐ Provides potassium, protein and B vitamins

▶ Cook the noodles in boiling, lightly salted water according to the instructions on the packet.
▶ Heat the oil in a wok and stir-fry the chicken for about 4 minutes. Add the garlic, beansprouts and spring onion, and cook for about 3 minutes.

▶ Add the beaten eggs, stirring continuously until set before adding the sugar, lemon or lime, soy sauce, sweet chilli sauce and oyster sauce.
▶ Finally, add the noodles and stir until heated through.

Singapore noodles

Preparation: 45 minutes, including 30 minutes marinating; cooking: 20 minutes
Makes 4 portions   Provides beta-carotene, fibre, iron, protein, B vitamins including folate, vitamin C and zinc

These noodles can be made spicier with added chilli and curry powder. If preferred, replace the prawns with pork or more chicken. For extra flavour, fry the beaten egg in ¹/₂ tablespoon of sesame oil.

▶ Mix together the marinade ingredients in a bowl, cut the chicken into thin strips, add to the bowl and marinate for at least 30 minutes.

▶ Heat ¹/₂ tablespoon of oil in a frying pan, add the egg and fry to make a thin omelette. Remove from the pan and cut into ribbons. Heat a tablespoon of oil in the pan or a wok and sauté the garlic and chilli, if using, for 30 seconds. Drain the chicken, add to the pan and cook for 3–4 minutes, then set aside.

▶ Heat the remaining oil in the wok. Add the baby sweetcorn and carrots and stir-fry for 2 minutes. Add the courgettes and beansprouts and cook for 2 minutes. Stir the curry powder into the stock and add to the wok. Return the chicken to the pan with the prawns, spring onions and egg, and fry for 2 minutes.

▶ Cook the noodles in boiling, lightly salted water according to the instructions on the packet. Drain, mix with the stir-fry and heat through.

150g (5oz) **chicken breast fillet**

2¹/₂ tbsp **vegetable oil**

1 beaten **egg**

1 **garlic clove**, peeled and chopped

¹/₄ tsp finely chopped **red chilli** (optional)

75g (2¹/₂oz) **baby sweetcorn**

75g (2¹/₂oz) each **carrots** and **courgettes**, cut into thin strips

75g (2¹/₂oz) **beansprouts**

¹/₄ tsp **mild curry powder**

4 tbsp **strong chicken stock**

90g (3oz) small **peeled prawns**

3 **spring onions**, thinly sliced

150g (5oz) **Chinese noodles**

Marinade

1 tbsp each **soy sauce** and **sake** (rice wine)

¹/₂ tsp **sugar**

1 tsp **cornflour**

2 tbsp **vegetable oil**

1 **onion**, peeled and finely chopped

250g (8oz) lean **minced beef**

½ tsp **dried thyme**

salt and freshly ground **black pepper**

400g (14oz) **potatoes**, peeled and boiled for 12 minutes, then mashed together with 25g **butter**

1 tbsp chopped **fresh parsley**

1 tbsp **tomato ketchup**

½ tsp **Worcestershire sauce**

plain flour for dusting

Gravy

1 tbsp **vegetable oil**

1 **onion**, peeled and thinly sliced

1 tsp **demerara sugar**

2 tbsp **water**

1 **beef stock cube**

400ml (14fl oz) **boiling water**

1 tbsp **cornflour**

1 tsp **tomato purée**

a few drops **Worcestershire sauce**

½ tsp **mustard powder**

Minced beef croquettes

⟳ Preparation: 15 minutes; cooking: 25 minutes　✎ Makes 12 croquettes　⚡ Provides iron, potassium, protein, B vitamins, vitamins C and E and zinc　✳ Suitable for freezing

I think this dish is probably my kids' favourite minced meat recipe and their dad loves it too! The mashed potato gives these croquettes a lovely soft texture

▶ Heat 1 tablespoon of the vegetable oil in a saucepan and fry the onion for 3–4 minutes. Add the beef and fry for a further 3–4 minutes. Stir in the thyme and season with salt and pepper. Cook for 1 minute more.

▶ Stir the mixture into the mashed potato with the parsley, tomato ketchup and Worcestershire sauce. Season to taste. Cool, then place in the fridge until cold.

▶ Using your hands, form the mixture into 12 croquettes, dust with flour and refrigerate for at least 1 hour.

▶ Heat the remaining vegetable oil in a large frying pan and sauté the croquettes for about 5 minutes or until golden and cooked through.

▶ To make the gravy, heat the oil in a saucepan and, over a low heat, cook the onion for about 8 minutes until softened. Stir in the sugar and 1 tablespoon of water. Dissolve the stock cube in the boiling water and add.

▶ Mix 1 tablespoon of cold water with the cornflour and stir into the beef stock Pour into the saucepan. Stir in the tomato purée, Worcestershire sauce and mustard powder. Bring to the boil and simmer for 3–4 minutes. Season to taste. Serve with the croquettes.

Beef tacos

Preparation: 10 minutes; cooking: 15 minutes   Microwave on high, or conventional oven at 180°C/350°F/gas 4   Makes 4 portions   Provides beta-carotene, fibre, iron, protein, B vitamins including folate, vitamin C and zinc

Children seem to love Mexican-style stuffed tacos. Taco shells are readily available in most good supermarkets. Try filling them with a variety of delicious ingredients. Beans make a great filling, and this is a good way of getting them into your child's diet.

▶ Heat the oil in a saucepan, add the onion and garlic and sauté for about 2 minutes. Add the peppers and continue to cook, stirring occasionally, for 3 minutes. Add the minced meat and cook, stirring, until browned.

▶ Stir in the chopped tomatoes, mild chilli sauce and stock, then simmer uncovered for 15 minutes. Stir in the red kidney beans and cook for 3 minutes. Stir in half the coriander (if using) and heat through. Season to taste.

▶ Meanwhile, warm the taco shells in the preheated oven for 2 to 3 minutes, or in a microwave on full power for 1 minute. Remove the shells from the oven, line with the lettuce, spoon in the beef mixture and garnish with the remaining coriander.

1 tsp **vegetable oil**

1/2 small **onion**, peeled and finely diced

1 **garlic clove**, peeled and crushed

30g (1oz) each **red pepper** and **green pepper**, cored, deseeded and finely diced

150g (4oz) lean **minced beef**

200g (7oz) **canned chopped tomatoes**

1 tsp **sweet** or **mild chilli sauce**

100ml (3½fl oz) **chicken stock** (see page 52)

100g (3½oz) **canned red kidney beans**

salt and freshly ground **black pepper**

1/2 tbsp chopped **fresh coriander**

4 **taco shells**

4 **lettuce leaves**

Minute steak with teriyaki sauce, mushrooms & beansprouts

Preparation: 45 minutes, including 30 minutes marinating; cooking: 12 minutes   Makes 3 portions   Provides iron, potassium, B vitamins including folate, vitamin C and zinc

Minute steak is made from very thin slices of tender steak, preferably fillet steak. You need cook the steak for only one minute on each side. These steaks are also good served with the gravy from the recipe Chicken with gravy and mashed potato with carrot on page 165.

▶ To make the marinade, mix together the sugar, soy sauce, lime juice, beef stock and cornflour mixed with water. Add the steaks and leave to marinate for 30 minutes. Reserve the marinade.

▶ To make the sauce, heat the sesame oil in a wok and stir-fry the mushrooms and garlic for 5 minutes. Add the spring onion and beansprouts and cook for about 1 minute. Stir in the marinade and cook for 3–4 minutes until thickened slightly.

▶ Heat a large frying pan with a few drops of vegetable oil. Pat the marinated steaks dry with some kitchen paper and fry each steak for 1 minute on each side. Serve with the stir-fried vegetables and sauce.

300g (10oz) **minute steaks** (very thin steaks)

Sauce

1 tbsp **sesame oil**

100g (3½oz) **oyster mushrooms**, sliced

100g (3½oz) **chestnut mushrooms**, sliced

1 **garlic clove**, peeled and crushed

4 **spring onions**, thinly sliced

150g (5oz) **beansprouts**

a little **vegetable oil**

Marinade

1 tbsp **brown sugar**

2 tbsp **soy sauce**

1 tbsp **lime** or **lemon juice**

100ml (3½fl oz) **beef stock**

1 tsp **cornflour**, mixed with 1 tsp **water**

3 tbsp **soy sauce**

4 tbsp **mirin** (sweet rice wine)

1 tsp **sesame oil**

1 **garlic clove**, peeled and crushed

2.5cm (1in) piece fresh **root ginger**, grated

300g (10oz) **fillet steak**, cubed

1 tsp **cornflour**

Beef teriyaki skewers

Preparation: 1 hour 5 minutes, including 1 hour marinating; cooking: 10 minutes

Makes 4 portions   Provides iron, protein, B vitamins including B12 and zinc

Marinating the beef not only gives it a wonderful flavour, it also makes it more tender. You can serve the skewers with or without vegetables.

▶ Combine all the ingredients except the cornflour in a bowl and marinate for at least 1 hour. While the steak marinates soak four bamboo skewers in water to prevent scorching when under the grill. Preheat the grill to high.

▶ Thread the beef on to the skewers, reserving the marinade. Transfer the skewers to the grill (or barbecue) and cook for 4–5 minutes on each side.

▶ Meanwhile, mix the cornflour to a paste with 1 tablespoon of the marinade then pour into a pan with the remaining marinade. Heat for 2 minutes, or until thickened. Serve as a dipping sauce.

375g (12oz) lean **beef frying steak**, cut into strips

1 tbsp **corn oil**

1 small **onion**, peeled and sliced

1 tbsp **sesame oil**

1 **garlic clove**, peeled and crushed

1 **carrot**, peeled and cut into strips or stars

125g (4oz) **broccoli**, cut into florets

125g (4oz) **baby sweetcorn**

125g (4oz) **mangetout** or **courgette**, cut into strips

1 **red pepper**, cut into strips

Marinade

1 tbsp each **sake** and **oyster sauce**

2 tbsp **soy sauce**

1 tsp **light brown sugar**

Beef stir-fry with oyster sauce

Preparation: 45 minutes, including 30 minutes marinating; cooking: 25 minutes

Makes 4 portions   Provides beta-carotene, fibre, iron, protein, B vitamins including folate, vitamins C and E and zinc   Suitable for freezing

This quick Oriental dish uses oyster sauce, but there are other good, ready-made stir-fry sauces available – check they are additive-free.

▶ Combine the marinade ingredients in a bowl. Add the beef strips and leave for 30 minutes.

▶ Remove the beef and set aside, reserving the marinade.

▶ Meanwhile, heat the corn oil in a wok or frying pan. Add half the onion and stir-fry until softened. Add the beef and stir-fry until cooked, then remove and set aside.

▶ Heat the sesame oil in the wok and stir-fry the remaining onion and the garlic for 2–3 minutes. Add the carrot, broccoli and sweetcorn and stir-fry for 3–4 minutes. Add the mangetout and red pepper, then stir-fry for a further 3–4 minutes.

▶ Return the beef strips to the pan, pour in the marinade and stir-fry for 2–3 minutes more. Serve with rice.

Marinated lamb cutlets

⟳ Preparation: 1 hour 5 minutes, including 1 hour marinating; cooking: 14 minutes
🍴 Makes 2 portions   🥕 Provides iron, potassium, protein, B vitamins and zinc

*I've never had any problems getting children to eat these lamb cutlets.
Make sure you trim away any visible fat from the meat.*

▶ Whisk the marinade ingredients together, then pour into a dish and marinate the lamb cutlets for at least 1 hour. Preheat the grill.

▶ Grill for 6–7 minutes on each side. Trim the fat from the lamb cutlets and cut into slices. Serve with boiled potatoes and vegetables.

4 **lamb cutlets**

Marinade

1 tbsp **lemon juice**

1 tbsp **soy sauce**

1 tbsp **soft brown sugar**

1/2 tsp **herbes de Provence**

1 tsp **vegetable oil**

salt and freshly ground **black pepper**

Small leg of lamb with rosemary

⟳ Preparation: 8 minutes; cooking: 1 hour 10 minutes   🔥 200°C & 180°C/400°F & 350°F/ gas 6 & gas 4   🍴 Makes 6 portions   🥕 Provides iron, potassium, protein, B vitamins and zinc

Children tend to like traditional roasts of lamb or chicken. This dish would make a good centrepiece for Sunday lunch, accompanied by roast pototoes.

▶ Make about 12–14 holes in the lamb with a small sharp knife. Push a slice of garlic into each hole, with a little chopped rosemary. Brush the lamb with the oil and season with salt and pepper. Place on a trivet in a roasting tray.

▶ Roast the lamb in the preheated oven for 20 minutes at 200°C, then for 50 minutes at 180°C (or 180°C and 160°C in a fan oven). Baste the lamb a couple of times with juices and fat during cooking and turn it over a couple of times.

▶ Once cooked, remove from the oven and keep warm on a warm plate. Pour the excess fat out of the tray and keep the juices.

▶ To make the gravy, place the tray on the hob and bring the juices to the boil. Pour in the wine and add the sprigs of rosemary. Cook for about 1 minute. Pour in the stock and the redcurrant jelly or honey, then bring to the boil.

▶ Mix the cornflour with a little water to make a paste and add enough to thicken the gravy. Season with salt and pepper and strain through a sieve. Carve the lamb and serve with the gravy.

1.5kg (3¼lb) **leg of lamb**

2 **garlic cloves,** peeled and sliced

2 sprigs **rosemary,** chopped

1 tbsp **vegetable oil**

salt and freshly ground **black pepper**

Gravy

200ml (7fl oz) **red wine**

2 sprigs **rosemary**

300ml (10fl oz) **beef stock**

1 tbsp **redcurrant jelly** or **honey**

1–2 tbsp **cornflour**

1 tbsp **water**

salt and freshly ground **black pepper**

5 **Granny Smith** (or other) **apples**

1½ tbsp **ground cinnamon**

2 tbsp freshly squeezed **orange juice**

450g (15oz) **granulated sugar**

375g (12oz) **plain flour**

½ tsp **salt**

3 tsp **baking powder**

4 **eggs**

½ tsp **almond essence**

2 tsp **vanilla essence**

250ml (8fl oz) **sunflower oil**

icing sugar for dusting

Annabel's apple cake

Preparation: 25 minutes; cooking: 1 hour 30 minutes   180°C/350°F/gas 4
Makes 8 portions   Provides potassium and vitamins B12 and E
Suitable for freezing

Apart from how simple it is to prepare, the beauty of this truly delicious apple cake is that it will stay moist for as long as a week, because it is made with sunflower oil rather than butter.

▶ Peel and slice the apples thinly and place in a bowl. Toss with the cinnamon, orange juice and 100g (3½oz) of the granulated sugar.

▶ In a separate bowl mix together all the dry ingredients (the flour, salt and baking powder and the remaining sugar). Add the eggs one at a time (this can be done in an electric mixer on a low setting, if you wish), then add the almond and vanilla essences along with the oil.

▶ Grease a deep ring tin or other decorative moulded cake tin, such as a Cathedral mould. Pour in a third of the batter, then half the sliced apple mixture, then a third more of the batter, followed by the rest of the apple mixture. Finish with the remaining third of batter.

▶ Bake in the preheated oven for about 1½ hours or until a toothpick inserted comes out clean. When mostly cool remove from the pan and cool further.

▶ To serve, dust the top of the cake with sieved icing sugar.

10g (¼oz) **butter**

375g (12oz) **apples**, peeled, cored and thinly sliced

2 tsp **soft brown sugar**

410g (14oz) **canned prunes**

Crumble topping

150g (5oz) **plain flour**

a generous pinch of **salt**

75g (2½oz) **demerara sugar**

100g (3½oz) cold **butter**, cut into pieces

50g (1¾oz) **ground almonds**

Apple & prune crumble

Preparation: 10 minutes; cooking: 32 minutes   190°C/375°F/gas 5
Makes 6 portions   Provides fibre, iron, potassium and vitamins A, C and E
Suitable for freezing

If apple and prune is not to your child's taste, many other different fillings can be used with this wonderful crumble topping. Try rhubarb or apple and blackberry instead.

▶ To make the topping, mix the flour together with the salt and sugar, then rub in the butter using your fingertips, until the mixture resembles breadcrumbs. Finally, rub in the ground almonds.

▶ Melt the butter in a pan, add the sliced apples, sprinkle over the sugar and cook for 2 minutes. Spoon the apples into an ovenproof dish, about 20cm sq and 6cm deep.

▶ Stone the prunes, reserving the juice. Mix the prunes and 6 tablespoons of the prune juice from the tin with the apples. Cover the fruit with the crumble topping and sprinkle over a little water.

▶ Bake in the preheated oven for about 30 minutes or until the topping is golden.

Seriously strawberry lollies

⟳ Preparation: 3–4 hours, including freezing time   ✂ Makes 6 lollipops
🥄 Provides calcium and vitamin C

The one food that children are almost guaranteed to like is ice lollipops. These are made with ingredients that are actually good for your child: puréed strawberries, yogurt and fresh fruit juice. The three-tier version looks very attractive, but you can make up a single fruit flavour if you prefer.

▶ Put the sugar and water in a saucepan and boil for about 3 minutes until syrupy. Set aside to cool.

▶ Quarter the strawberries and purée in a hand blender. Press through a sieve to remove the seeds.

▶ Combine the strawberry purée with the cooled syrup and orange juice and pour into six ice lolly moulds until about a third full. Freeze until solid. When the first layer is set, pour in yogurt to a depth of 2.5cm (1in) and freeze. Once this layer is frozen, pour in the purée, syrup and juice mixture almost to the top and insert a stick in each lollipop. Freeze again.

▶ When ready to eat, run the mould under the hot tap for a few seconds to loosen the lollipops.

Variations

▶ Mix 450ml (15fl oz) strained freshly squeezed orange juice with 125ml (4fl oz) pineapple juice or exotic fruit juice. Add the strained juice of three passion fruits. Pour into the moulds and freeze.

▶ Cook a selection of fresh or frozen berries with a little sugar. Purée and sieve, then mix with enough caster sugar and blackcurrant or cranberry juice to sweeten.

1½ tbsp **caster sugar**

50ml (1¾fl oz) **water**

200g (7oz) **strawberries,** hulled

juice of 1 **orange** (about 75ml/2½fl oz)

300g (10oz) **strawberry yogurt** or **strawberry fromage frais**

TIP It's easy to make your own healthy ice lollies by pouring fruit juice or fruit smoothies into ice-lolly moulds.

Base

250g (8oz) **digestive biscuits**

125g (4oz) **butter**

Filling

225g (7½oz) **caster sugar**

3 tbsp **cornflour**

675g (1½lb) **cream cheese** such as Philadelphia

2 **eggs**

1 tsp **vanilla essence** or grated zest of ½ **lemon**

225ml (7½fl oz) **whipping cream**

75g (2½oz) **sultanas** (optional)

American-style cheesecake

⏱ Preparation: 15 minutes; cooking: 1 hour 🌡 180°C/350°F/gas 4 🥄 Makes 8–10 portions 📈 Provides calcium and vitamins A and B12 ❄ Suitable for freezing

This is a foolproof recipe for delicious cheesecake.

► To make the base, break the biscuits into pieces, put into a plastic bag and crush with a rolling pin. Melt the butter in a pan over a low heat and stir in the crushed biscuits.

► Line a 23cm (9in) spring-clip cake tin with baking paper and grease the sides. Press the crushed biscuit mix over the base of the tin using a potato masher.

► To make the filling, mix together the sugar and cornflour. Beat in the cream cheese until smooth, then add the eggs and vanilla essence. Beat until smooth.

► Slowly whisk in the cream until the mixture thickens slightly. Stir in the sultanas, if using. Pour the cheesecake mixture over the biscuit base. Bake in the preheated oven for 1 hour.

175g (6oz) **butter** (at room temperature)

75g (2½oz) **icing sugar**, sieved

225g (7½oz) **self-raising flour**, sieved

½ tsp **salt**

½ tsp grated **orange zest**

60g (2oz) **plain chocolate chips**

Chocolate chip & orange cut-out cookies

⏱ Preparation: 1 hour 15 minutes, including 1 hour chilling; cooking: 10 minutes 🌡 180°C/350°F/gas 4 🥄 Makes 25–30 cookies 📈 Provides vitamin A ❄ Suitable for freezing

Children love interestingly shaped biscuits and will enjoy helping you cut them out. The subtle orange flavour combines well with the chocolate chips to make these very "moreish".

► Put all the ingredients except the chocolate chips in a food processor and mix until blended together. Alternatively, beat the ingredients together by hand.

► Stir in the chocolate chips. Knead the dough until pliable and form it into a ball. If you have time, wrap it in cling film and set aside in the fridge for about 1 hour.

► Roll out the dough to a thickness of ½cm (¼in) and cut into shapes using a variety of cookie cutters. Arrange on a lightly greased baking tray (or one sprayed with non-stick cooking spray) and bake in the preheated oven for about 10 minutes.

Chocolate profiteroles & choux pastry mice

Preparation: 10 minutes; cooking: 35 minutes plus decoration

200°C/400°F/gas 6   Makes 20 profiteroles

Provides vitamin A   Suitable for freezing: undecorated

▶ To make the pastry, put the butter and water in a saucepan and slowly bring to the boil. Remove from the heat and sift in the flour, then stir to combine. Beat the mixture vigorously with a wooden spoon until it comes away from the sides of the saucepan, then allow it to cool a little.
▶ Add the eggs, a little at a time, until the mixture is soft and smooth and has a dropping consistency (you may not need to add all the egg).
▶ Fit a size 8 plain round nozzle into a piping bag and pipe small round mounds of the mixture on to a greased baking sheet. Bake in the preheated oven for 20–25 minutes. Remove and leave to cool.
▶ Whisk the double cream with the icing sugar until thick and fluffy. Cut a slit in the profiteroles and fill with the sweetened cream.

▶ Melt the chocolate in a heatproof bowl set over a saucepan of simmering water, or in a microwave on full power for 1 minute. Stir in the butter, allow it to melt and combine to make a smooth mixture. Leave it to cool slightly.
▶ Spread a little of the chocolate mixture over the top of each profiterole with a palette knife. If liked, the profiteroles can be decorated to look like mice: add a pair of flaked almond ears, a chocolate chip nose, glacé cherry eyes and a red liquorice tail.

Choux pastry

90g (3oz) **lightly salted butter,** cut into small pieces

200ml (7fl oz) **water**

90g (3oz) **plain flour**

3 **eggs,** lightly beaten

Cream filling

600ml (20fl oz) **double cream**

2 tbsp **icing sugar**

Chocolate icing

175g (6oz) **high-quality plain chocolate,** broken into small pieces

90g (3oz) **unsalted butter,** cut into small pieces

To decorate as mice (optional)

flaked almonds

chocolate chips

glacé cherries

red liquorice laces

TIP *The pastry will expand during cooking, so do not make the pastry mounds for the profiterole mice longer than 4cm (1½in).*

Chewy apricot & chocolate cereal bars

Preparation: 15 minutes plus refrigeration time   Makes 10 portions

Provides fibre, iron, magnesium, potassium, B vitamins including folate and vitamin A

Great for special treats, these are popular with adults and children alike. They are fun for children to make themselves as they require no oven cooking.

▶ Combine the oats, puffed rice, chopped apricots and nuts (if using) in a mixing bowl.
▶ Put the butter, golden syrup and white chocolate into a small saucepan and heat gently until melted. Stir the mixture into the dry ingredients until well coated.

▶ Press the mixture into a shallow 28 x 18cm (11 x 7in) lined tin, using a potato masher to level the surface. Place in the fridge to set. Cut into bars and store in the fridge.

150g (5oz) **rolled oats**

50g (1¾oz) **puffed rice** (Rice Krispies)

100g (3½oz) **dried apricots,** chopped

60g (2oz) **pecan nuts,** chopped (optional)

100g (3½oz) **unsalted butter**

125g (4oz) **golden syrup**

85g (2½oz) **white (or plain) chocolate,** broken into pieces

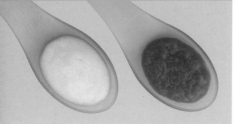

Menus: first tastes

Start with one meal of solids a day, building up to three meals a day by week five or six of weaning, when the third solid meal can be introduced at tea or supper time. It may be a good idea to offer half the usual milk feed before the solids, then finish the meal with more breast milk or formula (see page 29). Some babies may need an extra milk feed or a little cooled boiled water during the day.

	Weeks 1 and 2			Weeks 3 and 4			
	Early a.m. and breakfast	**Lunch**	**Mid p.m. and bedtime**	**Early a.m.**	**Breakfast**	**Lunch**	**Mid p.m. and bedtime**
Day 1	Milk	Milk First fruit purée (apple) *see page 36*	Milk	Milk	Milk First fruit purée (apple) *see page 36*	Milk First veg purée (carrot) *see page 37*	Milk
Day 2	Milk	Milk First veg purée (carrot) *see page 37*	Milk	Milk	Milk First veg purée (carrot) *see page 37*	Milk First veg purée (potato) *see page 37*	Milk
Day 3	Milk	Milk Fruity baby rice (pear) *see page 37*	Milk	Milk	Milk Fruity baby rice (pear) *see page 37*	Milk First veg purée (sweet potato) *see page 37*	Milk
Day 4	Milk	Milk First veg purée (potato) *see page 37*	Milk	Milk	Milk First veg purée (potato) *see page 37*	Milk Butternut squash purée *see page 39*	Milk
Day 5	Milk	Milk First fruit purée (apple) *see page 36*	Milk	Milk	Milk First fruit purée (apple) *see page 36*	Milk Avocado purée *see page 38*	Milk
Day 6	Milk	Milk Sweet potato purée *see page 39*	Milk	Milk	Milk Sweet potato purée *see page 39*	Milk Creamy veg purée (carrot) *see page 37*	Milk
Day 7	Milk	Milk Mashed banana *see page 36*	Milk	Milk	Milk Mashed banana *see page 36*	Milk First veg purée (sweet potato) *see page 37*	Milk

Menus: exploring tastes

You can now offer a wider variety of flavours and textures. Let your baby's appetite guide you as to whether you give one or two courses of solids. I have suggested some simple desserts to give at lunchtime and you can include something similar at supper or give fresh fruit, yogurt or fromage frais. Offer a drink of water or well-diluted juice from a beaker with lunch and supper.

	Breakfast	Snacks	Lunch	Snacks	Supper	Bedtime
Day 1	Milk Cereal Mashed banana *see page 36*	Milk	Potato, leek & pea purée *see page 48* Apple & pear, with raisins & cinnamon *see page 45*	Milk	Fish with carrots & orange *see page 51*	Milk
Day 2	Milk Banana, prunes and yogurt plus toast fingers, lightly buttered	Milk	First chicken casserole *see page 53* First fruit purée (apple) *see page 36*	Milk	Tomato & cauliflower gratin with cooked carrot sticks *see page 49*	Milk
Day 3	Milk Cereal First fruit purée (apple & pear) *see page 36*	Milk	Braised beef with carrot, parsnip & potato *see page 53* Fromage frais	Milk	Cheesy leek, sweet potato & cauliflower *see page 47*	Milk
Day 4	Milk Well-cooked scrambled egg with toast Yogurt	Milk	Lentil & vegetable purée *see page 49* Apricot & banana custard *see page 46*	Milk	Trio of root vegetables *see page 47*	Milk
Day 5	Milk First fruit purée (apple) *see page 36*	Milk	Fish with carrots & orange *see page 51* Peach, apple & strawberry purée *see page 45*	Milk	Sweet potato, carrot & broccoli purée *see page 49*	Milk
Day 6	Milk Apricot, pear, peach & apple compôte *see page 45* Fromage frais	Milk	Chicken with sweet potato & grapes *see page 52* Yogurt	Milk	Fillet of cod with a trio of vegetables *see page 50*	Milk
Day 7	Milk Cereal with milk Mashed papaya or banana *see page 36*	Milk	Tomato & cauliflower gratin *see page 49* Chunks of soft, ripe fruit such as pear or peach	Milk	Spinach, potato, parsnip & leek purée *see page 48*	Milk

Menus: 9 to 12 months

Most of these recipes are found in the 9 to 12 month section, but dishes from previous chapters are also suitable. You can substitute a selection of finger foods, such as strips of roast chicken, cheese, fruit and rice cakes, for cooked meals. Serve the snacks with a drink of breast milk or formula between main meals, perhaps mid-morning and mid-afternoon.

	Breakfast	Lunch	Supper	Snacks
Day 1	Fruity baby muesli *see page 63* Yogurt	Quick chicken couscous *see page 66* Fruit	Cheesy pasta stars *see page 64* Exotic fruit salad *see page 63*	Milk Sandwiches *see page 95* Dried fruit
Day 2	Scrambled egg with toast First fruit purée (apple) *see page 36*	Fillet of fish mornay with vegetables *see page 65* Fruit	Tomato & tuna pasta sauce *see page 64* Fruit	Milk Vegetable fingers and toast strips with dips Yogurt
Day 3	Cereal Fruit Fromage frais	Baby's bolognese *see page 67* Fruit	Easy mashed vegetable duo *see page 62* Banana	Milk Sandwiches *see page 95* Grated apple
Day 4	Toast with yeast extract or jam Fruit	Flaked cod with tomatoes & courgettes *see page 66* Yogurt	Creamy chicken & broccoli *see page 67* Fruit	Milk Sandwiches *see page 95* Fruit
Day 5	Apple & date porridge *see page 63* Fruit	Fruity chicken with carrots *see page 67* Fromage frais	Cheesy pasta stars *see page 67* Apple purée *see page 36*	Sweet potato, carrot & broccoli purée *see page 49*
Day 6	Raisin toast fingers Apple & pear purée *see page 36*	Braised beef with carrot, parsnip & potato *see page 53* Yogurt	Steamed vegetable fingers and cheese sticks Fruit	Milk Cheese on toast Fruit
Day 7	Cereal Juicy pear & prune purée *see page 44*	California chicken *see page 66* Fruit	Cauliflower gratin (variation) *see page 49* Fruit	Milk Sandwiches *see page 95* Yogurt

Menus: 12 to 18 months

Your child is now able to join in family meals and many of these recipes are suitable for the whole family. Choose your preferred accompaniments to the main courses, perhaps pasta, potatoes, bread or rice, and a selection of vegetables. Your child should also drink at least 400ml (14fl oz) of milk daily, which can be given with his snacks. You can now give him full-fat cow's milk.

	Breakfast	Lunch	Supper	Snacks
Day 1	Toast with yeast extract or jam Yogurt Fruit	Turkey balls & pepper sauce *see page 82* Fruit	Orzo with colourful diced vegetables *see page 79* Apricot & pear purée *see page 43*	Milk Raisin toast fingers *see page 85* Yogurt
Day 2	Cereal Fromage frais Fruit	Shepherd's pie *see page 83* Raspberry frozen yogurt *see page 84*	Courgette & tomato frittata *see page 76* Fruit	Milk Toasted ham & cheese sandwich Dried fruit
Day 3	Scrambled egg with toast Fruit	Chicken sausage snail *see page 81* Yogurt	Pasta cartwheels (variation) *see page 77* Banana	Milk Creamy avocado dip & vegetable fingers *see page 62* Fruit
Day 4	Pancake or waffles with bananas & maple syrup *see page 76* Yogurt	Turkey balls & pepper sauce with rice *see page 82* Fruit salad	Pasta & sauce with hidden vegetables *see page 78* Fruit	Milk Baked beans with toast Fromage frais and fruit
Day 5	Boiled egg with fingers of toast Fromage frais Fruit	Finger picking chicken & potato balls *see page 83* Banana	Tomato & tuna pasta sauce *see page 64* Fruit	Milk Vegetable fingers and other finger foods Ice-cream
Day 6	Cereal Yogurt and fruit	Bow-tie pasta with ham & peas *see page 79* Fruit	Mini veggie bites *see page 77* Fruit	Milk Baked beans with toast Banana
Day 7	Yogurt pancakes with maple syrup *see page 84* Fruit	Pasta cartwheels with cheese & broccoli *see page 77* Ice-cream	Joy's fish pie *see page 80* Fruit	Milk Vegetable fingers or Root vegetable chips *see page 76* Dried fruit

Menus: 18 months to 2 years

Shared family meals are not always possible, so I have included recipes in this weekly menu that can be prepared in advance or frozen, so that your toddler can eat the same food as you but at an earlier time. At this age, most children tend not to eat much at one sitting and to be physically very active, so between-meals snacks with milk are especially important.

	Breakfast	Lunch	Supper	Snacks
Day 1	Cereal Cheese Fruit	Annabel's vegetable rissoles *see page 99* Frozen yogurt with fresh berries *see page 113*	Chicken bolognese *see page 102* Fruit	Milk Sandwiches *see page 95* Yogurt
Day 2	Scrambled eggs with cheese & tomato *see page 94* Apple purée *see page 36*	Bow-tie pasta with spring vegetables *see page 96* Fruit	Shepherd's pie *see page 83* Fruit	Milk Baked beans with toast Fromage frais
Day 3	Pancakes or waffles with bananas & maple syrup *see page 76* Yogurt	Honey & soy salmon skewers with rice *see page 109* Fruit	Salmon starfish *see page 100* Fruit	Milk Cheese on toast Dried fruit and rice cakes
Day 4	Cereal Summer berry milkshake *see page 113*	Tender strips of griddled chicken with steamed vegetables *see page 110* Frozen yogurt with fresh berries *see page 113*	Tuna melt *see page 109* Fruit	Milk Raisin & oatmeal biscuits *see page 112* Fruit
Day 5	Apple, mango & apricot muesli *see page 94* Yogurt	Mini pizzas *see page 97* Jelly and ice-cream	Chicken kebabs with honey & citrus marinade *see page 102* Fruit	Milk Raw vegetables and other finger foods Banana muffin *see page 112*
Day 6	Banana muffin *see page 112* Fromage frais Fruit	Honey chicken *see page 101* Fruit	Courgette & tomato frittata *see page 76* Ice-cream or Mock fried egg *see page 116*	Milk Sandwiches *see page 95* Fruit
Day 7	Toast with yeast extract or jam Fruit Yogurt and honey	Macaroni cheese *see page 107* Fruit	Diana's chicken & sweetcorn rissoles *see page 110* Fruit	Milk Raisin and oatmeal biscuits *see page 112* Summer berry milkshake *see page 113*

Menus: 2 to 3 years

This menu plan shows a progressively wider choice of recipes that will accustom your child to new tastes. As with the other menu charts, you can substitute a few healthy convenience foods, such as pizzas, cooked chicken pieces or fish fingers, and vary or omit desserts, but do aim to keep snacks nutritious and provide milk, fruit juice or water with them.

	Breakfast	Lunch	Supper	Snacks
Day 1	Apple, mango & apricot muesli *see page 94* Yogurt and honey	Pasta with courgettes, peppers & sausages *see page 123* Fruit and ice-cream	Teriyaki chicken stir-fry *see page 126* Fromage frais	Milk Sandwiches *see page 95* Fruit
Day 2	Boiled egg with fingers of toast Fruit Fromage frais	Tomato soup *see page 120* Fruit	Annabel's tasty meatballs *see page 127* Ice-cream	Milk Banana muffin *see page 112* Natural yogurt and honey
Day 3	Cereal Energy-boosting smoothie *see page 146*	Chinese noodles with chicken & beansprouts *see page 124* Jelly and ice-cream	Mini baked potatoes *see page 121* Yogurt	Milk Baked beans with toast Fruit
Day 4	Porridge Raisin toast Fruit	Annabel's vegetable rissoles *see page 99* Sticky toffee pudding *see page 130*	Golden turkey fingers *see page 125* Yogurt	Milk Cheese and vegetable sticks Fruit
Day 5	Toast with yeast extract or jam Yogurt Fruit	Heart-shaped chicken nuggets *see page 125* Fruit	Annabel's pasta salad *see page 122* Raw vegetables & dip Ice-cream	Milk Cheese on toast Summber berry milkshake *see page 113*
Day 6	Cereal Yogurt Fruit	Golden turkey fingers *see page 125* Peach & berry compôte *see page 146*	Hungarian goulash *see page 127* Fruit	Milk Cheese on toast Dried fruit
Day 7	Muffins with creamy scrambled eggs *see page 142* Fruit	Caramelized chicken breast *see page 125* Fruit salad *see page 147*	Mini baked potato *see page 121* Salad Fruit	Milk Sandwiches *see page 95* Seriously strawberry lolly *see page 177*

Menus: 3 to 7 years

At this age, children love to help prepare their meals and there are many simple things they can do, such as cut sandwich shapes or cookies. Although I have suggested fruit after most meals, it is fine to offer occasional treats such as cheesecake or trifle. If your child eats lunch at nursery, pre-school or school, just balance her evening meal at home accordingly.

	Breakfast	Lunch	Supper	Snacks
Day 1	Poached or fried egg with fingers of toast Cereal Fruit	Spaghetti with special tomato sauce *see page 153* Salad Yogurt	Paella *see page 166* Fruit	Milk Vegetable sticks with hummus Chocolate chip, raisin & sunflower seed cookies *see page 149*
Day 2	Apple, mango & apricot muesli *see page 94* Yogurt Fruit	Beef teriyaki skewers *see page 174* Salad Fruit	Egg-fried rice with chicken & prawns *see page 170* Seriously strawberry lolly *see page 177*	Milk Cheese on toast Chewy apricot & chocolate cereal bar *see page 179*
Day 3	Porridge with honey or jam Thinly sliced cheese or miniature cheeses Fruit	Sticky salmon with rice and vegetables *see page 162* Seriously strawberry lolly *see page 177*	Singapore noodles *see page 171* Exotic fruit salad *see page 63*	Milk Baked beans with toast Chocolate chip & orange cut-out cookies *see page 178*
Day 4	Muffins with creamy scrambled egg *see page 142* Toast Fruit	Chicken satay *see page 168* Fruit	Fish & oven-baked chips *see page 163* Jelly and ice-cream	Milk Sandwiches *see page 95* Fruit skewers *see page 147*
Day 5	Yogurt pancakes with maple syrup *see page 84* Fromage frais Fruit	Mini baked potatoes *see page 121* Fruit	Beef stir-fry with oyster sauce *see page 174* Sticky toffee pudding *see page 130*	Milk Vegetable and cheese sticks Raisin & oatmeal biscuits *see page 112*
Day 6	Cereal Cheese Energy-boosting smoothie *see page 146*	Sloppy Joe with rice *see page 153* Fruit	Turkey pasta salad *see page 145* Jelly & ice-cream	Milk Cherry tomato & mozzarella salad *see page 144* Dried fruit
Day 7	Waffle & maple syrup Fruit Yogurt	Sticky mango chicken *see page 169* Apple & prune crumble *see page 176*	Butternut squash risotto *see page 159* Fruit	Milk White chocolate & cranberry cookies *see page 149* Fruit

Menus: snacks and party food

Snacks form an important part of every young child's diet, so it's important to have a selection of healthy snacks ready for when your child is hungry. Encourage children to eat healthily now and you will lay the foundation for a lifetime of healthy eating. For special meals, such as a birthday tea, you could make up an individual picnic box for each child rather than laying a table.

Healthy snacks

Recipes for snacks

Pineapple, coconut & banana smoothie
see page 112

Chunky tomato & cream cheese dip/Creamy avocado dip & vegetable fingers
see pages 94 and 62

Mock fried egg (vanilla yogurt & tinned peach half)
see page 116

Raisin & oatmeal biscuits
see page 112

Banana muffins
see page 112

Seriously strawberry lollies
see page 177

Raspberry frozen yogurt
see page 84

Root vegetable chips
see page 76

Sandwiches
see page 95

Scrambled eggs with cheese & tomato
see page 94

Mixed salad with dressing from Annabel's pasta salad
see page 122

Toasted tuna muffins
see page 142

Tuna melt
see page 109

Mini pizzas
see page 97

Toasted seeds with honey & soy sauce
see page 142

Turkey pasta salad with honey & soy dressing
see page 145

Pasta salad with prawns
see page 145

Pitta pockets with tuna, egg & tomato
see page 142

Chocolate chip, raisin & sunflower seed cookies
see page 149

Energy-boosting smoothie
see page 146

Fruity cranberry shake
see page 146

Other ideas

Boiled egg with toast fingers

French bread

Cheese on toast

Toasted raisin bread fingers with cream cheese

Toasted sandwiches

Miniature cheeses & cheese slices

Dried fruit

Fresh fruit & fruit salad

Wholegrain breakfast cereal with milk

Baked beans on toast

Glass of milk or fresh orange juice

Popcorn

Yogurt

Rice cakes, crispbreads, bread sticks

Vegetables on their own or with a dip

Party planner

Prepare in advance

Parcel birthday cake
see page 129

Heart-shaped chicken nuggets
see page 125

Chunky tomato & cream cheese dip (cut crudités the day before the party)
see page 94

Character fairy cakes (decorate the day before the party)
see page 128

Chocolate choux pastry mice (decorate the day before the party)
see page 179

Chewy apricot & cereal bars
see page 179

Jelly boats (cut in half and decorate on the day)
see page 85

Shortbread cookies
see page 131

White chocolate & cranberry cookies
see page 149

Chocolate orange mini muffins
see page 130

My favourite brownies
see page 148

Make on the day

Sandwich selection
see page 95

Annabel's pasta salad
see page 122

Chicken kebabs with honey & citrus marinade
see page 102

Chicken satay
see page 168

Pasta with courgettes, peppers & sausages
see page 123

Golden turkey fingers
see page 125

Mini pizzas
see page 97

Fresh fruit platter with chocolate-dipped fruit

Fruit skewers
see page 147

Index

Bold type indicates illustrations

Acknowledgments

Author's acknowledgments

I am indebted to the following people for their help and advice during the writing of his book: Dr Margaret Lawson, Senior Lecturer in Paediatric Nutrition, Institute of Child Health; Dr Stephen Herman FRCP, consultant Paediatrician, Central Middlesex Hospital; Dr Barry Lewis FRCP, FRCPH, Consultant Paediatrician; Luci Deniels, State Registered Dietitian; Simon Karmel; David Karmel; Evelyn Etkind; Jane Hamilton; Marian Magpoc; Letty Catada; Jo Pratt; Joy Skipper; Jacqui Morley; Lara Tankel; and Mary Jones. I would especially like to thank Nicholas, Lara and Scarlett Karmel, and all the other discerning young tasters who have eaten their way through the recipes in this book. Thanks also to Dave King for the beautiful photography, and Daniel Pangbourne for the lovely portrait of myself and Scarlett. And thanks to all the team at DK who have worked on this project.

Dorling Kindersley would like to thank: Lyndel Costain for advice on nutrition; Annaïck Guitteny for photographic assistance; Bethany Heald and Dagmar Vesely for food styling; Clare Louise Hunt for prop styling; Stokke for the loan of the Tripp Trapp highchair; Katie Dock for editorial assistance; Alyson Lacewing for proofreading; and Hilary Bird for the index.

Many thanks to all our models:

Louix Ball, Hanni Blaskey, Henry Boag, Clara Boucher, Jordan Chan, Susan Colyer, Connor Fitzjohn, Hebe Harvey, Thomas Leman, Scarlett McKelvie, Lavinia McKelvie, Luc McNally-Drew, Alexandra Mellor, Emilia Momen, Alexander Moore-Smith, Ella Moriarty, Jacob Moriarty, Sophie Moriarty, Patrick Moriarty, Ethan Myers, Sabina Netherclift, Sabina Regan, Finnegan Regan, Mike Rogers, Felix Rogers, Max Salzer, Georgia Sargent, Harvey Sidebottom, Erin Somes, Gabrielle Somes, Ben Somes, Kai Takahashi.

Picture credits

Picture research: Anna Bedewell.
Picture librarian: Romaine Werblow.
The publisher would like to thank the following for their kind permission to reproduce their photographs:
page 7: Daniel Pangbourne
page 12: Corbis/George Shelley
page 59: Bubbles/Chris Miles
page 73: Mother & Baby Picture Library/Ian Hooton.
All other images © Dorling Kindersley. For more information, see www.dkimages.com.

Useful websites

Annabel Karmel
www.annabelkarmel.com
The top destination for recipes, books, and advice on weaning, feeding children, and family food from Annabel Karmel. See her Make it Easy feeding and food preparation range.

akTV
http://annabelkarmel.tv
The Annabel Karmel online internet TV channel with step-by-step videos of recipes, advice, and top tips.

Babycentre
www.babycentre.co.uk

National Childcare Trust
www.nct.org.uk

National Childminding Association
www.ncma.org.uk

Tesco Baby Club
www.tesco.com/babyclub

Allergy

Allergy UK
www.allergyuk.org

Anaphylaxis Campaign
www.anaphylaxis.org.uk

Equipment

Amazon
www.amazon.co.uk

Babies R Us
www.babiesrus.co.uk

Mothercare
www.mothercare.com

Nutrition and health

British Dietetic Association
www.bda.uk.com

British Nutrition Foundation
www.nutrition.org.uk

Food Standards Agency
www.food.gov.uk

NHS Direct
www.nhsdirect.co.uk
24-hour helpline 0845 4647

Vegan Society
www.vegansociety.com

Vegetarian Society
www.vegsoc.org